Japanese Flowering Cherries

'Oshokun'. From Sano IV (1961).

Japanese
Flowering Cherries

by
WYBE KUITERT
with
Arie Peterse

Foreword by Roy Lancaster

Timber Press
Portland, Oregon

To Noriko & Kense

Published in 1999 by

Timber Press, Inc.
The Haseltine Building
133 S.W. Second Avenue, Suite 450
Portland, Oregon 97204, U.S.A.

Printed in Hong Kong

Library of Congress Cataloging-in-Publication Data

Kuitert, Wybe.
    Japanese flowering cherries / Wybe Kuitert with Arie Peterse; foreword by
Roy Lancaster.
        p.   cm.
    Includes bibliographical references and index.
    ISBN 0-88192-468-7
    1. Japanese flowering cherry. I. Peterse, A. H. II. Title.
SB413.C5K85   1999
635.9'77373—dc21   98-34246
                                                                    CIP

Contents

Foreword

For several years in the 1960s I would pass each day, on my way to and from work, a large specimen of *Prunus sargentii*. It grew in a garden beside the road, its branches soaring above the boundary wall in a great wave, which in spring carried an abundance of pink single blooms ahead of the coppery emerging leaves. I enjoyed it then, delighting in its exuberance and charm, and was always sad to see its brief spring beauty fading to be replaced by the lush dark canopy of summer foliage. Come autumn, however, my eyes again searched eagerly for this tree as its leaves, encouraged by the cooler nights, changed from green to a blaze of bonfire shades that burned ever brightly and then were gone, leaving only the bare branches dark against the sky. Imagine then my joy when, in October years later on my first visit to Japan, I saw this cherry in the wild, its leaves staining red the black forest and lighting like flares the gray mist of a Hokkaidō dawn.

I have enjoyed the Japanese flowering cherries ever since, as a boy, I lay on the lawn at home trying to catch the falling petals of a pink-flowered tree that probably was 'Kanzan'. 'Kanzan' was then, and still is in many areas, the most popular and commonly planted of these trees. Bold and brazen in the sheer exuberance and predictability of its blooming, 'Kanzan' was in part responsible for opening my eyes to the variety of Japanese cherries in the gardens of England and available in the many nurseries of the day.

It was at the nursery of Hillier and Sons in Winchester and later at the Hillier Arboretum near Romsey in Hampshire that the ornamental riches of this group really caught my imagination. To Western gardeners, the Japanese flowering cherries rank with the magnolia, the peony, and the lily in the aristocracy of garden flowers. They offer something special, and yet appreciation of their quality and charms is not by any means a prerogative of the wealthy and the privileged. They are just as much admired by ordinary people, whether they call themselves gardeners or not, for their beauty transcends class and race and touches the souls of all people.

That cherry blossom inspires is not surprising given its exotic appearance and reliability. No matter what the weather, its appearance each spring and in strength is virtually guaranteed. Its fragility and brief appearance meanwhile remind the poets in us that beauty is fleeting and life should be lived to the full. I have seen the young and old of Japan relaxing in their parks and gardens beneath the cherry trees' boughs, and memories of my childhood are never far away when I see them in bloom.

A person of my acquaintance who knew Japanese flowering cherries well was the foreman of the old Hillier nursery at West Hill in Winchester in the 1950s and 1960s. Ronald Hoskins, a Welshman, had worked many years for the firm and knew the names of every plant under his charge. The nursery was situated on a shallow chalk soil that suited well the large collection of cherries found there. Mr. Hoskins knew them all, their characteristics and their names, and he never tired of extolling their merits. He was also responsible for preparing cherry specimens in pots for the firm's impressive exhibits at the Chelsea Flower Show in London. This internationally famous show takes place each year in the second half of May when most Japanese cherries are past flowering, so it was Mr. Hoskins' responsibility to keep them in cold storage until shortly before the big day. Judging when to start and terminate the cold storage treatment was critical to their success and no one did it better than he. In doing so over many years he had come to know his Japanese cherries intimately, and it was from him that I first learned the differences in petal, sepal, bract, and leaf that characterize each sort, such as the occasional little green carpels in the center of the exquisitely formed flowers of 'Ichiyo', the beautifully fringed leaves of 'Shirotae', and the fragrance of 'Jo-nioi'—perhaps the strongest scented of all cherries. Mr. Hoskins also taught me to observe the different habits of each tree, and I think there are no more suitable trees for a lawn, especially 'Shirotae' and 'Shogetsu' with their broad-spreading to semi-pendulous crowns. Likewise, the perfect fountain of *Prunus pendula* and its selections so slender branched and delicate of flower.

The precocious pale-blushed *Prunus* ×*yedoensis,* the resilience and reliability of *P.* ×*subhirtella* 'Autumnalis', and the curious cream and chartreuse flowers of *P.* 'Ukon' are all to be admired and cherished, though we might not have space for them all in our gardens. And then there are their histories, stories to tell and be told as I myself was told one day in the Benenden garden in Kent of that doyen of Japanese flowering cherry enthusiasts and friends, the late Captain Collingwood Ingram.

"Cherry" Ingram, as he was known to his many gardening friends, was in his 100th year, and I had been invited by a mutual friend to accompany him around his garden. Despite his great age, he was alert and eager to talk, and among his many fascinating recollections I heard again the familiar story of his finding of the great white cherry 'Tai Haku' and its poignant aftermath.

Over many years I have been aware of the frequent confusion and misunderstanding concerning the correct names and identities of the Japanese flowering cherries. During this time it has been my privilege to meet or work with several Western authorities on the subject, including the late Sir Harold Hillier; Mr. John Bond, for many years Keeper of the Savill and Valley Gardens, Windsor; Mr. Roland Jefferson, lately of the U.S. National Arboretum, Washington, D.C.; and the late Mr. Geoffrey Chadbund of L. R. Russell, Richmond Nurseries, Windlesham, Surrey. I have also been fortunate enough to visit some of the best collections of Japanese cherries in the West, including those of Lady Jelena De Belder and her late husband, Robert, at Kalmthout and now Hemelrijk in Belgium.

All these authorities and many others in Europe and North America have made and in some cases continue to make an important contribution to our knowledge and appreciation of the Japanese flowering cherries grown in Western cultivation. To their names we should now add those of the authors Dr. Wybe Kuitert and Mr. Arie Peterse. Mr. Peterse I met several years ago when we discussed his work on the identification of those hybrids and cultivars grown in British and European cultivation. I was given a copy of his key, tried it out, and it worked very well, confirming how diligently and with what great care and sensitivity he has observed the detailed characteristics of these trees. I am therefore delighted that these two dedicated Dutchmen have combined their knowledge and expertise in producing this beautifully illustrated, detailed, helpful, and sorely needed account that I believe will become the standard work on this important and most popular group of gardening trees.

ROY LANCASTER

Preface

The Japanese flowering cherries can be found in a wide range of species and varieties in the forests of their homeland, but hundreds of forms also are found in cultivation. Some of these cultivated cherries exist as a single monumental specimen or a small group of trees in specialized collections, and they hardly deserve to be given status as a cultivar (cultivated variety). Others are well described and seen often in many parts of the world. Cultivars such as those related to the hybrids *Prunus* ×*yedoensis* or *P.* ×*subhirtella* have a clear standing in the systematic classification of Japanese flowering cherries.

Confusing names, however, have been applied to a group of centuries-old garden cultivars, known in Japan as *sato-zakura,* meaning literally "village-cherries" or cultivated (garden) flowering cherries. Well-known *sato-zakura* forms are 'Ama-no-gawa' and 'Kanzan', but a thorough search in western Europe showed about fifty other forms locally often not known by name or wrongly labeled. It is mostly the confused nomenclature of this loosely defined group that has precluded a definitive English reference on Japanese flowering cherries.

Japanese researchers have suggested a range of parents for many of the *sato-zakura,* such as the three varieties of *Prunus serrulata,* namely, var. *spontanea,* var. *speciosa,* and var. *pubescens,* but also the peculiar *P. apetala* and even a Chinese cherry, *P. pseudo-cerasus.* (The identity of *P. pseudo-cerasus* is discussed in chapter 1, "The Borders of Civilization," and the identities of *P. serrulata* and other cherries are discussed in detail in chapter 4.) Strictly speaking, hardly any of the *sato-zakura* has a clear breeding history, and a hybrid between a known seed parent and an unknown pollen parent already has an unusually well defined family-tree status.

In spite of their uncertain parentage, most semi-double flowered forms have some constant botanic characteristics, and these characteristics seem to point to the Oshima cherry (*Prunus serrulata* var. *speciosa*) as a parent. Therefore, these forms were grouped together as cultivars in 1916 by the Japanese botanist Manabu Miyoshi and by his American colleague Ernest H. Wilson in two separate publications. Miyoshi grouped them under *P. serrulata* and was followed in the West by Ingram (1929, 1948). Wilson's solution of *P. lannesiana* was used in Japan, resulting in some communication problems between East and West. The more deviating *sato-zakura* forms with pubescent leaves or umbellate inflorescences either were included in this group and described under one of these two species names, or, depending on the cherry authority, were given a genus name. This has led to some peculiarly ostentatious Latin names for good and simple garden cultivars.

Jefferson and Wain (1984) proposed lumping all the garden cultivars under a Sato-zakura group and applying the original Japanese cultivar names to solve at least the nomenclature problem. The garden form 'Ama-no-gawa' would have become correctly named *Prunus* (Sato-zakura group) 'Ama-no-gawa'. This nomenclature was not universally accepted; after all, *sato-zakura* is not a taxonomic term but an ethnobotanic concept. Furthermore, since the academic solution of Jefferson and Wain did not include descriptions, it did not help the gardener or horticulturist. In fact, of the studies discussed so far, only that of Miyoshi gave descriptions that are extensive enough to be conclusive, at least in most cases.

The Flower Association of Japan, for which the word *flower* means first "flowering cherries," prepared a detailed descriptive manual in 1982 of almost two hundred species, varieties, hybrids, and cultivars of Japanese flowering cherries. An English version came out also. One of the researchers in the association was Mr. T. Kawasaki, who published *Nihon no Sakura* (Flowering cherries of Japan) in 1993. This persuasive work gives evidence of an even more thorough understanding of Japanese flowering cherries and attempts to roughly classify almost 350 cherries in a few family-tree-like groups. The book appeared only in Japanese and has been an important aid to the present study. Both of these Japanese sources did not attempt to clear up identification problems and other confusions that exist in the West.

As helpful as these publications are, the present book would not have been written without the help of a report prepared in 1987 by Mr. Arie

Peterse, son of a flowering-cherry nurseryman, for the Wageningen Botanic Gardens in the Netherlands. The merit of this unpublished report is that it concisely describes the almost fifty *Prunus serrulata* cultivars that Mr. Peterse could trace in Ireland, the United Kingdom, the Netherlands, Belgium, and Germany; it even gives a key for their classification. Mr. Peterse's understanding of Japan's garden cherries matches that of the best cherry botanists in Japan. His initial set of fifty garden forms formed the starting point for this book and was expanded with many other descriptions and remarks on Japanese flowering cherries that either circulate as phantom names or are actually cultivated in the West.

The classification key, which was designed by Mr. Peterse, has been adapted and improved to include growing characteristics of lusher climates, such as that of Japan.

Among the ancient sources consulted some require special mention. *Kokon-yōran-kō* (Notes on a survey of old and new) is an encyclopedic work compiled by Yashiro Hirokata (1758–1841) from written sources and hearsay. It treats religious matters, the humanistics, diseases, foods, instruments, geography, botany, zoology, and so forth. Appearing in 303 volumes from 1821 to 1842, it has a complicated bibliography. The cherry information in it is based on *Igansai-ōhin* (Matsuoka 1758) and *Kafu*, an 1803 scroll by Sakurai Sessen. *Kokon-yōran-kō* illustrates 136 cherries.

Another primary source, *Hana-no-kagami* (A paragon of flowers) consists of two scrolls of cherry flower paintings. The complete set of eighteen scrolls shows eighteenth-century scenes from the Yokuon-en garden and is titled *Yokuon-en gaki* published in 1822; it is now in the Tenri University Library. At my disposal was a hand-painted copy by Kano Yoshinobu (late 1880s) from the collection of Ozawa Suien, showing 125 cherries; this copy is kept in the Diet Library. Further I could study (in a private collection) Horiyoshi San'yo's hand-painted *Jakufu* (1861), which is a copy of Sakurai Sessen's 1803 *Kafu* and illustrates 250 cherries in the garden of the daimyo Seihō Ichihashi. This copy, which was owned by Manabu Miyoshi and has his handwritten annotations, probably was a source for his *Ōka zufu* (1921). Other cherry illustrations of the Edo period are comprehensively discussed and partly given as illustration in a bibliographic overview in Sano (1990, pp. 285–300).

Working on the book, I soon realized that a strictly taxonomic perspective would be too plain to make the flowering cherries of Japan understood.

Their recorded plant history spans twelve centuries and reads as an ethnobotanic story that demonstrates their richly varied botanic origin. Seen in this light, the *sato-zakura* are truly the classic garden cherries of Japan, and even Japan's wild cherries would not have become as wild as they are without human interference. Reflected in the names, folklore, and horticultural qualities of these plants is the cultural history of a country that stretches from boreal Hokkaidō to sub-tropic Okinawa, a country that had its horticultural exchanges with China, Korea, and Western nations. Many centuries of close observation and intense pleasure with flowering cherries as garden plants have led in Japan, and later in other parts of the world as well, to a very refined appreciation, and consequently to a perplexingly rich nomenclature.

The present book gives a history of each garden form under its respected old name as proposed by Jefferson and Wain. The latest opinions of Japanese botanists and of Miyoshi (1916), Ingram (1948), and others are given in the descriptions when relevant. Opinions on parentage are given also, but assigning the cultivars to a wild parent species in most cases adds more to the confusion than to the resolution of problems, as family relations are hardly ever straightforward. Indeed, for daily practice it is advised to present the *sato-zakura* garden forms such as *Prunus* 'Ama-no-gawa' without a species name. To make for a complete guide, other common flowering cherries of Japan as well as some successful Western nursery cultivars have been included. The Cherry Name Index not only gives the page numbers where a particular plant is discussed, but is also structured to solve synonym and homonym problems with names.

Now that the world is becoming one large village, it is hoped that this book will bridge some gaps in the understanding of the cherries of Japan.

Acknowledgments

First, I want to thank Mr. Arie Peterse for teaching me how to look at cherries, for lending me many splendid slides, and for his pleasant company while traveling through Japan. In a way this book commemorates the late Dr. Onno Wijnands, director of the Wageningen Botanic Gardens, because he suggested that we cooperate to make this book.

I acknowledge the help of the Flower Association of Japan and specifically Mr. S. Iwai, Mr. Y. Takishima, and Mr. H. Wada in the association's Tokyo office, who were always friendly when answering questions or helping with introductions. The expert on varieties in the field, Mr. H. Tanaka of the association's Yūki Experimental Station in Ibaraki, helped greatly, as did the association's researcher, Mr. T. Kawasaki, who kindly presented scientific material and gave his time to discuss the cherries.

At the Tama Forest Science Garden in Tokyo, Mr. T. Katsuki and Mr. Y. Nishiyama introduced the garden's cherry collection, while Mr. E. Iwaki and Mrs. H. Morishima showed the collection of the National Institute of Genetics in Mishima. In Kyōto I was helped by Mr. T. Sano, who kindly presented valuable source material, and by Professors Y. Tsukamoto, S. Yazawa, and H. Maruyama, who helped me trace sources in the various libraries of the Kyōto University. Mr. S. Takabayashi, director, and Mr. S. Matsutani of the Kyōto Botanic Garden showed me the garden's cherry collection and allowed me to use material for research. Mrs. C. Teune of the Botanic Garden of Leiden University, the Netherlands, not only donated precious source material, but also helped with introductions. Professor Y. Kobayashi, trustee of the Flowering Cherry Association of Japan, gave kind advice, as did Mr. Roland M. Jefferson, formerly attached to the U.S. National Arboretum, Washington, D.C. The ForestFarm nursery in

Williams, Oregon, United States, gave me an overview of current cherries in American nurseries, while Mr. P. Schalk of the Martin v.d. Bijl Nurseries in Opheusden, the Netherlands, reported on the state of the art in this country. The staff and curator Mr. J. J. Bos of the Wageningen Botanic Gardens maintain a splendid flowering cherry collection in the Belmonte Arboretum and helped with source material and with solving various practical problems.

Mr. Matthi Forrer and Mr. Ken Vos (Rijksmuseum v. Volkenkunde, Leiden, the Netherlands), Ms. Judy Glattstein (The New York Botanical Garden, United States), Lady Jelena De Belder and family (Arboretum Kalmthout and Hemelrijk, Belgium), and Mr. Gilles Baud Berthier (Musée Albert Kahn, Boulogne, France) helped with this project.

Finally, Ms. Noriko Nakamura gave this research her daily support and was of great help in collecting cherries and making many study drawings; a selection of these is gratefully used to illustrate this book.

Research was made possible in the Netherlands by the Wageningen Agricultural University and in Japan by the Kyōto University of Art and Design, the International Research Center for Japanese Studies, and the Japan Society for the Promotion of Sciences.

The reader will note throughout the book various traditional Japanese family crests that take flowering cherries as a motif.

The photos were taken by the author, Mr. Arie Peterse, and Mr. Kense Kuitert at the following cherry collections: Yūki Experimental Station of the Flower Association of Japan, Ibaraki; Tama Forest Science Garden of the Forestry and Forest Products Research Institute (FFPRI), Japanese Ministry of Agriculture, Forestry, and Fisheries, Tokyo; Botanic Gardens of the Agricultural University, Wageningen, Netherlands; Opheusden, Nursery Peterse, Netherlands; Uryuyama Campus Forest and surroundings of the Kyōto University of Art and Design, Japan; Kyōto Botanic Garden of Kyōto Prefecure, Japan; Ninna-ji Temple and Hirano Shrine, Kyōto, Japan; and Arboretum Kalmthout, Antwerp Province, Belgium.

WYBE KUITERT

About Japanese Cherry Names

The *International Code of Nomenclature for Cultivated Plants* supports the use of fancy names for cultivars, in our case the old Japanese names. These have priority over the more recently invented Latin attributes that are given as synonyms in the Cherry Name Index and in the descriptions. To determine priority of names, we have relied on the thoroughly historical nomenclature study of Jefferson and Wain (1984) and on other, Japanese, sources.

The spelling of Japanese names in Roman alphabet now commonly uses the Hepburn system. 'Kanzan' is the Hepburn romanization, whereas 'Kwanzan' has become an obsolete spelling. In some cases we have become so used to older spellings that they were never adapted to the Hepburn system. Therefore one finds Ohwi, Shimidsu, and Koidzumi, for example, although at present one would rather spell these names as Ōi, Shimizu, and Koizumi.

Much Japanese is written with Chinese characters that are often pronounced in imitation of the Chinese. For example, the two characters that read as *Guan-shan* in Chinese become *Kan-zan* in Japan's "Chinese" reading. The vernacular Japanese reading of the same characters is *Seki-yama*, so that 'Kanzan' and 'Sekiyama' are synonyms of a linguistic origin. Cherry names were often used in literary prose, and playing with the characters of these names has given many synonyms as described in the text.

Vowels should sometimes be prolonged in pronunciation. For instance, 'Fugenzo' should be pronounced with a prolonged *o* as 'Fugenzō'. In the descriptions, when the cultivar name is explained, we have indicated whether such a prolonged pronunciation is required. It is, however, hardly distinguished by English ears, and for practical reasons, it is perfectly all right to omit the macron ¯ in daily usage. Vowels are pronounced in Japanese as follows:

> *a* as the *a* in *father*
> *e* as the *e* in *get*
> *i* as the *i* in *macaroni*
> *o* as the *o* in *hot*
> *u* as the *u* in *flu*

More pronunciation rules would be necessary for those wanting to study the Japanese language, but for horticultural practice the above is sufficient. By pronouncing consonants in Japanese names as they are pronounced in English, an English speaker could communicate with a Japanese-speaking plantsman or plantswoman.

Japanese cherry names occasionally are very long, because of an intricate origin or cultural plant history. The Japanese language does not use hyphens or spaces between the words. Thus 'Raikojikikuzakura' becomes a tongue-twister even more cumbersome for the Japanese botanist trying to translate it into English. Literally the name means "the-chrysanthemum-flowered-cherry-from-the-Raikoji-Temple." In such cases, names are hyphenated to ease the reading, 'Raikoji-kiku-zakura'. There is no taxonomic reasoning behind this.

The *s* in *sakura*, the Japanese word for flowering cherry, becomes a *z* in the middle of a word, such as in 'Kiku-zakura'. Some nurseries omit the suffix *-zakura*, which obviously leads to shorter names but which may create confusion as the same folk name is sometimes applied to cultivars of *Prunus mume* or another *Prunus,* the flowering peach. In a rare case the suffix decides the identity of a cultivar: 'Kumagai' is a different cherry than 'Kumagai-zakura'. The suffix *-zakura* should therefore not be omitted.

Garden forms are referred to throughout the text by their cultivar name, such as 'Ama-no-gawa', to smooth the reading, rather than with a botanically complete name such as *Prunus serrulata* Lindley 'Ama-no-gawa'. The descriptions include the scientifically acceptable nomenclature with its author(s).

CHAPTER 1

The Natural and Cultural History of Japan's Flowering Cherries

The Native Habitat of Japanese Flowering Cherries

Climate

The mild and gentle climate of Japan has four clearly distinct seasons that favor plant life and flowering cherries in particular. There are about 2000 mm of precipitation a year, including the rainy season in June. The watering of plants is generous, and the extra rainy spell in early summer falls exactly in the growing season of the cherry.

Summer in Japan is hot and humid. Infestations of plant lice, caterpillars, and bugs shave many cherry trees in this season. Some trees are almost leafless at the end of summer, which is not pleasing to view but is not harmful to the tree. The insects stop the early summer growth by eating the leaves. It is likely that this cessation of growth benefits the ripening of the wood and fruits, and it may even support the development of the winter buds of the cherry.

Autumn helps the final maturing of cherry buds in Japan. The weather is dry and bright, so that buds develop with dry and tight scales that protect the new growth of coming spring.

Japan's winters are mild with a few days or weeks of temperatures just below 0°C. No severe, enduring frosts occur in most parts of the country so that the soil is never deeply frozen. Root growth of the shallow-rooting cherry slows down but hardly seems to stop in winter. Above the ground the cherry has a distinct period of rest, awaiting the warmer days of spring.

Buds of *Prunus*×*yedoensis* 'Yedoensis', popular in Japan as 'Somei-yoshino', begin to develop at 2 to 9°C, and they are out after twenty days of temperatures above 15°C.

Among the sunny spring days of Japan, a few rainy days occur and nights are still rather cold and crisp. This is the ideal climate in which the blossom is at its best.

Geology and Topography

The geology and topography of Japan give us more clues in understanding the cherry, its distribution, and its tremendous variability. The archipelago of Japan offers as many opportunities for regional or local diversification of cherry forms as it has islands. Japan also has a young volcanic geology with earthquakes and eruptions that again offers change and renewed opportunities for plants to adapt, improve, and show new forms. The region at Mount Fuji and the neighboring bay with islands such as Ō-shima is known for its cycles of damage and revival of the flora with periodic eruptions. In other regions the hilly geology, combined with the large amount of rain and the almost tropical summers, makes a constantly changing landscape because of soil erosion, land slides, and the formation of new soils.

Alpine regions, called "the Japanese Alps" in English by the Japanese, are found in the center of Honshu, the main island. These mountains are surrounded by a vast belt of foothills. In the foothills the mountains are never very high, averaging about 300 to 1500 m. It is here that erosion is most prominently doing its work. Short and many-branched rivers, with a highly irregular flow, run through deep valleys that only widen after entering the narrow coastal plains for their final short course to the sea. There the beds are broad and meandering, up to 900 m wide for the Ōi-gawa River at Mount Fuji.

In the mountains, the slopes of the valleys are steep, often 30 degrees or more. Walking through the winding valleys and over the ridges, one may see the landscape change every half hour or so. Depending on topography and exposure to the sun, north-facing sides are cool, whereas south-facing sides are warm and sunny. The air may be fresh or chilly in a deep valley shaded by giant, broad-leaved evergreens, and hot and dry on the same day on top of the neighboring ridge. In the humid air of early spring these differences in microclimate are most dramatic and favor or prevent the ger-

Figure 1. Map of Japan with selected cities and islands important in cherry ecology and history.

mination, growth, and competitiveness of plant seedlings such as the cherry. As a consequence, vegetation types can occur in intricate mosaic-like patterns; the flora of both colder and warmer regions can often be studied within close distance.

Within a distance of a few hundred meters completely different types of vegetation may, for example, be found on Abukuma Sanmyaku, an east-west extending mountain range in Ibaraki Prefecture. This mountain range has a legal status as Natural Forest and is introduced for its cherries (Sano 1990, pp. 112–113). On the south side of this range grow *Actinodaphne lancifolia,* nagi (*Podocarpus nagi*), and *Prunus spinulosa* at the northern extreme of their range of distribution that centers on southern, warmer temperate regions. The north-exposed slopes of this range show Japanese red pine (*Pinus densiflora*) and Japanese beech (*Fagus crenata*) with katsura tree (*Cercidiphyllum japonicum*) and hornbeam maple (*Acer carpinifolium*), which belong to the cooler north.

Such vegetation patterns are not rare in Japan, but this site deserves closer study because there also occurs a natural hybridization between two cherries, the Japanese mountain cherry (*Prunus serrulata* var. *spontanea*) and the Edo-higan cherry (*P. pendula* f. *ascendens*). The latter has a distribution from Honshu southward, including Korea, Taiwan, and parts of China. Japanese mountain cherry is found between narrower latitudes on the southwestern half of Honshū, southern Korea, and Kyūshū, the southern, large island of Japan. Where their regions overlap, the species usually hybridize as is nicely illustrated in this forest in Ibaraki. The active hybridization, here in process, typically demonstrates how classification problems in taxonomy can be generated by nature. Ascending or spreading, pink or white, early or later flowering cherries—before or at the same time of the unfolding foliage—all cherry types are found in this area, and all show botanic details that range between the extremes of both species. The young geology and the intricate natural features of Japan's topography offer opportunities for such hybridizations.

Site and Soil

The soil and other conditions of the natural home of cherries in Japan give gardeners important clues to making a given cherry feel at home wherever one gardens. Cherries of the alpine regions, such as the Fuji cherry (*Prunus incisa*) or the Japanese alpine cherry (*P. nipponica*), are found on slopes of young volcanoes. The soil is coarsely granular, rather lean, and well drained; trees have a strong regenerative power and often appear in stands.

Cherries such as the Japanese mountain cherry (*Prunus serrulata* var. *spontanea*) and the Oshima cherry (*P. serrulata* var. *speciosa*), both frequently seen as parent to classic garden forms, find their natural home on the lower mountainous foothills. Their sites in the wild are always open and airy with much sunshine and fresh air. The Japanese mountain cherry also can be found on the mountainous slopes and close to the ridges or even on top of them among species such as Japanese red pine (*Pinus densiflora*), southern Japanese hemlock (*Tsuga sieboldii*), and rarely even Japanese umbrella pine (*Sciadopitys verticillata*).

The Japanese mountain cherry (*Prunus serrulata* var. *spontanea*) tolerates drier soils that can be of a firm and sticky consistency, whereas the Edo-higan cherry (*P. pendula* f. *ascendens*) and the Oshima cherry (*P. serrulata* var. *speciosa*) are happier in a looser soil near fresh, running water. Subterranean water never seems to be very far away for these two, which are found only on the lower slopes. If they can compete with the natural vegetation, they are also found in the plains, but then usually helped by human intervention. Farther down the slope where fallen leaves and dead branches accumulate, the soil is loose in structure, well aerated, often rich in leaf-mold, relatively poor in minerals, and slightly acidic. This soil is preferred by most garden cherries as their far-reaching roots can easily penetrate it. More will be said about light, moisture, and air requirements in chapter 2.

Wild Flowering Cherries of Japan

Flowering cherries are grouped under the genus *Prunus*. The seven Japanese species are introduced below in their systematic context. The systematics presented in this volume are based on (but do not follow the nomenclature of) Ohwi (1965) and Kawasaki (1994). Ohwi elevated the three varieties of *Prunus serrulata* to specific status and presented the garden form 'Takasago' as the species *Prunus sieboldii* (Carrière) Wittmack. I follow Kawasaki's grouping of flower cherries, except for his separating of *P. apetala* from the alpine cherries and his treatment of *P. maximowiczii* as a flowering cherry.

An understanding of the way in which the wild flowering cherries are related helps one grasp the forms and names, and should be studied by anybody who wants to identify an unknown tree. To make the story complete, other *Prunus* species seen in Japan, such as plums, peaches, and the downy cherry, are mentioned briefly. Some of these play an important role in the history of the flowering cherry. We should also mention here that Ohba (1992b) made a persuasive proposal for separating cherries from plums on the generic level. Such a separation would result in thirty-three new names of Japanese flowering cherry species and intraspecific taxa under *Cerasus*. Chinese researchers already use *Cerasus* for cherries and are likely to be followed by the Japanese.

All plums seen in Japan are native to China. They are distinguished by a flower stalk that is extremely short or almost absent. Flowers stand alone or in groups of two or rarely three. Fruits have a flattened stone with a furrow. Most often seen is *Prunus mume* Siebold & Zuccarini, which has been cultivated in Japan since the early centuries of the Christian Era. The fruits are quite astringent like the sloe and resemble small yellowish or green apricots. They are salted and eaten as pickles, are made into a good vinegar, or are used in making a plum liquor. Many varieties are in cultivation either for the flowers or the fruits, or for both.

What is called Japanese plum in English and known botanically as *Prunus salicina* Lindley is closely related to the European *P. domestica* Linnaeus. It flowers a month or more after *P. mume* and bears its fruits on longer stalks. This "Japanese" plum is, in fact, a native Chinese plant, called *sumomo* ("vinegar peach") in Japan, where it has been cultivated since ancient times.

The sweet Japanese apricot, known in Japanese as *anzu* and in Latin as *Prunus armeniaca* var. *ansu* Maximowicz, also is native to China but has been cultivated in Japan since times beyond memory.

The peach, *Prunus persica* (Linnaeus) Batsch, is found in Japan in many cultivated forms with delicious juicy fruits. Its flowers range between white and an intensely deep pink color. Flowering peaches, called *hanamomo*, are popular garden plants in Japan.

The cherry plums are distinguished from the plums (and peaches) proper. The three cherry plum species seen in Japan are native Chinese plants. The cherrylike fruits lack the furrow in the stone, and the leaves are rather short-stalked. The downy cherry, *Prunus tomentosa* Thunberg, has small, bright red cherries and very downy leaves. *Prunus japonica* Thunberg is a twiggy shrub with attractive little white or pink flowers; it is native to China in spite of its Latin name. The third member of this group, *P. glandulosa* Thunberg, also is a low shrub grown for its flowers; the double white form 'Alboplena' is quite well known in the West.

Four species of bird cherries are found in Japan. These are distinguished by the panicle cluster with its many flowers. All are deciduous: *Prunus buergeriana* Miquel, *P. grayana* Maximowicz, *P. padus* Linnaeus, and *Prunus ssiori* Fr. Schmidt. *Prunus grayana* is grown in parks and cities in northern Japan and has some fall color.

Although it is not a bird cherry, *Prunus maximowiczii* Ruprecht also has short panicles with four to seven flowers. Its deciduous leaves resemble those of the alpine cherries. This tree is found deeply hidden in mountainous regions in northern Japan, up to Sakhalin and the Amur area in Russia, with related species in China.

Cherry laurels, *Prunus zippeliana* Miquel and *P. spinulosa* Siebold & Zuccarini, are evergreen trees with flowers also in panicles.

All cherry plums and bird cherries have cherrylike fruits with a round stone that has no deep furrow. Japanese flowering cherries have the same kind of fruits and three to seven flowers that are set in branched clusters of two types, umbels or corymbs. Looking at regions of distribution, and checking details such as the cluster type, calyx, and leaves, one can arrange the seven Japanese flowering cherry species in systematic order in four groups as described below.

The Bell-flowered Cherry

The bell-flowered or Taiwan cherry, **Prunus campanulata,** is cultivated throughout southern Japan up to Tokyo. It is found in the wild on the southern Ryukyu Islands, in China, and in the mountains of Taiwan at altitudes between 500 and 2000 m. It represents the most eastern species of a group that includes cherries found in the Himalayas. It flowers very early with a deep red blossom in umbels.

Spring Cherries

The spring cherries, **Prunus pendula** f. *ascendens* and its relatives, are Japanese flowering cherries with flowers in umbels and a typically urceolate calyx. This calyx is clearly pitcher-shaped with a distinctly narrow mouth. The flower stalks, calyx, and often parts of the leaf are quite pubescent.

Figure 2. 'Inu-zakura' ("dog's cherry") is often found in old lists of garden cherries. It was the folk name for either the cherry laurel *Prunus spinulosa* or the bird cherry *P. grayana*. From an 1891 reprint of Matsuoka (1758).

These plants flower early in the cherry season (but later than *P. campanulata*), in Japan around the spring equinox, about 20 March, when day and night are equally long. The Edo-higan cherry (*P. pendula* f. *ascendans*) grows into a large tree and is found throughout Japan and on the Korean peninsula, with very similar cherries in central China and Taiwan as well. A weeping form of this cherry, *P. pendula,* was described before the ascending form was discovered. Both forms are wild. *Prunus ×subhirtella* is a hybrid between *P. pendula* f. *ascendens* and *P. incisa;* it has the same calyx as *P. pendula* f. *ascendens* but coarser leaf serration. A difference is that sets of chromosomes are diploid with *P. pendula* and triploid with *P. ×subhirtella.* The hybrid *P. ×yedoensis* is grouped under the spring cherries because of its calyx and because the ascending *P. pendula* was one of its parents.

Mountain Cherries

The mountain cherries **Prunus serrulata** and **P. sargentii** are distinguished by a slender, funnel-shaped calyx and long, narrow sepals. The three varieties of *P. serrulata* have their flowers mostly in corymbs, although a rare individual of *P. serrulata* var. *speciosa* might have them in umbels. The Japanese mountain cherry, *P. serrulata* var. *spontanea,* is found in the southern half of Japan and the southern half of the Korean peninsula. Most remarkable is the bright red, young foliage that appears with the flowers that are pinkish in bud, but expand to white. Leaves show a whitish or glaucous backside. The Korean mountain cherry, *P. serrulata* var. *pubescens,* is wild on the Korean peninsula, in northeastern and eastern China, and throughout Japan, excluding Kyūshū and the islands south of it. Its leaf does not have a whitish backside, but parts of the plant have a distinctive pubescence. The Oshima cherry, *P. serrulata* var. *speciosa,* is an insular form closely related to the two mountain cherries above. It is found on Ō-shima Island and neighboring islets and coasts of Japan, where deep volcanic troughs meet with the main island of Honshu. Here it is perfectly adapted to the young and active volcanic geology of the region. The Oshima cherry has a typical bristled, aristate serration of the leaves. *Prunus sargentii* is found in northern Japan in mountainous regions to very high altitudes. It differs from *P. serrulata* in its umbels. In its other botanic details it is an enlarged version of the Japanese mountain cherry, so that *P. serrulata* var. *sachalinensis* is a convincing name. Roughly speaking *sato-zakura,* or garden cherries, belong to this group and are understood as selections of one of the four mountain cherries above, or as hybrids with at least one of the four as parent.

Alpine Cherries
The alpine cherries, ***Prunus incisa, P. nipponica,*** and ***P. apetala,*** are found at high altitudes in the mountains of inner Japan or in the northern regions. Most typical is the double serrated, incised edge of the leaves. These cherries have few flowers per umbel, and all of them make shrubs or only small trees. The Fuji cherry, *P. incisa,* grows on the lean, young volcanic soils close to the top of Mount Fuji. The Japanese alpine cherry, *P. nipponica,* is found in mountains on altitudes above 1500 m in mid-Japan. Farther north it is found in a wide region on mountains and in plains of Hokkaidō and Sakhalin. It has a red, shiny bark reminiscent of *P. serrula,* though less brilliant. The clove cherry, *P. apetala* (Siebold & Zuccarini) Franchet & Savatier has a long, clove-shaped, and pubescent calyx, and tiny petals in its flowers. Its botanic name comes from the Latin *apetala* ("without petals"). In Japanese it is called *chōji-zakura.* The shape and serration of its downy leaves are very similar to the two cherries above. Though not exactly alpine, it is found in the mountainous landscape along the Japan Sea coast.

All the wild flowering cherries are quite variable and, except for *P. apetala,* good garden plants. As such they are described in more detail with their varieties and cultivars in chapter 4.

The Unknown Origin of Japanese Garden Cherries

No fewer than 193 cherries are described in the *Manual of Japanese Flowering Cherries* by the Flower Association of Japan. Cherry researcher T. Kawasaki (1994) listed 346 names, not counting synonyms, in his index. The richness of cherry species, varieties, forms, cultivars, and clones is due to the intricate geology of the Japanese archipelago that had, and still has, many isolated primary forest areas where cherries continue to generate new forms because of their great variability. Furthermore, the wild flowering cherries of Japan are also able to interbreed easily. Even their hybrids, and hybrids of hybrids, are usually fertile. Though triploids are sterile as a rule, even triploid cherries produce fruit with fertile seeds, again promising new forms.

Figure 3. The clove cherry (*Prunus apetala*) has a clove-shaped calyx and is best classified close to the Fuji cherry *(Prunus incisa)*. Photo by author, 13 April 1997, Yūki Experimental Station of the Flower Association of Japan, Ibaraki Prefecture.

Ingram (1942) traced the following hybrids from his cherry seedlings with *Prunus incisa* as one parent and *P. sargentii, P. serrulata* var. *speciosa, P. serrulata* var. *spontanea,* and *P. serrula* var. *tibitica* as the other. The latter cherry gave hybrids with *P. serrulata* var. *spontanea* and with a garden variety of *P. serrulata* as well. Ingram further reported hybrids from crossing *P. canescens* with *P. avium* (Hillier?). By keeping pollen he procured vigorous hybrids of *P. incisa* and *P. campanulata* and reported a hybrid from crossing *P.* ×*yedoensis* with *P. campanulata.* Ingram also procured seeds from *P. incisa* × *speciosa* × *P. sargentii* and *P. incisa* × *speciosa* × *P. campanulata*. Natural hybrids of *P. apetala* × *P. serrulata* var. *pubescens* and *P. incisa* × *P. pendula* f. *ascendens* are reported by Ohba (1992a), and horticultural hybrids of *P. campanulata* × *P. serrulata* var. *speciosa* and *P. campanulata* × *P. pseudo-cerasus* are reported by Kobayashi Yoshiō (1992). An impressive list of hybrids and hybrids of hybrids (of hybrids) is given in Kawasaki (1994, pp. 333–337). Flowering cherries are notoriously promiscuous.

A visit to the Tama Forest Science Garden in Tokyo is a very bewildering experience when one sees the garden's almost three hundred cherries in the blossom season. A visit, or better a few visits throughout the year, to see the fall colors, and autumn-bloomers or winter-bloomers as well, gives an impression of the enormous range of forms of the Japanese cherries. Yet, one has not seen them all.

Traveling through Japan, one may see a cherry that has a striking blossom never seen before. Old trees in the countryside, far from nurseries or famous gardens, must have started as just one peculiar plant brought from the forest by an unnamed person in forgotten times; as a consequence it is of singular genetic stock. Only one specimen usually is planted, although sometimes a few are planted close to each other or a young tree is trained to replace the old one when it dies. Such countryside cherries have a profound meaning to the history of the place where they stand and are planted in memory of an event. They are usually given richly colored names full of sacred lore or wistful memory. Descriptions of these folk cherries appear in magazines or papers of local horticultural clubs and sometimes also in scientific journals, but usually the trees are not propagated for wider cultivation. Rather, it is felt they should stay where they are, telling their unique story. Thus, the vast Japanese countryside has originated some famed and useful ornamental cherries thanks to nameless villagers who, upon finding a peculiar cherry in the forest, planted it in commemoration at a road crossing, or brought it to their village temple, or donated it to a local mayor who could in turn present it to his feudal lord. Such valuable donations, not to be expressed in money, were freely generated by the lush and generous nature of Japan. The practice of introducing peculiar plants to cultivation has continued from the primary forests of early civilization to today. In the 1960s, for instance, a chrysanthemum-flowered form of *Prunus incisa* was found among a wild stand and is now in cultivation as 'Fuji-kiku-zakura'.

Besides such random discoveries from wild material, the actively bred garden forms came into cultivation around the beginning of the seventeenth century. Certain nurseries came to specialize in cherries, and dwarfed or standard trees would be trained in the nursery for ten years or so before being sold. The concept of a clonal and named cultivar was valid for mass sales, but for a wealthy or high-ranking person a unique seed-grown hybrid selected from full-grown nursery trees was essential. As a matter of business politics such a plant was only made once and not reproduced as a cultivar; parents of such a precious nursery product were not recorded. The nurseryman had to, and wanted to, guarantee the tree's uniqueness, and the proud owner wanted to show off with an unequaled and spectacular tree. Many valuable cultivars known today originated in this feudal situation, where plants served other purposes than satisfying a plant-systematic curiosity. They existed only in one garden, where they were not known as a hybrid of designated parents. Only after the collapse of the feudal society in the 1860s were these trees grown as clonal cultivars.

With such an unspecified systematic status, most cultivated cherries are now known as *sato-zakura* ("garden cherries"). They are distinguished from the botanic cherries found in the wild that are loosely known as *yama-zakura* ("mountain cherries"). This set of terms makes the plant history of the flowering cherries more easily understood, although in a botanic-scientific sense the terms are too general to be useful. Wild cherries are in the process of being classified by botanists. The process is largely concluded but not completed, and it might never be due to the fickle nature of cherries, especially in areas where several acknowledged species overlap and continue to generate new forms and varieties.

Garden cherries were genetically fixed when they were brought under human control. Names were attached and stories gave these cherries an added meaning that is "horti" and "cultural" in the widest sense of the word *horticultural*. Most garden cherries have been cultivated in Japan for many centuries. One classic, 'Fugenzo', has been propagated since the fifteenth century, and its generations can be counted by tens. In propagating these generations in various regions, mutations and adaptations to climatic or growing conditions have occurred, resulting in differing clones.

Good nurserymen of old would keep the parent stock of a particularly successful cultivar as the "mother tree" in a corner at the back of their yard. The source of their commercial success could often receive wider recognition, and the clone was given a name. 'Shiro-fugen' is, for example, in some parts of the world the name of a distinct clone of 'Fugenzo', although in other regions it is only used as a synonym of 'Fugenzo'. In the modernized nursery world the mother tree is the sanitized, virus-free tree in the garden of an experimental station where it is often given a number, rather than a name. Virus-free material, giving healthy, more robust plants, has become the standard for flowering cherries in the West, but not yet in Japan.

Over the many centuries of cherry propagation, various clones of a cultivar came in circulation, creating a wider range for the identity within which a cultivar should be defined. Another mechanism that has widened the cultivar definition is that some cultivars have been propagated from seed. A cherry such as 'Ito-kukuri' is reasonably true to seed, although plants from seedlings have some variability. Such a seedling could be taken in clonal cultivation in Japan under the same old name or under a new name.

Taking a closer look at the garden cherries, we have tried to define the cultivars broadly to include all related clones and local strains. Some of the resembling forms are retained under their respected old name, although they might be directly related as a filial form. This happens particularly with the semi-double, pink-flowered garden cherries.

Human Activity and Flowering Cherries

Before turning to the cultural plant history of cherries in Japan, we should explain the role of humans in cherry ecology. Some species profited greatly from human activities, leading in time to the formation of the garden forms.

Cherries such as the Japanese mountain cherry (*Prunus serrulata* var. *spontanea*) and the Oshima cherry (*P. serrulata* var. *speciosa*) prefer a light and open location. In nature these conditions occur whenever a large, old tree falls and the forest floor becomes exposed to full light. Then it only takes the dropping of a bird that has eaten cherry fruits to ensure the *Prunus* a new generation. Birds play an important role in spreading flowering cherries throughout Japan. In fact, the spreading of certain cherries throughout the larger Far East has been connected to the routes of migratory birds.

Another animal helping the cherry to spread was man. The early country dwellers in Japan chose to settle at the lower end of the foothills of the mountains. Here they were safe from floods that threatened in the plain.

The clear and sweet water that came in abundance from the mountains was good for the household and could be controlled here for irrigating the rice fields. South-facing slopes gave the warmth of the sun in winter and secured in the heat of summer fresh air currents that came down from the mountain at the back. At the lower end of the slope the forest was cleared, a yard for vegetables was fenced in, and a well was dug. Cherries got a chance at this new, manmade forest edge where birds deposited seeds in their droppings.

Farther from the villages, the so-called *sato-yama* ("village-mountain") was a well-exploited farmers' wood that gave fruits and timber for various household uses. Forestry methods on the *sato-yama* resulted in a more open structure of the forest canopy, which gave opportunities for cherries. The *sato-yama* was most commonly exploited as coppice for charcoal and firewood. Depending on the region, wild cherries such as the Oshima cherry (*Prunus serrulata* var. *speciosa*), the Japanese mountain cherry (*P. serrulata* var. *spontanea*), or the Korean mountain cherry (*P. serrulata* var. *pubescens*) would inevitably appear. In fact, there is a connection between the Oshima cherry and maintenance of forest on Ō-shima Island as firewood coppice (Sano 1990, p. 116). Orchards for persimmons, peaches, or chestnuts and fields for *Aleurites cordata* (grown for the oil in the seeds) gave cherries opportunities to settle in the *sato-yama*. A cherry wood at Miko in Fukui-ken, for example, was started after the *Aleurites cordata* fields were established in 1742 (Sano 1990, p. 118). Stands of cherries in such secondary forests are composed of often old, thick trees that are much older than the surrounding trees of different species, indicating that the cherries were left to grow, while other trees were felled (Yamamoto and Takahashi 1991). Agricultural management of the paddy fields in the plains was usually too intensive to leave any room for cherries, but in cemeteries, yards around a religious structure, or a corner at a roadcrossing, cherries would develop, enhancing the meaning of such sites as physical or spiritual landmarks.

These kinds of ecological mechanisms gave the cherry chances that it did not have in unspoiled nature. Moreover, cherries were appreciated and were not removed as were other weeds. Until modern times, village people would actively help the cherry by saving wild seedlings and planting them along roads and at edges of orchards or fields. Small areas planted with a few cherries would be cared for as if they were private gardens, as can be seen in old photographs of Japan's countryside.

Figure 4. Typical secondary *sato-yama* forest with dominant presence of deciduous oaks and the Japanese mountain cherry (*Prunus serrulata* var. *spontanea*) coming up here and there. *Rhododenron decandrum* is in the foreground. Photo by author, 10 April 1997, Uryuyama campus of the Kyōto University of Art and Design.

Japanese mountain cherries are found in the wild as single specimens, though never completely isolated. Only when helped by humans do they grow in stands, which are often visited as picnic spots in spring. The practice of maintaining such cherry woods by adding wild seedlings is becoming history. With villagers turning to their television sets, and agricultural labor done with machines on a larger scale than history has ever seen, the semi-wild cherry stands are collapsing throughout Japan. For example, the cherry woods of *Prunus serrulata* var. *spontanea* at the village of Yoshino have a nationwide fame that traces back to poetry of the eighth century. The deteriorating health of the mostly old trees has drawn attention to the stand and replanting has begun. However, the old, small-scale, agricultural world of Japan with its incredibly labor-intensive management will never return. Other, more ecologically tuned strategies for maintaining famous cherry stands must be developed.

What is behind this love of the cherry? History shows that it was not only the beauty of the flowers, but also a more abstract appreciation that helped wild cherries and generated large numbers of garden varieties over the centuries. Their most fascinating cultural history is given in the following sections.

The Borders of Civilization

Flowering cherries are present in the earliest written history of Japan. These early notions would establish in later centuries the essence of the cultural meaning of cherries. A closer look leaves us nevertheless in doubt about their botanical identity, although some cherries were introduced from China or Korea because of their fruits.

In the early centuries of the Christian Era, Japan was sparsely populated by a peaceful, isolated people who grew rice and millet. In the fifth century a wave of immigrants from the continent came to Japan to escape the war and conflict that troubled the Korean kingdoms and China. Japan promised a better livelihood because it was potentially rich and had a mild climate but was still undeveloped and sparsely populated.

The immigrant Chinese and Koreans with their superior culture became leaders in religion, politics, trade, business, and in the opening up of natural resources by agriculture. Silkworm and horse-breeding are typical introductions of the period, as are more complicated ceramic industries,

Figure 5. Semi-wild stands of the Japanese mountain cherry (*Prunus serrulata* var. *spontanea*) on the hills of Yoshino still attract crowds of tourists when in bloom. In winter the ascending shape of this tree is simply splendid. Photo by author, 15 April 1996, Yoshino.

road building, and public works for irrigation. Immigrants introduced horticultural plants along with the mulberry for the silk industry. Turnips and gourds, but also *Acorus* and *Celosia* were newly cultivated plants.

The development of the country in this period was accompanied by the clearing of the shady primary forests of evergreen oaks and trees such as the nagi (*Podocarpus nagi*). This gave new opportunities for light-loving plants such as the mountain cherries. As followers of civilization, the cherries entered a period of expansion after the influx of the immigrants and sprung up wherever people had settled. Whether these cherries were actually imported by the fifth-century immigrants or whether they were already in Japan when the immigrants arrived is not clear at present. Nonetheless, the flowering of the trees became associated in later centuries with the new civilization.

In time one of the immigrant clans became closely related to the Japanese court because it provided brides to several generations of the early emperors. A power struggle between the inner court and members of this clan ended with the adoption of far-reaching political reforms that loosely unified the country. Japan rose as a stable confederation of clans, called Yamato in the seventh century.

The ensuing Nara period (710–794) started with the founding of Nara as a capital city for Yamato, and for the first time Japan witnessed civilization on an urban scale. The city had its avenues and markets; huge temples were constructed after Chinese architectural styles. Civilization became based on Buddhist ideology, and the country was ruled by a centralized bureaucracy modeled after the great Chinese dynasties. Chinese-style officials produced the first histories of Japan such as *Kojiki* (Record of ancient matters) in 712 A.D. and *Nihon Shoki* (Chronicle of Japan) in 720 A.D. These chronicles obviously were designed to legitimize the power of the imperial house during the Nara period. In a strict sense they are mythologies rather than histories. They begin with the creation of the land by the gods, who gave birth to the first emperor, thus founding the imperial house at a time that, in these sources, is dated back many centuries. In these oldest written sources of Japan we come across a plant called "cherry."

The "Chronicle of Japan" describes, for instance, an imperial banquet that supposedly took place in the eleventh month of the Chinese calendar in the year 402 A.D. When the emperor Richū was offered rice wine, a cherry flower fell in his cup. Surprised by this wonderful flower, the emperor ordered a courtier to find out from where it came. It was discovered that the cherry was plucked on a nearby mountain, and the emperor, delighted about this unusual event, named a palace after the flower and bestowed a similar name upon the diligent courtier as a reward. The mountain is given in the text as (*Wakigami*) *Wakinokami no Muronoyama* in the Nara region. The eleventh month in the old Chinese calendar is about January in modern count, being the flowering time of the first *Prunus mume*. The early date of Richū's cherry flower suggests that we have to take it as a literary rather than a literal statement. Indeed it was fashionable among Chinese and Japanese men of letters to have a *Prunus mume* flower floating in a cup of rice wine. Its faint fragrance and taste of nectar added to the refined enjoyment of the wine. Changing the word for plum into cherry proves that the cherry had attained a new, important meaning.

In a few other instances the cherry appears in these chronicles in events that are located in the first half of the fifth century, around the time of the Korean and Chinese immigrants. These stories were made up three centuries after the fact, and in each case the cherry is referred to with an imperial event or an emperor. Archaeology and Chinese contemporary histories of Japan show that "emperors" in the fifth century were a kind of manorial lord living in large wooden structures better called manor-houses than imperial palaces. Since these chronicles were written in Chinese, they followed Chinese models of thinking in presenting the Japanese lords as true emperors.

To write the word *cherry* in Chinese, the character *ying* is used in these chronicles, which in modern Japanese pronunciation reads as *sakura*, suggesting a flowering cherry. Chinese dictionaries of the period, however, explain the meaning of *ying* as "tree with many fruits." Thus *ying* obviously referred to Chinese fruiting cherries such as the downy cherry (*Prunus tomentosa*) or a more mazzard-like cherry such as *P. pseudo-cerasus*, rather than to the typical flowering mountain cherry of Japan. It is believed that *P. tomentosa* had been introduced to Japan by this time and had become a common garden tree of which the sweet fruits were eaten. (See Morohashi (1968), referring to the dictionary *Wamyō ruijushō* compiled before 935 A.D. by Minamoto no Shitagō (911–983)). In modern Chinese, *P. pseudo-cerasus* is called *ying tao,* but that does not exclude the possibility that it was called simply *ying* and already introduced to Japan in these early centuries rather than, or with, *P. tomentosa*.

Figure 6. Spring begins with many promises in early March when the plum (*Prunus mume*) comes in flower. Photo by author, 8 March 1996, Kitano Shrine, Kyōto.

By the way, the modern botanic identity of *P. pseudo-cerasus* Lindley has been questioned in the West, but is clearly established with Lindley's herbarium type, shown with a description in Miyoshi (1916). More extensive descriptions are found in the Flower Association of Japan (1982) and Kawasaki (1994).

Apart from early sources such as the chronicles, cherries are mentioned in poetry. In reality, the plant that inspired the poets most of all was the Chinese plum, *Prunus mume,* which had been introduced with its literary meaning in these early centuries of Japanese civilization. Famous poets, however, also wrote about cherry flowers in a different imagery that assures

Figure 7. The downy cherry (*Prunus tomentosa*) is believed to have been among the earliest plant imports to Japan. It is an easy garden plant, producing many delicious fruits that disappear even before a proper photo can be taken. Photo by author, 5 August 1997, Obihiro.

the yearly coming of spring in an endless peaceful cycle of the seasons. The imagery used reminds readers of a lover one does not want to forget and in other poems enforces the assuring presence of the new ruling emperor in the new capital Nara. As far as one may see cherries in bloom, the emperor's rule extends. Physically speaking, the views of the original readers of these poems extended to the hills that surrounded the plain with its civilized world around the capital. The hills, with their cherries springing up where civilization butted against the manmade edge of wild mountain forests, were seen as an assuring and protective belt around Yamato. Names of hills and cherries in poetry carry, therefore, an extended, almost magical meaning that interprets the landscape as a guardian of the nation. Among the names of the hills we find Yoshino, which in time became Japan's pre-eminent cherry hill. (For examples of this kind of poetry, see *Man'yōshū* 1047 or 1429.) Moss and the eternal process of aging that it demonstrates when growing on old rocks were used in a similar imagery of ensuring eternal rule of the emperor (see W. Kuitert, "L'Art des jardins japonais et les mousses" [Moss and the art of Japanese gardening, in French], in *Mousses, Bonkei, Bonsaï: Un secret séculaire du jardinier japonais* [Brussels, 1989], p. 7).

This kind of poetry was produced by Nara bureaucrats in an academic setting in the palace halls. They tried to beautify their words in imitation of Chinese models, as they did for the texts of the mythologies. They were not trying to express their emotions or make notes of botanic observations. A writer who never had seen the plant could compose a poem about it of the highest formal quality. Following the Chinese literary model, cherry blossoms are therefore often mentioned in the same sentence as the bright green foliage of willows in spring. The typical Far-Eastern weeping willow, *Salix babylonica*, was brought to Japan in the eighth century from China via Korea.

Apart from songs written after the Chinese model, a few truly Japanese songs from earlier times had been handed down by oral tradition. They now (the eighth century) were written down with Chinese characters in a complicated writing system that was revolutionary for its time and eventually developed into the spelling of the Japanese language as it is known at present. In these more authentic songs, the cherry represents female beauty. The word for cherry was written as a cumbersome and unsettled set of differing Chinese characters that read as *Sa-Ku-Ra*. Apparently there existed a notion of *sakura* as a cherry that was beautiful because of its blossom, and this must be taken as evidence of the existence of wild flowering cherries in Japan at least as early as the eighth century.

Historical references from these early centuries give us no information about the botanical identity of the cherries. Records in the eighth-century chronologies are vague events or legends located in the first half of the fifth century. They refer to the cherry with an early emperor whose power was secured by cultural innovations introduced from the continent. The cherry is more or less consciously associated with a novel, enhanced imperial power at the time of the great wave of immigrants. Poetry of the period makes this older meaning contemporary by invoking an ensuring protection for the country by hills with cherries flowering in spring. Cherries in bloom form the almost euphoriant border of a new, expansive civilization.

Aristocratic Plants in the Capital of Peace

Nara functioned as a capital city until 784 A.D. when the court moved and a new city was built where modern Kyōto now sits. The new capital was called Heiankyō (Capital of Peace). Peace would last for the almost four centuries of the Heian period (794–1185). A stable political structure with tributary agricultural provinces ensured a flourishing urban culture. Over time the Chinese fashion was molded into truly Japanese, highly refined expressions. The process meant a growing cultural self-consciousness mainly among a small elite group at the court, which benefited flowering cherries as well. First evidence of the new status of the cherry dates from 834 when the emperor Ninmei had a cherry planted in front of the main hall of the imperial palace instead of the usual plum tree (*Prunus mume*), which traditionally was planted with a citrus tree (see *Sandai Jitsuroku,* 901, a collection of historical facts compiled by several noblemen-politicians, including Michizane Sugawara). Two centuries later this commonplace historical fact was repeatedly cited in such works as *Kinpimishō* (1213) and Akikane Minamoto's (1160–1215) *Kojidan.*

Wider use of the cherry came later. For example, an index of native plants is striking for the absence of cherries. This source, *Honsō wamyō* (Japanese names of plants), appeared in 918, almost one century after a cherry had been planted in front of the imperial palace hall (see also Saito 1978, p. 135, referring to the index *Honsō wamyō).* It is possible that this singular cherry was appreciated as a magic imperial symbol rather than as garden plant, which could explain the absence of the cherry in this plant list. But one needs to understand that writing itself was an act of magic; hardly anything was written at the time for the simple purpose of recording daily life.

With the increasing use of the phonetic writing system for native, spoken Japanese, expressions in literature turned to a truer depiction of emotions and to a more descriptive view of the world. The latter half of the Heian period produced many diaries written in phonetic Japanese. These diaries give us an idea of how the ruling classes perceived the world around them. From this time on, the history of the cherry leaves the veils of myth and legend and enters the light of documented history.

The diary of Teika Fujiwara (1162–1241), a nobleman at the imperial court, is an example. It speaks of cherries in quite some detail. The author's notes picture a narrow world of problems about what clothes to wear and what colors they should be at obligatory courtesy visits. The diary also tells about the weekly bath and the monthly appointment with the hairdresser. In between are remarks about an early cherry that flowered even before the plum (*Prunus mume*) and another late flowering, pink double cherry. The diary refers to transplanting and grafting cherries (Uehara Keiji 1977, pp. 2, 33). The word the author uses for the cherry is the native Japanese word *sakura,* meaning flowering cherries.

Teika Fujiwara had a countryside retreat planted with flowering cherries. The retreat was located at Arashiyama, a scenic opening in the hills that surround the valley of the Capital of Peace. The area had been famous for centuries prior as the site of aristocratic picnics in autumn when the wild maples would be at their best. It was reached by passing through fields; the city only occupied part of the plain opposite Arashiyama. Today the entire plain has become an urban area, and Arashiyama is widely known for its cherries, which probably originated with the cherries of Teika Fujiwara.

Not long after the death of Teika Fujiwara, the area was chosen as a site for an imperial residence. Construction began in 1255. A spacious garden was laid out with a pond fed by water from the river that runs between the hills of Arashiyama. To heighten the beauty in spring, numerous cherries were brought from the Yoshino region at Nara, about seventy kilometers to the south, and planted among the maples on the foothills of Arashiyama

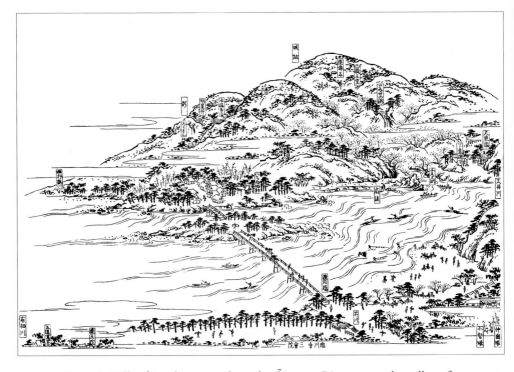

Figure 8. Hills of Arashiyama, where the Ōi-gawa River enters the valley of Kyōto. The Hōrin-ji Temple can be seen tucked between the hills just above the hamlet at the point where the bridge reaches the opposite riverbank. The cherries 'Arashiyama', 'Horinji', and 'Tagui-arashi' originate from this area. From Akisato Ritō (1780).

at the back of the estate, adding to Fujiwara's cherries. In spring the landscape would form a background of blossom clouds for the spacious pond garden at the palace.

It can be assumed that the villagers of Yoshino had selected particularly nice cherries to fill the imperial cherry order. The trees would have been young yet beautiful, suggesting that they offered deep foliage colors rather than spectacular flowers. In later centuries the Arashiyama area would produce such garden cherries as 'Arashiyama' and 'Tagui-arashi'. These single-flowered forms show a remarkable red coloring of bud scales, bracts, calyx, and sepals, and must be judged as selections from the Japanese mountain cherry. A rare form, known as 'Horinji', comes from this area and has the same deep coloring of calyx and sepals.

The planting of large numbers of cherries as background scenery was a general principle in the design of a nobleman's garden. (For details of the design and the symbolic meaning it carried, see W. Kuitert, *Themes, Scenes, and Taste, in the History of Japanese Garden Art* [Amsterdam, 1988], pp. 46–54.) It is also seen in the *Tale of Prince Genji,* a romance written around 1000 A.D. by a noblewoman. It describes the fictional garden of the prince thus:

> [It was] a very pleasant arrangement of lakes and hills. The hills were high in the southeast quarter, where cherry trees were planted in large numbers. The pond was most attractively designed. Among the plantings in the forward parts of the garden were cinquefoil pines, red plums, cherries, wisteria, Kerria, and rock azalea, most of them trees and shrubs that are enjoyed in spring. . . . The branches caught in mists from either side were like a tapestry, and far away in the private gardens a willow trailed its branches in a deepening green, and cherry blossoms were rich and sensuous (after Seidensticker 1982).

For the nobility, clouds of cherry blossom as a background to village scenery must have been an archetypal landscape imagery similar to that found in the poems praising the emperor with his power extending as far as cherries are in bloom. The imagery was re-created on a smaller scale in private gardens for the nobility. In the foreground of Genji's garden, it is a combination of cherries and willows that heralds a virtuous ruler in the classic Chinese manner.

Making a garden was a rare undertaking for which planting material was collected from the wild or from other gardens. Growing and selling plants in nurseries did not exist. Cherries were brought to the garden from mountains that would have been named in poetry. These must have been the mountain cherries of the region around the capital cities Nara and Kyōto, cherries such as *Prunus serrulata* var. *spontanea* or var. *pubescens.*

Besides Arashiyama, cherry sites of the old legends and classic poems became popular at the court as destinations for excursions. Chariots pulled by oxen and an entourage on foot would travel to the place, taking a few days for more remote sites, and have an extensive picnic that also could last several days before returning. Favorite among the emperor and the nobility were the cherries from the hills of Yoshino close to Nara that brought back the melancholic memories of the older dynasty of Yamato.

Poems about a double-flowered cherry in Nara appear beginning in the mid-eleventh century in such works as *Honchō monzui* (1037–1046), a compilation of poems in Chinese by Akihira Fujiwara. *Shikawakashū* (compiled 1151–1154) by Akisuke Fujiwara and *Shasekishū* (1279–1283), also refer to this cherry. 'Nara-no-yae-zakura', the "double-cherry-from-Nara", still cultivated in this city, is likely the same, unchanged form. (For more details, see the description of *P. serrulata* var. *pubescens* in chapter 4.) It is a small-flowered, double form of *Prunus serrulata* var. *pubescens* with deeply bifid petals tightly set together, giving a precisely regular fringe of the flower. A wild stand of this double-flowered form of *Prunus serrulata* var. *pubescens*

Figure 9. 'Nara-no-yae-zakura', the "double cherry from Nara," is a form of the Korean mountain cherry *(Prunus serrulata* var. *pubescens)*. Photo of a clone known as 'Yono-no-yae-zakura' by Arie Peterse, 30 April 1996, Mishima.

was reported from Yono in Mie Prefecture, and a selection with an excellent, erect tree shape is known as 'Yono-no-yae-zakura' (synonym *P. leveilleana* Koehne 'Nara-zakura') in Kokuritsu Idengaku Kenkyujo (1995, p. 82).

Entering the fourteenth century, cherries are fully established as garden plants in aristocratic circles in the capital. Yoshida Kenkō (see Inamura Toku 1981) commented in 1330:

> Trees to plant at the house are pine and cherry. As pine the five-needled one is preferred (*Pinus parviflora*) and for cherries the single-flowered forms. Originally, double cherries were only found in the city of Nara, but recently these are found everywhere. However, of old, the cherries from Yoshino and the cherry in front of the main hall of the imperial palace were all single-flowered. These double ones are grotesque, badly misshapen and distorted. Therefore it is better not to plant these. They are late in flowering, present a disastrous sight, and because of the bugs they are not to be preferred.

Conservative on the point of its appreciation of double-flowered cherries, this comment nevertheless shows us that the triumph of the garden cherries in Japan had begun.

Contact with the Eastern Provinces: More Garden Cherries

Economic progress had brought a group of warlords to power in the eastern provinces. Headed by their leader-general, the shogun, they turned to threaten the Capital of Peace from their strongholds in the city of Kamakura. When they finally occupied the capital, present-day Kyōto, in 1336 A.D., the ruling emperor fled to Yoshino, where he set up a temporary court in a local temple. Thus, the cherries of Yoshino became intimately associated with the mythical imperial power as the fleeing emperor continued to be revered as the true spiritual leader of the country. Even so, the warlords asserted their power over the country by installing their emperor. What interests us at this point is that they even brought their own cherry and in 1357 planted it in front of the main hall of the shogun's palace or the old imperial palace in Kyōto. Quite precise accounts of cherries are now found in the diaries of priests in Kyōto, whose temples were sponsored by the military rulers. Although it is not clear which palace the sources deal with, it is a fascinating idea that no plant could express the claim to power better than a cherry from Kamakura, the birthplace of the shogun and his men (see *Entairyaku,* a cumulative collection of historical records 1308–1360, quoted in Yamada 1941, p. 121; see also Kayama 1938, pp. 6, 16).

Off the coast at Kamakura lie Ō-shima Island and the neighboring Izu Islands. I am convinced that the cherry brought from Kamakura must have been a form of the Oshima cherry, although strictly speaking this remains hypothetical. Kamakura lies about four hundred kilometers east of Kyōto: cherries were therefore moved about the country over long distances. Hitherto isolated plant material of the highly variable Oshima cherry was brought to Kyōto, while Yoshino cherries had been brought to the city about a century earlier. Cherry populations that had developed separate identities during their evolution were brought together and could start to hybridize, a process that would lead to several distinct cultivars in the following centuries. Remarkable names of peculiar cherries and a rare, short description appear frequently in historical sources.

'Kirigaya' (synonym 'Mikuruma-gaeshi') is one such example. This cherry is mentioned in *Inryōken-nichiroku* (also known as *Kikei-nichiroku*), a journal kept by priests of one of the subtemples of the monastery Shōkoku-ji in Kyōto during the mid-fifteenth century. The 'Kirigaya' records are dated 1429–1443. This cherry was brought from Kamakura as explained by Yamada (1941, pp. 122–123), who suggested that it was this cultivar that was planted in the palace grounds. Another precise account of the grafting of a double-flowered cherry with red leaves and the donating of plants to several temples is given in an entry dated 1360 A.D. in the temple records of Horyu-ji (*Ikaruga-kagenki*) (Yamada 1941, pp. 125–126).

With new garden discoveries and an elite disposed to the gentle art of gardening, it is no surprise that cherries caught the attention of the literati even more. The bold deed of planting a cherry from the eastern provinces of Kamakura in Kyōto's palace grounds incited a veritable debate. This strengthened the image of the cherry as a symbol of expanding civilization, political power, or even of the country of Japan. A Buddhist priest of the Zen sect, Keisan Ōsen (1429–1493), proposed cherries as a symbol of Japan. Though Japan was hardly an established nation when compared with neighboring China, the priest felt confident enough to state (see Ōsen's original text in Satō 1935, pp. 352–355):

Our country is the country of *sakura*. However, most people speak simply of "the flowers" [*hana* in Japanese—W. K.] when they mean to say *sakura*. That our country is the *sakura* country has the same precious meaning as the peony has for Chinese Loyang, or the crab apple [*Malus halliana* Koehne—W. K.] for Sichuan in China.

Interestingly, this idea of the cherry as Japan's flower was repeated by Matsuoka (1758) with the same comparison to China.

Ōsen's account kept in the records of his monastery Shōkoku-ji in Kyōto (*Hekizan-nichi-roku*) even proves the existence of a cherry named 'Fugenzo' as early as 1459, for the horticulturist, this priest's detailed report is simply exciting:

> The best among the cherries is 'Fugendo' [*sic*]. People say that there is a temple hall in Kamakura where Saint Fugen is enshrined, but there is also a cherry in the compound and it is called therefore 'Fugendo' after the name of the hall, which is Fugendo [meaning Hall of Fugen—W. K.]. Others call this cherry 'Fugenzo', meaning 'Fugen's elephant', because the big and white flowers resemble the nose of the white elephant on which Fugen rides, moreover because the words for "flowers" and for "nose" in Japanese both have the same pronunciation [*hana* for both—W. K.]. Whatever of these two explanations is correct, this cherry is now found in western Kyōto, and it really is an excellent flowering cherry; it is called 'Fugenzo', but sometimes also 'Fugendo'.

Apart from the play of words we also have a statement here that 'Fugenzo' originates from Kamakura. The Oshima cherry parentage of both 'Kirigaya' and 'Fugenzo' is backed up by this kind of documented evidence.

Temples, especially the ones that were frequented by the ruling class, gained a standing that matched that of warlords' residences. The number of prestigious gardens in Kyōto increased, and from about the fifteenth century on gardening existed as a trade. Garden designers were from a lowly standing and often employed by rulers as a kind of spy to spot famous stones and plants. These would change hands through diplomatically forced donation or simple confiscation. A gardening manual of this ancient period was written by gardeners living in and around the Ninna-ji Temple, close to Arashiyama, along a road that led through the plain to the city. From the end of the seventeenth century cherries enter the written history of this area, and Ninna-ji is still famous for a plantation of classic garden forms including the green-flowered or cream-flowered cherries such as

Figure 10. Partying people under the cherries of Ninna-ji Temple, where 'Asagi', 'Gyoiko', and 'Ukon' originated. From Akisato Ritō (1780).

'Gyoiko'. One also may see unique cherries that only exist here and were never widely cultivated. The nearby nursery of the house of Sano has specialized in cherries since the beginning of the twentieth century.

Along a similar route connecting Arashiyama and the inner city of Kyōto lies the Hirano Shrine. This Shinto shrine keeps another set of typical Kyōto cherries. The recorded history of this collection also begins in the seventeenth century. Some forms in the Hirano Shrine are famous, but known here under different names. 'Shogetsu' is found as 'Nadeshiko' here, and a form that appears to be 'Kanzan' is called 'Okame', although this name is usually reserved for a hybrid of *Prunus incisa* and *P. campanulata*. Typical Kyōto garden cherries such as 'Imose' and 'Kinugasa' are found in the shrine's compound.

The region of Ninna-ji and the Hirano Shrine, between the Japanese mountain cherries at Arashiyama and the center of the city, must—with its gardeners passing by—have been an increasingly interesting cherry hybrid area since the fourteenth century when Oshima cherries were planted in the garden of a Kyōto palace.

Kyōto was the imperial and most powerful city up to the seventeenth century, remaining the most important region in garden cherry history during this time. With evolving political situations and a growing number of named cultivated forms, cherries became more and more a precious symbol of power, a plant that excited the desire of emperor, courtier, priest, and warrior alike. The cherry openly represented all the best aesthetic, poetic values, but kept hidden a political meaning that was to be interpreted in a more disastrous way in the future.

Cherries for Townspeople—From Shogun to Commoners

In the seventeenth century Japan became a unified state under a strictly organized class of warlord-politicians governed by a new dynasty of shoguns. Edo, east of Kamakura, became the new capital city; centuries later it would develop into modern Tokyo. This dynasty is referred to as the Edo period (1600–1868) because of the typical urban culture of Edo that dominates its history. Trade with foreign countries was strictly limited, and the country was closed from the outside world; only via Nagasaki, at least officially, could plants leave the country and surprise plant lovers at the rococo courts of Europe. Eleven Korean missions, each lasting more than a year, visited the shogun in the first half of the Edo period, and it is not unthinkable that they brought plants as gifts. For spiritual and cultural influences, however, the country was in self-chosen isolation.

Within this walled-in world a political system was set up aiming at stability. The power of temples had dwindled, and the emperor with his court was only supported by the new government as a spiritual leader who in turn supported the new government's worldly power. Each province was ruled by a feudal lord called a daimyo, who was a vassal of the shogun. Each daimyo had to maintain a state residence in the new capital, and thus the daimyos came to compete with increasingly luxurious estates. At the beginning of the nineteenth century more than a thousand such estates were found in Edo, all with spacious gardens. To maintain these, the number of gardeners and nurserymen increased enormously, as did the growing artistic quality of their work. The high standing of the horticultural craft of Edo has never before and never since been surpassed in Japan. The garden trade, professed by gardeners of name and fame, took profit from the donation of wild selections of cherries by nameless persons as well as the active breeding of new forms. By this time, the flowering cherry was generally known and much admired, in part because of the wealth of references in Japanese folklore. Many well-known historical figures were associated often with the ornamental cherry.

The unified state of the Edo period meant peace and prosperity in trade, as well as for the common citizen. Richer merchants or shop owners had space for a garden or for some plants in the courtyards of their shops. Townspeople of lesser standing often had a flowering tree at the back of their house. The German Engelbert Kaempfer (1651–1716) visited Japan in the service of the Dutch at the end of the seventeenth century and reported:

> If there be not room enough for a garden, they have at least an old ingrafted plum, cherry, or apricock tree. The older, the more crooked and monstrous this tree is, the greater value they put upon it . . . . to make it bear larger flowers, and in greater quantity, they commonly cut it to a few, perhaps two or three branches. It cannot be denied but that the great number of beautiful, incarnate, and double flowers, which they bear in the proper season, is a surprisingly curious orna-

ment to this back part of the house, but they have this disadvantage, that they bear no fruit (Kaempfer 1712, book 5, chapter 4, p. 425).

With this last remark Kaempfer was the first Westerner with the later often-repeated complaint about the lack of edible fruits on Japanese flowering cherries.

For the average commoner living in the cramped streets of Edo, a garden was a dream rather than something that had been seen from the inside. Nonetheless, nurseries and hawkers vending plants became part of the city scene, and in nooks and corners bonsai and other potted plants were cherished. A printing industry produced cheap books on plants and gardening, and these could be borrowed from traveling book-lenders as well. Without possessing a garden, the general public was informed on garden plants through books such as *Kadan-kōmoku* (Flower bed catalog) by Mizuno Motokatsu (1681). It contains a rare illustration and treats flowers, shrubs, and trees. It also lists forty flowering cherries with short descriptions, most still known today as names for cultivated cherries.

櫻 *Je, jo, O,* vulgò *Sákira.* Cerafus flore fimpli-ci, fructu auftero.

Jamma Sákira. Cerafus fylveftris flore pleno.

Ito Sákira. Cerafifera frutefcens, ab imo ramofa.

Niwa Sákira. Cerafus pumila, flore albo pleno.

Eadem, flore fimplici incarnato.

Ko fjoï Sákira. Cerafus arbor mediocris, flore incar-nato duplo, rofæ mediocris magnitudine.

Figure 11. A first report from the West on Japan's flowering cherries ("*Sákira*"). The botanic report reached Europeans in the early eighteenth century, but the author's Latin was too concise and the beauty of Japanese flowering cherries was left beyond the reader's imagination. From Kaempfer (1712, book 5, p. 799).

At the end of the seventeenth century a second popular catalog on garden plants appeared titled *Kadan-jikin-shō* (Flower bed embroideries) but sometimes read as *Kadan-chikin-shō*. Written by Ihee Itō (1656–1739), the third generation of the Itō nursery family, this booklet appeared in 1695 and it functioned as a first sales catalog, advertising also for the other nurseries in Itō's village of Somei, just outside Edo. In the nineteenth century the gar-

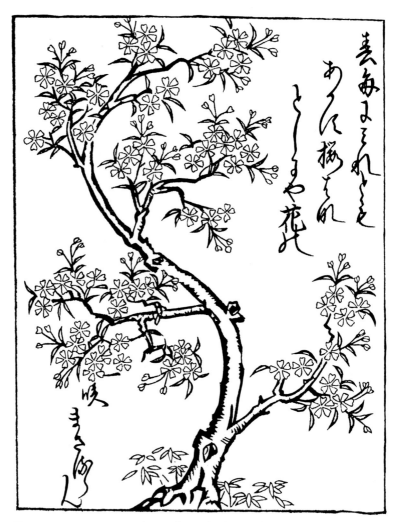

Figure 12. A mountain cherry from the horticultural treatise *Kadan-kōmoku* (Flower bed catalog). From Mizuno (1681).

deners of Somei would introduce the hybrid *Prunus×yedoensis,* known in Japan as the "Yoshino cherry from Somei," or 'Somei-yoshino', and the Takagi nursery, also in Somei, came to play an important role in cherry history.

Like the earlier book by Mizuno (1681), Ito's book gives short descriptions, including one for each of forty-four cherries, but has no illustrations. Cherry descriptions in both these seventeenth-century horticulture books are too short to be decisive about the identity of the cherries described. Some cherries, however, have such distinctive characteristics that, no matter how brief the description, if it is supplemented with a continuous string of records, we may assume that we are dealing with the same cultivar. 'Fugenzo' is a clear example of such a well-documented garden form.

The city of Edo expanded fast and uncontrolled, and soon was with its one million inhabitants larger than London or Paris. Men and women came from the countryside in search of a better life and a job, but many settlers ended up in shabby quarters along the banks of the city's rivers where no taxes were levied. Here the poor and unemployed gathered, and some riverside quarters became famous as districts of prostitution, gambling, and certain liberal forms of theater.

To the shogun's government, the riverside communities were eyesores that needed a policy to control their growth. One of the solutions was mass cherry planting, which was explained with the slogan that cherries purified the river water. The idea was begun by the shogun Yoshimune Tokugawa (in power 1716–1745), who had an enlightened concern for the welfare of the state and the well being of its citizens. He showed a keen interest in the ways of the ordinary people and sponsored sports and the training of martial arts. He supported various scientific experiments, including some with medicinal herbs, and the cropping of Korean ginseng roots, sweet potatoes, and sugar cane. In these years cherries were planted along the Tamagawa River at Koganei and along the Sumida River after the embankments had been improved. Plants used in this operation were so-called Yoshino cherries that were propagated from seeds of the Japanese mountain cherry (*Prunus serrulata* var. *spontanea*) originally collected on the mountains of Yoshino and at another famous cherry site, Sakuragawa, in modern Ibaraki Prefecture. The enormous Japanese mountain cherries that were described and photographed at Koganei at the beginning of the twentieth century by cherry researchers such as Manabu Miyoshi and Collingwood Ingram might well have been remnants of this eighteenth-century planting operation.

Figure 13. Clients gathering in a nursery in the village of Somei. Potted plants for sale are on the racks. National Museum of Ethnology, Leiden, Netherlands, from *Ehon Edo Zakura,* 1803.

Figure 14. A few very old trees of 'Somei-yoshino' (*Prunus ×yedoensis*) with typical heavy side limbs low on the stem can be found in the Somei cemetery, once the site of the gardens of the Somei nurseries in old Edo. Photo by author, 28 April 97, Tokyo.

The citizens of Edo, from landless commoners to rich merchants, knew the imperial history of Yoshino's cherries, and the planting of these cherries confirmed for them the ruling of the shogun. A tourist guidebook to the old province, *Yamato-meguri-ki* (by Ekken Kaibara, 1709), not only discusses herbs, animal life, and minerals, but also the cherries of the Yoshino mountains in the old Yamato region. It tells how the village children at the wayside sold cherry saplings to tourists and pilgrims. This continuous planting must have greatly supported the upkeep of the wood. Ekken's book is full of melancholy of imperial glory forlorn when it comes to the emperor's forced exile to Yoshino in 1336. Ekken's readers, most of whom had never left Edo, would have felt the melancholic memory of glorious periods before the shogun came to power with his daimyos.

Figure 15. Urbane ladies attended by servants on their way to a cherry picnic; Japanese mountain cherries in the background. Painting by Katsushika Hokusai. National Museum of Ethnology, Leiden, Netherlands.

Mass planting of cherries as at Sumida gave an opportunity for the simple joy of a free party under the cherries in the shogun-sponsored picnic site. "Viewing the flowers" (*hanami*) became a popular spring outing for anyone from beggar to emperor. Such picnics became the theme of illustrative paintings and woodblock prints, and these show us that the classic combination of wine and women accompanied the longing for spring in a gentle outdoors.

Not only the new cherry-picnic sites, but even the historical places for imperial outings—Arashiyama and in time Yoshino—became popular party spots where there was ample room for letting loose the emotions and passions that were restricted in urban society with its demands. Cherries in blossom became loosely associated with the loosening of the shackles of convention, and they became a symbol for women. The word *hana* (flower), understood as cherry blossom, gained an attached meaning of women or, more accurately, expressed the playful side of womanhood. Districts with brothels such as Yoshiwara in Edo were often planted with flowering cherries.

Early Cherry Collectors

A man of letters, Kassho Naba (1595–1648) was the first to write a text exclusively on cherries. He was not interested in Japan alone, but was one of a small group of intellectuals who studied Chinese classics and kept a lively diplomatic correspondence with Korean government officials. Unlike the popular horticultural books of the time, which included lists of cherries more as a registration of existing forms, Naba's *Ōfu* (Cherry list) of 1707 was not meant for publication, nor did it intend to present cherries as merchandise; rather it was a private statement of an intellectual who knew his classics, including classic cherries. It sets a pattern of appreciating cherries followed by daimyo garden lovers that would continue to appeal to the cultured elite over the centuries to come, well past the Second World War.

Naba's list is interesting because it presents a picture of the cherry in 1707 that is not biased by commerce or nationalism. It gives names and short descriptions of cherries that formed the starting point of the explosive wealth of garden forms that appeared in the following centuries. The cherries of Kassho Naba include 'Fugenzo', 'Higan-zakura', 'Ise-zakura', 'Ito-zakura', 'Kirigaya', 'Kumagai-zakura', 'Mazakura', 'Niwa-zakura', 'Shio-

花見の圖

Figure 16. Townspeople on their way to, or already partying under, the flowering cherries at Asukayama, just outside the city of Tokyo, not far from Somei. From the magazine *Shinsen Tōkyō saijiki* of *Fūzoku gahō* 157 (1898).

gama', 'Taizan-fukun', 'Temari-zakura', 'Tora-no-o', 'Uba-zakura', 'Yama-zakura', and 'Yokihi'. Most of these, such as 'Fugenzo', 'Taizan-fukun', or 'Yama-zakura' (synonym *P. serrulata* var. *spontanea*), are of a clear botanic identity. 'Higan-zakura' must be *P. ×subhirtella,* 'Ito-zakura' is *P. pendula,* and 'Uba-zakura' is an old name for *P. pendula* f. *ascendens.* These are from more remote mountainous areas and were in cultivation at the time Naba listed them. 'Kumagai-zakura' is probably the double form of *P. incisa* var. *kinkiensis* that is still in cultivation. 'Niwa-zakura' denotes a group of Chinese *P. glandulosa* forms: double, single, white, and pink ones were found. It makes a shrub of about 1.5 m tall rather than a tree. Naba stated explicitly: "Niwa-zakura is not a type of sakura." It should not be understood as a flowering cherry.

Chinese influence on later Japanese garden cherries can be supposed because of Naba's mention of 'Mazakura'. This hybrid form has as one of its parents the Chinese *P. pseudo-cerasus*. The triploid 'Mazakura' is not a beauty, but it produces aerial roots and is easily propagated from cuttings. Therefore it has always been used as stock for grafting rather than as an ornamental. As a tree from which cuttings were taken, it would have stood in the corner of many nurseries, but it was never for sale and it is not mentioned in the catalogs of the Somei nursery owners. The Chinese genes in 'Mazakura' are found in 'Taizan-fukun', which also has *P. pseudo-cerasus* as one of its parents. 'Taizan-fukun' is rather easily propagated from rootstock and is more a garden lover's plant than a nursery product. It is not found in the Somei catalogs.

The list of Kassho Naba shows a collection of cherries from almost all over Japan as well as with influence from the continent. The collection must be valued as a rich genetic mixture, with the capacity to produce a large and varied number of cherry forms. And indeed, that is what happened in the centuries that followed.

Going beyond a simple listing is the systematic treatise by Joan Matsuoka (1669–1747). His pen name was Igansai, and his book on cherries, dated 1758, is better known as *Igansai-ōhin* (Igansai's cherries). More than 60 cultivars are described in this illustrated work, which became a standard for later books on the subject. Scientific curiosity speaks from a discussion of the botanic details of a cherry flower. Indeed, Matsuoka was not an amateur, but one of the first professional plant specialists sponsored by the daimyo. Some among these herbalists developed a special interest for cherries, such as this Matsuoka. In time also veritable cherry connoisseurs appeared among the daimyo sponsors.

An above-average taste for gardening was found in such daimyo politicians as Seihō Ichihashi and Sadanobu Matsudaira, whose gardens were renowned for their botanic collections. The latter, nicknamed the Old Epicurean of Shirakawa, owned a string of country estates and the botanical garden Yokuon-en in the Tsukiji quarter of Edo, which he had planted with many rare specimens. In this collection were numerous cultivars of ornamental plum trees and many "strange trees brought in by ship," which were probably exotic plants from China, Korea, and perhaps Russia or even Holland, the only European country that was allowed to trade with Japan.

No fewer than 224 garden forms of flowering cherries are listed in a

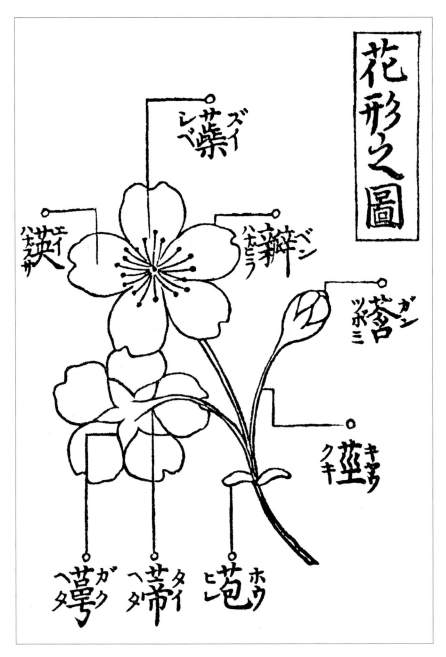

Figure 17. Cherry botany of the eighteenth century; bracts, calyx, and sepals are distinguished but no difference is yet made between pistils and stamens. From an 1891 reprint of Matsuoka (1758).

record of this garden, most of which are pictured in an illustrated catalog, *Hana-no-kagami* (A paragon of flowers) of 1822. This work does not include descriptions of the trees, but shows nicely how the flowering cherry was viewed by the connoisseurs of the time. First, they needed many cherry forms; thus the scroll shows many cherries that would be clones rather than different cultivars. Further, names were rich and suggestive,

Figure 18. A cultured lady hangs a poem she has written on the branches of a weeping cherry; the words for *flowering cherry* and *love* can be distinguished. A live cherry twig decorates her hair, and the pattern on her kimono is a five-petaled cherry flower. Peony flowers form the motif of her gorgeous sash. From a commercial poster, early twentieth century, Miki Shōten.

Figure 19. Cherry painter Katen Mikuma (1730–1794) lived in Kyōto, between Arashiyama and Ninna-ji, two areas noted for their peculiar cherries. From *Zoku kinsei kijinden* of 1798.

inviting poetic speculation or philosophic discourse. It was a custom of the day to hang pieces of paper on flowering branches on which one had written a poem or some appropriate words. There was no botanic interest nor thought about the responsibility for the conservation of a living collection. Cherries were freely used for an elegant garden pastime of the nobility.

Respectable cherry connoisseurs sponsored artists who specialized in flowering cherries. Among them were Katen Mikuma and his sister, Rokō Mikuma, who wrote and illustrated books about flowering cherries in the early nineteenth century. Their contemporary, Kōsetsu Sakamoto (ca. 1800–1854), painted flowering cherries for a foreign gentleman plant-lover, Philipp Franz Balthasar von Siebold (1796–1866). These painters

Figure 20. 'Asagi' and 'Fugenzo', a page from the illustrated album *Bai-ō-rui hana shashin* (True presentation of flowers of plums and cherries) by Kōsetsu Sakamoto. The album was brought to Europe by Philipp von Siebold. National Museum of Ethnology, Leiden, Netherlands.

worked for a gentleman's hobby and not to satisfy a modern scientific curiosity. Their paintings are usually not very helpful in tracing the identity of historical garden forms.

The appreciation of flowering cherries in Japan reached its peak in the first half of the nineteenth century. The enormous popularity these trees enjoyed during this period has never been equaled since.

The Nation's Flower

Japan had been closed to foreigners since the early seventeenth century. When American ships appeared in Japanese waters in 1853 demanding free access to the ports, the secluded, somewhat romantic world of the Edo period had to face reality. The shogun with his old feudal government could not meet the pending modernization of the country. A young emperor of the old lineage was installed by progressive imperialists as their new leader in 1868, Edo became known as the "East-Capital," Tō-kyō, and the country entered a period of cultural turmoil.

For the cherry this meant at first a change for the worse. Many cherry trees and garden cultivars were lost in the upheavals that followed. In time, however, the cherry was again pushed forward as the one and only symbol of the nation. This time it was viewed as an optimistic symbol for a nation that was quickly modernizing after European models. Health care and medicine were modeled after the Germans and motorized transportation was influenced by the English. England had its rose and France its lily, while Japan's flower was the cherry.

The cultural confusion of the time was well expressed with the exact opposite emotion. For some the cherry was seen as a symbol of the old feudal society, and thus, in an iconoclast drive, cherries were destroyed and burnt with Buddhist images and temples. Newspapers reported frequently on the cutting down of cherries at places that once were famous and popular for their trees. A majestic weeping cherry at Maruyama in Kyōto was to be sold at an auction as carpentry wood for woodblock stamps. A physician and intellectual leader named Hakutaka Akashi bought the live tree for five *ryo* so he could preserve it. Five *ryo* was the equivalent of 150 kilos of rice, a much more precious commodity than at present, showing not only the value of cherry wood but also the determined affection of men such as this Akashi for cherries. He was a close friend of Anthonius Bauduin (1822–

1885), a Dutchman who actively promoted the redevelopment of the Ueno area in Tokyo as a public park.

Ueno played a crucial role in the new, brighter meaning that the cherry gained. In a superstitious belief, the Ueno area was of utmost importance for the city of Edo. The site was northeast of the shogun's palace, in the exact location from which it was believed that evil spirits could influence the well-being of the country's ruler and therefore the people ruled. To control the problem, the shogun's family temple was built on this site in the early seventeenth century. The temple was named after the Eizan-ji Temple in the old imperial capital Kyōto. The Eizan-ji Temple also stood in the same northeast direction and had successfully guarded Kyōto since its earliest history. A pond close to Ueno's Eizan-ji Temple was even compared to the vast Lake Biwa that stretches behind Kyōto's Eizan-ji Temple. In the late 1620s cherries had been brought from Nara's imperial cherry wood at Yoshino to embellish the pond and temple grounds and to reinforce the meaning of Edo as capital city. Now that the old feudal state was done away with, however, such superstitions could no longer be tolerated, although it did not seem right to build anything else on the land. The Ueno area was used a few times for trade fairs and eventually was opened as one of Japan's first public parks. New cherries had been added starting in 1876; planting material came from Edo nurseries.

In a park survey of 1884 an unknown, pink-flowered cherry form named "Yoshino" showed up. It probably originated from a cherry nursery called Ōkō-en in the village Somei and was sold by the nurseries of the Itō house since the 1860s. It was traded as "Yoshino" also in export nursery catalogs. This caused confusion with mountain cherries from the region Yoshino, and so it was renamed 'Somei-yoshino' in 1900. A year later it was described under *Prunus* ×*yedoensis* by the botanist Jinzō Matsumura (1856–1928). This cherry proved to be easily propagated and quickly became a commercial success. A 1916 report indicates that fifty thousand trees of 'Somei-yoshino' had been planted in Tokyo alone. Because it flowered before the foliage appeared, the effect of a full-grown tree was spectacular, showing bare clouds of flowers. More trees of 'Somei-yoshino' were planted in Ueno. The mass effect of a pink ceiling in the park amazed the crowds invited to an already exciting and novel institution: a public park.

Ueno's cherries soon gained national fame, not in the least because the flowers quickly shed their petals, which psychologically increased the magic of the full bloom. It triggered an effort among local government officials throughout the country to achieve the same effect in their province or town. Cherries were planted at every new public building. City halls, town halls, and village halls, schools, and later the national railway stations, often built in modern, European architectural styles, brought the new state in a tangible form to the otherwise unchanged countryside. At these buildings large numbers of the cherry *Prunus×yedoensis* were planted. As a symbol of progress and optimism, *P.×yedoensis* thus became the nation's flower par excellence.

Rare Garden Cherries Brought to Light

With the fall of the shogun and his feudal government, the daimyo politicians lost their social standing and often their estates. Throughout the country and in Edo as well, their spacious gardens were used as tea or mulberry plantations, or public parks. Other gardens were destroyed to become the well-located construction site for public buildings.

With the loss of its sponsors, horticulture could not be maintained at the incredibly high level it once was, and hundreds of cultivated cherries were in danger of becoming extinct. In Osaka many rare garden cherries were saved and planted along the Yodo River on the grounds of the new National Mint. This site has been opened to the public at every flowering season since 1883. It still is a major cherry attraction of the region, and some rare trees can be seen.

In Tokyo a father and son from the Takagi nursery, located in the Somei District, took steps to conserve many cherries. The third in line, grandson Magoemon Takagi, inherited and actively enlarged the family's collection. In about 1880 this collection drew the attention of Kengo Shimizu (1840–1907), mayor of the little town of Kōhoku in the outskirts of Tokyo. The cherry 'Shimidsu-zakura' is named after the mayor because he wisely planted an embankment along the town's river with cherries, and just as wisely turned away from the ever-present *Prunus×yedoensis*. Instead he approached the Takagi nursery and ordered a complete set of the collection's trees. In early spring of 1886 about eight kilometers along the Arakawa River were planted with a double line of cherries, about three thousand trees of seventy-eight cultivars. By the early twentieth century the trees had grown so big as to attract large crowds of tourists and day-trippers. The vis-

Figure 21. Cherries at the Yodo River in Osaka. The smoking chimneys of the National Mint, now famous for its *Prunus serrulata* cultivar collection, can be seen on the opposite bank. Woodblock print sold as a souvenir in the late nineteenth century.

itors enjoyed a blossom season that lasted many weeks longer than seasons elsewhere, including the more recently developed cherry sites that relied on *Prunus ×yedoensis* and the older picnic sites that had short-lived flowers of a mountain cherry.

The historical importance of the Arakawa planting is much greater than it seems to our modern mind. Japan's society was in a process of modernization, but the old feudal way of thinking was still in everybody's mind. That a nursery had stock of old plants once grown for a daimyo did not involve that these trees could be sold or given away. A profoundly felt reverence towards anything from daimyo standing prohibited any other action than an anxious conserving. The enlightened vision and persuasive powers of Shimizu brought these treasured and unique cherries to the outside world. Most of the Arakawa cultivars had never existed in more than one specimen in a daimyo's garden and two additional specimens in the back of its nursery to replace it. Valuable cherries such as 'Ama-no-gawa', 'Fukurokuju', or 'Jo-nioi' show up here in history for the first time. If these would not have been planted at Arakawa, they would have been forgotten in a nursery as rare trees not to be traded.

Of the hundreds of jealously kept daimyo cherries, a clearly defined selection of seventy-eight useful forms was thus brought to light and attracted public attention. Among the cherries found at Arakawa in the 1890s were large numbers of 'Asagi', 'Edo-zakura', 'Fugenzo', 'Gyoiko', 'Hoki-zakura', 'Ichiyo', 'Kanzan', 'Yokihi', and other easy-to-propagate cultivars. Fragrant cherries were planted such as 'Goza-no-ma-nioi', 'Hosokawa-nioi', 'Jo-nioi', 'Mikuruma-gaeshi', 'Senriko', 'Surugadai-nioi', and 'Taki-nioi'. Other cherries included 'Ama-no-gawa', 'Arashiyama', 'Ariake', 'Botan-zakura', 'Choshu-hizakura', 'Fukurokuju', 'Hata-zakura', 'Ito-kukuri', 'Kirin', 'Shiro-fugen' (probably at that time understood as something other than 'Fugenzo'), 'Shirotae', 'Shogetsu', 'Shujaku', 'Taizan-fukun', 'Uzu-zakura', 'Washi-no-o', and 'Yae-akebono'. (For a complete list of the seventy-eight garden varieties at Arakawa, see Flower Association of Japan 1982, p. 92.)

Seisaku Funatsu (1858–1929), the mayor's disciple in Confucianism, poetry, and letters, became the ultimate expert on Arakawa's garden cherries. Funatsu's love of cherries was motivated by a typical Far-Eastern piety for his master Shimizu. After the collection came to public attention, it was visited by an American plant explorer, Ernest H. Wilson. Photos of Arakawa can be seen in Wilson's *The Cherries of Japan* (1916). Before turning to Wilson, however, we will discuss the earlier acquaintance of Westerners with Japanese flowering cherries.

Japan's Cherries to the West

There is a difference between introducing a Japanese cherry to America or Europe and exporting and importing large numbers of trees for the trade. Most fascinating in garden history is the large public interest in cherries at the start of the twentieth century. In this section we will also discuss the earliest flowering cherries to arrive in the West in the latter half of the nineteenth century. These pioneers give some clues in understanding garden cherries such as 'Takasago'.

Figure 22. Seisaku Funatsu (1858–1929) was a Confucianist scholar and garden cherry expert. From Sakura No Kwai (1918–1921).

A substantial report on Japanese flowering cherries was given by Philipp von Siebold in his younger years. When he lived in Japan in the 1820s the cherry was a widely popular garden plant, close to the peak of its popularity. Von Siebold described the Japanese mountain cherry as *Prunus jamasakura,* a name still used in Japan. Referring to double-flowered cherries as "temple cherries," he named them *P. donarium,* because they had been donated to the temples where he saw most of the garden forms. It was unthinkable then that a foreigner would visit the cherry collection of a daimyo. Taking a horticultural use as the starting point for naming a plant is not done in botanic sciences and Von Siebold's cherry names were never completely accepted. In Von Siebold's first shipment of Japanese plants to reach Europe, there were no cherries. Many plants had died en route, and shipping techniques had to be improved. Learning from French plant hunters such as Louis Antoine de Bougainville, Englishman Nathaniel Ward developed a transportable glass house about 1830 for shipping plants overseas. From that time on, transport of tender plants over longer distances became more successful.

A double-flowered pink cherry was received and described by Frenchman A. Jacques in the autumn of 1832, but it did not create a great sensation. A weeping cherry in the 1846 and 1847 catalogs of Ellwanger and Barry Company in Rochester, New York, also went unnoticed by the gardening public. Years later, in 1862, Parsons and Company in Flushing on Long Island, New York, reported that "fifteen new double flowering cherries, one of them described . . . to be as large as a rose" were brought from Japan (quoted in Jefferson and Fusoni 1977, p. 3). Robert Fortune, a Scottish botanist, traveled in Japan from 1860 to 1862 and imported a "double Japanese cherry" in 1864, which later proved to be the successful garden cherry 'Takasago', also known as "Von Siebold's Cherry" or *Cerasus sieboldii* in these years.

Cherries needed more time to be understood in the West. For one thing, once imported, they seemed to have no suitable rootstock and thus propagation was a problem. For another thing, apparently healthy trees could suddenly wither away, without any clear fungus or insect damage. The opinion of gardeners whose experiences with cherries were limited was that even healthy trees were greedily attacked by caterpillars and only flowered for a short period. Another factor was that Japanese nurseries were not interested in exporting; getting plants out of the country involved a lot of trouble (see the letters sent by Russian botanist Carl Johann Maximowicz from Japan to *Gartenflora,* published in this magazine in 1863).

The biggest problem facing cherries during this period was that it was not fashionable to plant them. Landscape design was for the large estate. The designers of the mid-nineteenth-century gardens, often great dendrologists, dreamed of evergreen trees and of the geometric flower bed. Ivy and laurel were not considered boring plants, but gave a touch of life to the winter garden, whereas the rest of nature was still bare and dead. Flowers might be a designer's concern, but flowering trees formed only part of mixed coppices that made up the design of the scenic landscape styles. In the best case, cherries were a kind of undergrowth. It was unthinkable to plant a solitary flowering cherry. Moreover the complaint that flowering cherries did not produce edible fruits was heard everywhere. Westerners living in Japan had to import their cherry fruits from Australia, and the Germans referred to flowering cherries as *Falschkirschen* (false cherries). Even the scientific names of the early flowering cherries discriminated against them. In Latin they were called "pseudo-cerasus," a supposed but not a real cherry. Complaints on the discordantly barbaric Japanese names of garden forms accompany the rare article that appears on this poorly understood plant from a poorly understood, strange country far away.

Following the Industrial Revolution and the growing class of well-to-do citizens, gardening became a more common pastime in the last quarter of the century. Horticulture was a respectable science with international ambitions by that time, crossing borders and connecting continents. There was a lively production of magazines and journals and, helped by some singular imports, flowering cherries entered French and Belgian magazines to delight the reader in the 1870s. The *Revue Horticole,* for example, introduced three cherries by Carrière: *Prunus sieboldii* (synonym 'Takasago') in 1866 (37: 371), *Cerasus lannesiana* in 1872 (p. 198; 1873, p. 351, with illustration), and an article and lithograph of *Cerasus serratifolia* Lindley (synonym *Prunus serrulata* 'Alboplena') and its form *rosea* (synonym 'Ichi-hara-tora-no-o'; sold as *Cerasus sieboldii rubra* ca. 1869) in 1877 (pp. 389–390). *Flore des Serres* presented *Cerasus caproniana flore roseo pleno* (synonym 'Fukurokuju'?) by Louis Van Houtte in 1875 (21: 141, Taf. 2238). This same plant, "of unknown origin but available at Van Houtte's," was shown with less purplish flowers that same year in *Revue*

Figure 23. A *Prunus serrulata* cultivar named "*Cerasus caproniana flore roseo pleno*" (called *Cerasus Juliana floribus roseis* in *Revue Horticole* and probably the cultivar 'Fukurokuju') was offered by Louis van Houtte in Belgium in 1875. From *Flore des Serres* (1875), Wageningen University Library Special Collections.

Horticole (p. 390) as *Cerasus Juliana floribus roseis* and described by Carrière in the article *Cerasus Juliana Flore Pleno,* attracting the attention of *Gartenflora* as well. In 1876 *The Garden* (2: 486) introduced *Cerasus Juliana Hort. floribus roseis.* The same 'Fukurokuju'-like plant as in the French magazines was once more shown as *Cerasus pseudo-cerasus* Lindley in a beautiful engraving in Lavallée's *Icones* (1880–1885), and Philipp Franz von Siebold's nursery could show a flowering *Cerasus pseudocerasus odorata* var. *Reine de Paijs-Bas* at the international horticultural exhibition held in Amsterdam in 1877.

Botanists and specialist-horticulturists had discovered and acknowledged the qualities of the flowering cherry. The Western public at large was about to discover the exotic culture of Japan. Artistic circles in Paris found inspiration in a romantically exotic image of Japan as it was presented by Aimé Humbert in his extremely well illustrated travel report *Le Japon Illustré* (1870). Emile Guimet repeated the effort in his beautifully designed volumes *Promenades Japonaises* (1878, 1880). The art-loving public in the French capital started collecting Japanese woodblock prints that inspired the impressionist painters. The cherry was often present as a decorative motif in posters or other graphic illustrations.

The press showed a growing interest in reports on Japan, the land of *geisha* and *Fujiyama,* the consistent misspelling for *Fuji-san* (Mount Fuji), the volcano with an incredibly regular and splendid cone that became the foremost symbol of the Land of the Rising Sun. In the United States the journalist Lafcadio Hearn (1859–1904) introduced Japan to a large public by interpreting its enigmas in a way that had literary qualities. Hearn, who lived the latter part of his life in Japan, wrote of the first day of his arrival in April 1890. His first book, *Glimpses of Unfamiliar Japan* (1894), described it thus:

> And I see before me what is infinitely more interesting—a grove of cherry trees covered with something unutterably beautiful—a dazzling mist of snowy blossoms clinging like summer cloud-fleece about every branch and twig; and the ground beneath them, and the path before me, is white with the soft, thick, odorous snow of fallen petals. . . . Why should the trees be so lovely in Japan? With us, a plum or cherry tree in flower is not an astonishing sight; but here it is a miracle of beauty so bewildering that, however much

you may have previously read about it, the real spectacle strikes you dumb. You see no leaves—only one great filmy mist of petals. Is it that the trees have been so long domesticated and caressed by man in this land of the gods, that they have acquired souls, and strive to show their gratitude, like women loved, by making themselves more beautiful for man's sake? Assuredly they have mastered men's hearts by their loveliness, like beautiful slaves. That is to say, Japanese hearts. Apparently there have been some foreign tourists of the brutal class in this place, since it has been deemed necessary to set up inscriptions in English announcing that it is forbidden to injure the trees.

Cherries are a part of the dreamy world of Japan as seen through the eyes of Hearn. His bewildering cherry beauty is explained by *Prunus ×yedoensis,* which flowers before the leaves appear.

Hearn's influence on the image of Japan that was forming in the minds of Westerners was enormous. His intimate-romantic Japan is clearly recognizable in Puccini's *Madame Butterfly* or in other writers on Japan such as Eliza Skidmore (1856–1928), who would play a role in the cherry planting at Potomac Park in Washington, D.C. Hearn's prose speaks also through *The Flowers and Gardens of Japan* by Florence du Cane (1908). Du Cane quotes Ralph Adams Cram on the cherries of the Ueno park:

> Here the cherry trees are huge and immemorial, gnarled and rugged, but clutching sunrise clouds caught by the covetous hands of black branches, and held dancing and fluttering against the misty blue of the sky. Here and there a weeping cherry holds down its prize of pink vapour, until it almost brushes the heads of those who pass; here and there the background of bronze cryptomeria is flecked with puffs of pink, as though now and then the captive clouds had burst from the holding of crabbed branches only to be caught in their escape toward the upper air and prisoned by the tenacious fingers of the cedar.

Indeed, the praises of the typical reporter in BBC's *Gardener's World* for the program's mouthwatering plants fall far short of the prose of this author of the early twentieth century:

At the end of the road the path blurs in odorous mist, and in a moment we are enveloped in the rosy clouds. As far as the eye can reach stretches the low-hung canopy of the thin petals; the trunks of the trees are small and gray, and one forgets them, or never thinks to associate them with the mist of pale vapour overhead, hung in the soft air, impalpable, evanescent, a gauzy cloud, lifted at dawn and poised breathless close over the earth.

A little wind ripples above, and the air trembles with a snow of pink petals swerving and sliding down to the carpet of thin fallen blossoms, while darting children in scarlet and saffron and lavender crow and chatter, catching at the rosy flakes with brown fingers.

The light here is pale and pearly as it filters through the sky of opal blossoms, and it transmutes the small dusky people into the semblance of butterflies and birds, now gathering into glimmering swarms of flickering color, now darting off with shrieks of delight over the carpet of fallen petals.

Such was the Western public's image of Japanese cherries in the early twentieth century. The days of the "false cherry" were long gone, its lack of edible fruits was no point of discussion, and it was bad taste to even only hint at it.

The situation in Japan also had changed completely. With the waves of modernization, Western commodities had swept the country in an explosive growth of imports. In an attempt to balance the trade deficit, the Japanese government had actively begun setting up markets for exporting things Japanese. A system of trade fairs and shows, quality examinations, and charters was set up, and extra-territorial trade zones were opened in port cities such as Yokohama and Kobe where foreigners were allowed to set up trade agencies, banks, and finance and insurance companies.

An important role in the opening of Japan's botanical world was played by Louis Böhmer, who made an expedition through the country commissioned by the Japanese government in 1874. A few years later he set up a nursery for exporting Japanese plants in the free trade zone of Yokohama. Böhmer's price list of 1894 announces that "the Japanese cherries, plums, and peach flowers are a sight in this country." It offers *"Prunus cerasus* double jap[anese] (cherry)" for the wholesale trade at ten dollars per hundred saplings or sixty for a thousand to be grown in open ground. Being the only Western wholesale exporter, Böhmer doubled his prices within five years.

Japanese-owned nurseries widened their horizon as well. The Yokohama Nursery Company supported an expansionist policy, opening branches in 1890 in San Francisco, and soon after that in Chicago, New York, and finally London in 1907. It printed quotations from letters of satisfied Western clients on the first page of its catalog. Playing on the fashionable *Japonaiserie* craze, all catalogs of the period were extremely fine specimens of the art of printing and paper making. Lithographs, photos, copper engravings, covers printed with gold or made from the finest Japanese paper, bindings with colored silk floss—no design technique or material was left unused. Böhmer's catalogs were designed by the famous bookmaker–art-printer Takejirō Hasegawa.

At this point it is interesting to see what kinds of cherries were leaving Japan. The French nursery of Letellier fils in Caen received around 1895

Figure 24. Japanese nursery catalogs for Western gardeners in fashionable *Japonaiserie* book design.

a shipment of twenty-two cherry cultivars. One, *Cerasus Sieboldi flore albo pleno,* apparently was a double white cherry. Another, *Cerasus flore luteo virescenti pleno,* must have been 'Ukon'. Also received were weeping cherries named *pendula flore roseo pleno.* The Takagi nursery, which had conserved the increasingly famous cherry collection that went to Arakawa, was also actively exporting by now. In 1899 it offered the following cherries: 'Asahiyama', a low form used for making bonsai trees; 'Choshu-hizakura'; a light green cultivar, most likely 'Ukon'; 'Edo-zakura'; 'Fugenzo'; 'Ichiyo'; a fragrant cherry likely to have been 'Jo-nioi'; 'Ko-fugen' (later named 'Daikoku'); 'Mikuruma-gaeshi', a nameless slow growing, double dark pink form; *Prunus pendula* f. *ascendens;* and finally *P.* ×*yedoensis.* Takagi was able to offer splendid trees of at least eighty garden cherries from his preservation collection. Most of the selections that he offers are still commercially interesting, proving that he was a keen nurseryman indeed.

In spite of all these achievements, flowering cherries remained something remote from the general public. It would be left to the lovers of Japan or specialists in horticulture to import cherries. This was to change soon though, at least in the United States.

Cherry Diplomacy

American garden lovers were given a first-hand look at the art of Japanese gardening at the 1904 World's Fair in St. Louis, Missouri, where Japan exhibited an extensive garden in the native style. Two years later a historically important shipment of a hundred cherries, dispatched by the Yokohama Nursery Company, reached the United States. The order was made by David Fairchild (1869–1954), an administrator with the U.S. Department of Agriculture in Washington, D.C. The imported trees were successfully planted on the spacious grounds of his private estate.

Encouraged by this undertaking, Fairchild and his wife, Marian, decided to organize a planting of cherries on Arbor Day. Again cherries were ordered from the Yokohama Nursery Company. The trees were shipped to Seattle on the West Coast and then traveled by rail across the United States without any problem. On Arbor Day in March 1908, each public school in Washington, D.C., received its Japanese cherry. Trees were planted in the school yards, which attracted the attention of Mrs. William Taft, wife of the U.S. president.

The First Lady had visited Japan with her husband, who had success-fully concluded an important treaty with Japan in 1905. She developed an appreciation for the beauty of flowering cherries and began to include the idea for a mass planting of Japanese cherries in her plans for developing Potomac Park. Mrs. Taft was supported in this endeavor by Fairchild and Eliza Skidmore, a journalist who wrote about Japan. In April 1909 ninety trees of 'Fugenzo' were purchased from an American nursery. Then, in the summer of that year, it became clear that the city of Tokyo wanted to do-nate two thousand cherries for the Potomac Park. It is striking how eagerly Japanese officials reacted. In November of the same year Tokyo shipped two thousand large trees of ten varieties to Washington. That a gift of the country's flower with such a profound emotional meaning could be made to a great Western power was without doubt enthusiastically welcomed by any Japanese cooperating in the donation.

In the meantime in the United States, the increasing import of plant material had aroused a growing concern, and the U.S. Department of Agri-culture began inspecting imported plants for insect pests and diseases. The shipment from Tokyo proved to be severely infested. With great diploma-tic sensitivity, the Japanese side was informed that no other measures could be taken than to burn the trees. It was a matter of regret for both parties.

In Tokyo a second shipment of trees was prepared. Funatsu helped select new planting material from the banks of Arakawa. Trees were grafted and trained by the Agricultural Experiment Station of the Japanese Ministry of Agriculture. Thoroughly fumigated with hydrocyanic acid gas, the ship-ment of six thousand young trees arrived in Seattle in January 1912 and passed severe inspections without any problem. Three thousand trees were meant as a donation for New York, the other half of the shipment went to Washington, D.C. In Potomac Park, thousands of specimens of *Prunus×ye-doensis* were planted along the Tidal Basin, and eventually this plant became known as the "Potomac cherry." (For a history of the Potomac cherries, see Jefferson and Fusoni 1977.) On the peninsula farther south, two thousand fragrant and double cherries of the following varieties were planted: 'Ariake', 'Fugenzo', 'Fukurokuju', the green 'Gyoiko', 'Ichiyo', 'Jo-nioi', 'Kanzan', 'Mikuruma-gaeshi', 'Shirayuki', 'Surugadai-nioi', and 'Taki-nioi'.

In the United States a general appreciation of Japanese flowering cherries developed from a friendship between the countries that was profoundly felt in the early twentieth century. Of all the countries in the world, only the

Figure 25. Japanese flowering cherries at Potomac Park, Washington, D.C., in 1920. In the background are the Lincoln Memorial (above) and the Washington Monument (below). Photo by Crandall in 1920.

United States had a Potomac Park as a show garden for cherries on a scale that resembled the best of the cherry picnic places in Japan. Every spring the Park revived, and continues to revive, a nationwide awareness of the cherry.

In Europe the general public was slow to warm up to the cherry. No large-scale planting of cherries helped the plant present itself. It was through the world fairs that Europeans became acquainted with the cherry, as we will discuss later.

A Botanist's Discussion

The classification of Japan's flowering cherries started as any discussion among taxonomists—with some articles that drew little attention. Entering the twentieth century, Japanese flowering cherries played a role in diplomacy between the United States and Japan, inflating the meaning of the plant and its taxonomy, and making researchers rush to conclusions. It would take a whole book to tell the history of flowering cherry taxonomy, and that is not our purpose here (see Russell 1934, Ingram 1948, or Kawasaki 1982.) But in reconstructing the discussion on *sato-zakura*—garden forms, however, we can shed light on some human factors in cherry taxonomy as well as clear up a major classification problem.

Broadly speaking, garden forms are classified according to two schools, a Western one that lists them under *Prunus serrulata* Lindley and a Japanese one that lists them under *P. lannesiana* Carrière. The schools are discussed below.

In *Transactions of the Royal Horticultural Society* (1830), John Lindley described a flowering cherry that was brought from Guangzhou, China, in 1822 by Joseph Poole, a plant hunter for the Barr and Brookes nursery in Newington Green, London. A herbarium sheet with Lindley's cherry is kept in the Cambridge University Herbarium, but no flowers are found on it. However, in the Royal Botanic Gardens, Kew, an old tree of *Prunus serrulata* Lindley is found. It must be a descendant of the material that Poole brought; the characteristics of this old tree easily fit Lindley's description. In spite of the incomplete herbarium, the identity of *P. serrulata* presents no major taxonomic problem. It is a double-flowered, slightly less gorgeous strain of 'Ichihara-tora-no-o'.

Important in this context is an illustrated article by French botanist Élie-Abel Carrière (1818–1891) in 1877 about his *Cerasus serratifolia* Lind-

Figure 26. *Prunus serrulata* 'Albo Plena'. From Bean (1919).

ley *rosea*. The description and plate match perfectly the Japanese garden form 'Ichihara-tora-no-o'. The lower right-hand corner of the plate includes a picture of a less abundant and more white *C. serratifolia* that Carrière received in 1839 from England, a plant that was Lindley's *Prunus serrulata*. Carrière's article on rare garden plants (*Revue Horticole*, 1875, p. 400) makes it clear that *C. serratifolia* is another name for *C. serrulata* Lindley.

Carrière further tells us that both of these forms of *Cerasus serratifolia* came from Japan; no mention is made of China. Apart from Dejima at Nagasaki, Guangzhou, known then as Canton, was the only open port in the Far East from 1760 to 1842 (Fairbank 1953). Furthermore, Guangzhou was much more accessible than Dejima, which was open only to the Chinese and the Dutch. It is not surprising, therefore, to find Japanese goods, including plants exported from Guangzhou in these years.

Lindley's cherry would certainly have been an interesting plant for the

Figure 27. *Cerasus serratifolia* Lindley *rosea,* now known as the garden form *Prunus* 'Ichihara-tora-no-o'. Shown in the lower right-hand corner are flowers of *C. serratifolia,* now known as *Prunus serrulata* 'Albo Plena'. From an article by É.-A. Carrière (1877) in *Revue Horticole,* Wageningen University Library Special Collections.

Barr and Brookes nursery, but Lindley had described a cultivated plant to which Camillo Schneider added in 1906 the cultivar name 'Albo Plena'. Thereafter the plant was known in Europe as *Prunus serrulata* Lindley 'Albo Plena' Schneider. This cherry served Manabu Miyoshi in 1916 as the type for the large-flowered garden cherries.

The name *Prunus lannesiana* is forty years younger and takes us back to 1870 when a flowering cherry was sent to the Jardin d'Acclimatation in Paris by the French statesman and general Napoléon Auguste Lannes, the Duke of Montebello (1801–1874), whose father had fought with Napoléon Bonaparte. This plant was reportedly from Japan, but whether Lannes had traveled to the Far East or how he otherwise obtained this plant still remains a question. This cherry was a grafted pot plant less than half a meter tall when it was described by Carrière in 1872 and published under the name *Cerasus lannesiana*. A colored lithograph of the cherry appeared a year later.

No herbarium sheet was made, nor does a living specimen of this plant exist. Furthermore, it is doubtful that a flowering cherry could be correctly described from a potted plant. As a graft it would have been influenced by the rootstock; the young plant's flowering suggests a stock of 'Mazakura'. The description calls to mind 'Mikuruma-gaeshi' or a pink, single, and large-flowered garden form close to the Oshima cherry. Carrière's cherry had its flowers in umbels rather than corymbs, which is not a typical characteristic of the large-flowered garden cherries, all of which have corymbose inflorescences. Grouping garden cherries under the name *Prunus lannesiana* Carrière, as Wilson did, is not very convincing, but because this was the first single-flowered Japanese cherry described, it was easily interpreted by Western botanists as the "wild" parent form.

Ernest H. Wilson (1876–1930), a botanist at the Arnold Arboretum, Jamaica Plain, Massachusetts, had traveled extensively and many times through China from 1899 to 1909, for the Veitch nursery and later for the arboretum. "Chinese" Wilson, as he was nicknamed, not only botanized but also bought many plants from flower shops and nurseries. He imported many good cherries for the arboretum from the Yokohama Nursery Company in 1903 and 1904, but could visit Japan only ten years later in 1914 to do the field research on these cherries. On his travel he was at times accompanied by Gen'ichi Koidzumi (1883–1953), who had just published his extensive study on the Japanese rose family. Wilson visited the Arakawa collection and had discussions with Japan's best garden-cherry specialist,

Figure 28. *Cerasus lannesiana* as illustrated in 1873 by É.-A. Carrière. Because the plant resembles the Oshima cherry and most semi-double garden forms, the name *lannesiana* was assigned to the species by Ernest H. Wilson, although he had seen neither a herbarium specimen nor a living plant. With an article by Carrière (1872) in *Revue Horticole,* Wageningen University Library Special Collections.

Seisaku Funatsu. Wilson also met with Suzuki, manager of the Yokohama Nursery Company; Takenoshin Nakai (1882–1952), an expert on Korean plants and cherries; and the "godfather" of Japan's modern botany, Tomitarō Makino (1862–1955). Wilson's extensive travels and broad interviews with specialists enabled him to provide a superb overview of botanic species in *The Cherries of Japan* (1916). The Japanese horticultural forms, however, are presented in an abridged form, and Wilson's grouping of them under a doubtful *Prunus lannesiana* was unfortunate.

Manabu Miyoshi (1861–1939), a professor at the Imperial University in Tokyo and founder of ecology as a science in Japan, was instrumental in setting up a government policy to designate natural monuments. His activities in this field have often a touch of old-fashioned nationalism: the natural monuments he proposed are singular specimens of old trees, often memorials for a heroic military or imperial event. Each cherry is described and given *forma* status, resulting in an impractical list of more than a hundred "forms" of the Japanese mountain cherry. Miyoshi reportedly was not a very sociable character, and various discrediting stories still circulate in Japan. Even amiable Ingram stated that Miyoshi was "more of a 'museum botanist' than a horticulturist, and I have good reason to believe that he relied very largely on Mr. Funatsu for the vernacular names of the cherries he described with such meticulous care."

Wilson and Miyoshi were rivals, and both were determined to publish the first cherry monograph. The two do not mention each other in their books. Only twenty days before Wilson's book was published, Miyoshi's work on cherries appeared, full of typesetting errors. Written in German, Miyoshi's *Japanische Bergkirschen, ihre Wildformen und Kulturrassen* is a volume of the *Journal of the College of Science, Imperial University of Tokyo* (10 March 1916). Those twenty days were not a coincidence: the preceding volume on *Rosaceae* in the same journal was published by Wilson's guide Gen'ichi Koidzumi in 1913.

Miyoshi's opinion thus has twenty-days' priority over Wilson's. The horticultural cherries of Japan are described extensively by Miyoshi and accompanied by lithographic color illustrations. Miyoshi lumps all the garden cherries under *Prunus serrulata* as it was described by Lindley in 1830, giving a black-and-white photograph of the herbarium specimen kept in the Cambridge University Herbarium that confirms Lindley's description. According to the internationally prevailing taxonomy rules, Miyoshi's view on *sato-zakura* is correct. Nevertheless, Miyoshi was a loner in his time and never accepted as a true colleague by fellow botanists. Furthermore, because of Japan's warm feelings towards America at the time, it was Wilson's opinion that made a school in Japan. In Japanese sources, one finds most garden forms described as cultivars of *Prunus lannesiana* Wilson.

For most Japanese researchers it has always been strained if not illogical to group Japanese garden forms under *Prunus serrulata,* which is commonly believed to be a Chinese plant. Nonetheless, *P. serrulata* Lindley is merely a strain of the Japanese 'Ichihara-tora-no-o' that was sent not from, but via, Guangzhou to Europe. Uehara Keiji (1977, p. 9) spoke of Lindley's cherry as a "Japan-product" (*nihonsan*) sent from Guangzhou. Thus a Japanese garden form became the type for other garden forms and some wild Japanese cherry varieties.

Optimism in Cherry History

The decades before the Second World War were bright. Japan, self-confident after its internationally acclaimed victory in the Russo-Japanese war, presented itself to the world openly, and cherries were exported in large quantities. In England the great tree expert W. J. Bean of the Royal Botanic Gardens, Kew, helped to promote exotics from the Far East. A great variety of garden cherries came into permanent cultivation in Europe and North America. At world exhibitions in the West, Japan presented collections of bonsai trees and sometimes a complete Japanese-style garden. The Paris World Exhibition of 1900 had a separate pavilion dedicated to Japanese horticulture with garden books, chrysanthemums, bonsai, and other ornamental trees. Large cherry trees were planted opposite the tea salon.

The city of Düsseldorf had a Japanese garden with cherries in 1904, but the garden at the 1910 Japanese-British Exhibition in London really attracted the crowds. A garden of two hectares was laid out under the guidance of three professional gardeners brought from Japan. Many plants were imported directly from Japan, but the cherries in this exhibit came from English nurseries. These Japanese exhibitions were instrumental in catching the attention of the well-disposed gardening elite of Europe.

In France the cherry accompanied the *Japonaiserie* fashion in gardening. The painter Claude Monet, known for his wisteria bridge, replaced some apple trees with Japanese cherries in his famous garden at Giverny. Among

Figure 29. The Japanese Pavilion at the Paris World Exhibition of 1900, advertised with irises and flowering cherries. L'Exposition de Paris 1900, Kyōto University, Jinbunken.

his garden friends was Georges Clemenceau, president of France, who also could boast of a stand of double-flowered, pink Japanese cherries. The banker Albert Kahn had his *Village Japonais* in Boulogne, not far from the Rothschilds, who had their cherries in a garden in the same *Japonaiserie* style. In England Leopold de Rothschild had a Japanese garden, and others were found at Tully House, Tatton Park, Heale House and elsewhere in England as well as in Ireland and Scotland.

In the German cities of Berlin and Leverkusen, other European interpretations of Japanese garden art were found. Flowering cherries stood among the Japanese-style lanterns, garden bridges, and potted bonsai trees. With so much interest in Japanese gardening among the artistic elite, who frequently had a cultural link with Japan, it is no surprise that a general appreciation of flowering cherries developed in the 1920s and 1930s. Following colorful trends in flower gardening and a popular interest in the exotic, and floating on the waves of an oncoming modernism, cherries such as 'Kanzan' became commonplace garden plants that even appeared in roadside planting schemes of the British Garden City movement.

A bright feeling of internationalism and optimistic progress was felt in Japan in these days as well, and again the nation's flower helped in giving expressions to it. In Tokyo, an exhibition with cherries as a theme in artistic painting was held in a department store in 1914 to an unexpectedly enthusiastic appraisal by the public. Newspapers that only recently reported the successful planting of cherries at Potomac Park in the United States could hail again the glory of the country's flower.

Encouraged by this highbrow event that elevated popular cherry enthusiasm above the increasingly licentious and boisterous partying under the cherries of the Ueno park, a group of business leaders and scientists set up a cherry club called *Sakura Kwai*. The club held its first and founding conference on 23 April 1917 in the Tokyo Imperial Hotel. Flowering branches of forty-three cherries were displayed at this occasion, with books, paintings, and illustrations. Speakers gave their opinions on cherries for the assembled public: the mission was to spread a loving protection and a taste for the country's flower to the lowest classes of society. The conference took place in the large banquet hall of the splendid art-deco hotel building still under construction after a design by American architect Frank Lloyd Wright (1869–1959). Among prominent club members were the manager of the hotel, Mr. Hayashi, and a Tokyo City Park official,

Kiyoshi Inoshita (1884–1973), who would become an important figure in the postwar landscape architecture scene. Miyoshi was a board member, and Funatsu a regular member. The club's honorary president was the enlightened gentleman-scholar Yorimichi Tokugawa (1872–1925), son of a powerful daimyo family, and the president was an upper-level politician from the Ministry of Finance, the successful businessman Eiichi Shibusawa (1840–1931), who took part in missions to Paris and the United States. Frank Lloyd Wright was a member from the beginning and his repeated donations were used to plant cherries in Tokyo parks. Less than two years later David Fairchild and Ernest H. Wilson were paying members and contributed short articles published in English in the club's periodical. The future of the cherry seemed as bright and promising internationally as it could be.

The Sakura Kwai was visited by the cherry botanist Captain Collingwood Ingram (1880–1981) in 1926 just after it had chosen a new honorary president, Nobusuke Taka Tsukasa (1889–1959). Taka Tsukasa was of noble birth and had an old-fashioned gentleman-scientist's love of cherries as did many politicians in the old, feudal Edo period. He invited Ingram to speak to the Sakura Kwai, an invitation Ingram hesitated to accept:

> As I loathe public speaking and, moreover, regarded it as an impertinence for a foreigner to address a Japanese audience on their national tree, I was very diffident about accepting. But there was no escape; all arrangements had been made. My only solace was that probably not more than three percent of those present could understand a word I said!

Ingram's (1929) warning that many garden cherries would become extinct without an active policy of preservation was not as necessary as he thought. Several local collections in other parts of Japan were set up in these years such as the one at Matsumae in Hokkaidō. (Short histories of 150 such local cherry parks are found in Nihon Sakura no Kai 1990, pp. 146–170.)

Ingram's visit resulted in the return of a garden cherry believed to be extinct in Japan; the cherry was renamed 'Tai-haku' by Taka Tsukasa. After his return, Ingram received grafting material of 'Bendono', 'Fukurokuju', 'Ichiyo', and 'Shogetsu', which was sent to his home in Kent, England. Not far from London the nursery of Waterer Sons and Crisp in Bagshot raised the cherry 'Pink Perfection', which was obtained from a group of seedlings grown from seeds of the diploid 'Shogetsu'. The male parent was most likely a tree of 'Kanzan'. 'Pink Perfection' was released in 1935. The same nursery presented 'Pandora' a few years later, and more and more Western nurseries would come up with new flowering cherries bred from Japanese parents.

In the same year (1935) the Garden Club of America visited Japan and its gardens. Garden enthusiasm was booming among wealthy gardeners in the United States, and Japanese-style gardens became fashionable even in California. With the dark clouds of world history closing in after the financial crash and the outbreak of the Second World War, the cherry lost popular attention again.

The Second World War

Just as everything Germanic became ideology for the Germans in the Second World War, the ancient province of Yamato became ideology for the Japanese. The spirit of Yamato represented the nationalist attitude, and the cherries of Yoshino, as guardians of Yamato, became the symbol of Japan's frontier spirit in Chinese Manchuria. An old proverb, *Hana ha sakura, hito ha bushi,* claimed that cherry flowers were the best flowers, just as the daimyo class was the highest class in society during the Edo period. Thus cherries were now understood as a supreme expression of daring military courage.

Although the chrysanthemum remained the symbol of the imperial house, the most adventurous militarists in 1931 that were marching in Chinese Manchuria without the official consent of the Japanese government took the Yoshino cherry as their symbol. With the quickly changing cabinets, these military actions became more and more supported by the government, and it is hardly surprising that tens of thousands of Japanese cherries were planted in China and Korea.

Since 1933 primary-school textbooks had the seemingly innocent text: *"Saita, saita, sakura ga saita"* (It blooms, it blooms, the cherry it blooms). In fact, the slogan formed part of a conscious propaganda campaign to propagate the cherry as a symbol of Great Japan with all its aspirations. Textbooks were edited by the Ministry of Education, and all school buildings were built and maintained by the central government. Each school had its stand of *Prunus ×yedoensis,* now majestic trees as most had been planted around the turn of the century. Japanese educational programs start in

Figure 30. Page one of chapter one in a first-grade textbook on the Japanese language. Ministry of Education, Japan, 1917.

April, and as a rule of the thumb this cherry flowers in mid-Japan in the first week of April. The average schoolchild started the new year's lessons under flowering cherries in full bloom, and most first-term textbooks took cherries as their theme. Teachings of the mother tongue started with the cherry, and even secondary school biology lessons would begin with the anatomy of cherry flowers. At the close of the Second World War a generation of youngsters appeared at the lines of battle completely brainwashed on the point of cherries. The infantrymen in their uniforms with dark-pink collars sang the following song:

> Ten thousand flower sprigs,
> pink as the collar of a soldier's uniform,
> are blown in a storm of Yoshino.
>
> Being born as a son of Great Japan
> is to die in the turmoil of battle,
> shed as a petal wind.

This is no cynical soldiers' humor. The official war propaganda was so perfectly organized that the song was sung by serious soldiers convinced that this was the only honor left. The sinister association of a hero's death with cherry blossoms scattered by a wind, which could be divine for the kamikaze pilots, was coupled with the image of a quickly shedding cherry. It is *Prunus* ×*yedoensis* that shows this dramatic sudden shedding of the blossom. Any Japanese citizen knew from school days that cherries were glorious and magnificent in bloom, but that they had to shed their blossom without any mercy.

In the 1930s and 1940s botanists, historians, journalists, and priests of cherry temples wrote many books and articles on the meaning, history, and botany of Japanese cherries. Most of these sources only loosely used what was handed down as source material over the centuries; even respectable researchers tended to forget the ethical standards of science and interpreted the facts in a way that appealed to the politicians of the time. Although the question "How could this have happened to our cherry?" was also heard, these authors often traced a fabricated history that proved the ancient Yamato spirit of the cherry. Yamada (1941, pp. 375 ff.), for example, in an appendix to his edited series of newspaper articles on cherry history, tried carefully to answer the question of what happened to the meaning that flowering cherries now carried. Nevertheless, he also created much cherry mythology. Typical reasoning of the period is illustrated by 'Sumizome'. For Yamada this probably-seventeenth-century cherry originated as a garden form in the ninth century, giving it the same date as the classic poem from which its name was derived.

Among the mixed-up theories on the etymology of *sakura,* the Japanese word for cherry, a popular interpretation traced its origin to the Asama Shrine at Mount Fuji, which enshrines a mythical goddess named *Kono hana no sakuya hime.* A local tradition holds that the word *sakura* was derived from the word *sakuya* in the goddess's name, but it is clearly the other way round. Her name translates literally "goddess that makes the flowers (namely, cherries) bloom." The goddess is of local origin and emerged to make the spectacular flowering of the wild stands of *Prunus incisa* intelligible. These cherries were on the slopes of Mount Fuji before there was a goddess. Of course, *P. incisa* had escaped the attention of the average nationalist, who carried an image of *P.* ×*yedoensis* as the flowering cherry, but the *sakuya-sakura* etymology closely related the cherry to the mythical gods who created Japan. Also appealing to the Great-Japan ideology was the story's mention of a supreme symbol of Japan, Mount Fuji.

Another confusing discussion of the years under nationalist ideology concerns the origin of the national flower, 'Somei-yoshino', or *Prunus* ×*yedoensis.* It started with a fragmentary herbarium specimen of a cherry collected by a certain Père Taquet in 1908 on the Korean island of Cheju. It resembled *P.* ×*yedoensis* and was taken by Koizumi as proof that this plant came from Korea. Considering Japan's occupation of Korea, it was for some the ultimate proof that Korea was Japanese; for others it was difficult to think that this cherry did not originate from Yoshino in the Yamato region. No such cherries have been found since on Cheju. It was only in the 1960s that breeding experiments between the Oshima cherry (*P. serrulata* var. *speciosa*) and the Edo-higan cherry (*P. pendula* f. *ascendens*) gave similar cherries and led to the conclusion that 'Somei-yoshino' is a hybrid of these two, as Wilson had suggested before.

In the last years of the war, Japan was completely ruined but still desperately fighting. Lacking steel, it armed its soldiers with bamboo spears and the aircraft industry experimented with ceramic jet engines. An exhausted population drained of all its resources, and bereft of its sons who had lost their lives on the battlefield, was entangled in an equally desperate struggle for survival. Sprouts and flowers of the cherries of Yoshino were eaten by the villagers instead of enjoyed as part of the picnic setting.

The Cherry after the Second World War

After Japan's eventual defeat, cherries were no proud nation's flower. Miyoshi's volume, *Sakura, Japanese Cherry,* in a handy set by the Tourist Library that introduced many facets of Japanese culture to foreign visitors, was replaced by an innocent booklet on *kimono*-dress. The country was in ruin and the spiritual world of Japan in a profound state of trauma; it was an atmosphere that prevailed during the occupation by the U.S. forces in the following years.

Land for gardens and nurseries had been confiscated, often by authority of only local police officers, for growing vegetables. Again a period was entered in which many horticultural cherries were in danger of becoming extinct. Fully aware of the problem this time, a few nurseries managed to prevent serious damage to their collections through the years of the disastrous ambitions of Great Japan.

A nursery on grounds formerly owned by the Ninna-ji Temple in Kyōto had already been run for some generations by gardeners of the Sano house. Mr. Tōemon Sano III (d. 1934) had been collecting cherries from all over the country since the early 1920s. His wife and son, Sano IV, were able propagators. During the Second World War they managed to save a large part of the collection, planting numerous trees out in various locations in the neighborhood before the nursery was turned into a vegetable garden. Mr. Tōemon Sano IV published *Sakura; Flowering Cherries of Japan* in 1961, which lists and illustrates 101 wild and garden forms. Mr. Tōemon Sano V (b. 1928) still actively conserves and promotes cherries. He helped in the construction of the UNESCO Japanese garden in Paris, after a design by the sculptor Isamu Noguchi. The garden has a nice stand of 'Kanzan' holding its branches at about eye-level over a well-designed garden path.

Mr. Kamenosuke Koshimizu had nurseries in Angyō, Kawaguchi, and took over a cherry preservation collection from another nurseryman, a Mr. Matsumoto. Thus, Koshimizu was able to carry the cherries of Arakawa through the Second World War, helped by special permission to preserve cherries instead of growing vegetables. His collection list of 1970 gives hundreds of names.

These two collections were most instrumental in passing many famous garden forms to the present generation of cherry lovers. A duplicate set of Sano's collection went to the Kyōto Botanic Garden, where it suffered severely when it was transplanted to make room for the construction of a new conservatory; steps are being taken to restore the collection to its old glory, and in other parts of this garden nice specimens can be seen. The cultivars of the Kyōto area, such as seen in this garden, are less well studied than those of the Tokyo area with collections at Arakawa and in the Koshimizu nursery. The latter collection formed the basis of the cherries seen today at the National Institute of Genetics in Mishima, where, after the Second World War, various research was begun such as on the origin of *Prunus ×yedoensis*. The soil of the institute's garden is a deep, friable loam, giving the trees a healthy growth that is rarely seen in other collections.

Cherry research in Western countries was greatly helped with Collingwood Ingram's extensive study on flowering cherries. Appearing in 1948 as *Ornamental Cherries,* it treated flowering cherries from *Prunus avium* to botanic cherries from the Himalayas and garden forms of *P. serrulata*. Ingram included two forms of *P. ×yedoensis* among the fifty-one *sato-zakura* cultivars that he described. Descriptions are rarely illustrated, and some are too short to be conclusive. In Europe "Cherry" Ingram became a cherished visitor of cherry collections, where he would discuss the plants' ins and outs until his death at a venerable age.

In Japan enthusiasm for cherries revived in the 1960s, helped by the country's general optimism after the Tokyo Olympic Games. A group of researchers found their home in the Flower Association of Japan (Nihon Hana no Kai), which was formed in 1962 and was sponsored by the Komatsu power-shovel factories. Ever since, the association actively supports the setting up of new cherry plantings by local government bodies. Over the years it has sent more than 2.5 million cherry saplings all over Japan, and even to Turkey, Iran, Brazil, Mexico, China, and several western European countries. Today the association has a broad base of popular support. It has a large group of eminent researchers, including cherry specialists Yoshio Kobayashi, Yasaka Hayashi, and Tetsuya Kawasaki, who support research at the association's Experimental Station at Yūki in Ibaraki Prefecture. The association published its *Manual of Japanese Flowering Cherries* in 1982.

A second association not to be confused with the above was set up by a few Liberal Democratic Party (LDP) members of Parliament. It is the Flowering Cherry Association of Japan (Nihon Sakura no Kai) that carries on a similar policy of promoting cherry plantings throughout the world. It has sent more than 1.5 million trees throughout Japan, but also to Monaco, Korea, Peru, and even the slopes of Mount Kilimanjaro in Tanzania! Yes, the flowering cherries of Japan have completely recovered from war damage.

At a forestry research station at Asagawa in Tama, in the outskirts of Tokyo, a cherry preservation policy was established in 1966. It became a place where horticultural practice and botanical science could meet. Many identification problems were solved here by such researchers as Hayashi and Kobayashi who worked on their cherry publications. The Tama Forest Science Garden is a regional center of the Forestry and Forest Products Research Institute (FFPRI) of the Japanese Ministry of Agriculture, Forestry, and Fisheries. It is a large general arboretum including an impressive collection of wild and garden cherries that covers about six hectares. The garden is open to the public and is easily reached on foot from the train station Takao on the Chūō line that departs from Tokyo station. A visit in spring is recommended to the reader who has a chance to visit Japan.

CHAPTER 2

Cultivating and Propagating Cherries

Hardiness

Northern cherries such as the Japanese alpine cherry (*Prunus nipponica*) or the alpine Fuji cherry (*P. incisa)* are surprisingly hardy and therefore are often used in breeding experiments. Most forms of *P. serrulata* originated in the more temperate regions of mid-Japan, so that they adapt best to zones where winters are not too severe. In the United States they would do well in USDA zones 4 to 6. The hardy alpine ones would do well in USDA zone 3, comparable with mid-Sweden in Europe, but only if they are not exposed to drying east winds in frosty periods in winter or in early spring.

Prunus ×*yedoensis* tolerates a midwinter temperature of −20°C, and probably colder, without any problem. At that time the trees are dormant. Hardiness diminishes as the temperature rises and the sap inside the tree begins to run. Thus early spring, when buds start moving, is the most critical time of the year.

A Japanese laboratory test done in early spring, rather than midwinter, gave interesting data on hardiness (Kitamura et al. 1984). An alpine cherry, such as the Fuji cherry (*Prunus incisa*) in this test, is very hardy and develops flowers and leaf-sprouts after an early spring with a temperature of −15°C. The Oshima cherry (*P. serrulata* var. *speciosa*), cultivated throughout Japan for many centuries, showed a clear difference in hardiness depending on the origin of the planting material. Plants from northern nurseries were hardier than those from southern nurseries. This holds true for other cherries, so that it is advised in colder regions to obtain plants from well-established local nursery material. The cherries tested in this study were divided into three groups of hardiness. The most hardy group included 'Imose', 'Ito-kukuri', and 'Kanzan'. A second, rather hardy group included *P.* ×*yedoensis,* the Oshima cherry (*P. serrulata* var. *speciosa*), 'Ama-no-gawa', 'Ichiyo', 'Shogetsu', the chrysanthemum-flowered 'Najima-zakura', and 'Beni-shidare'. The least hardy group included 'Fugenzo', 'Kenroku-en-kiku-zakura', 'Tai-haku', and 'Taizan-fukun'. The study was carried out in early March without regard for the early or late flowering of the tested cherries. It only gives an idea of what might be expected in regions with severe frosts in early spring after the new growth has begun. Scientific research is not reliable by itself, as hardiness is influenced in the open field by many other factors that cannot be included in a laboratory test.

Cherry specialist Mr. Masatoshi Asari (1983) from Matsumae, Hokkaidō, adds to our list of hardy cherries the following well-known ones: 'Gyoiko', the Kurile cherry (*Prunus nipponica* var. *kurilensis*), 'Surugadai-nioi', 'Yae-beni-shidare', *P. pendula* f. *ascendens, P. sargentii, P. serrulata* var. *pubescens* and its cultivar 'Nara-no-yae-zakura', 'Jugatsu-zakura' (*P.* ×*subhirtella* 'Autumnalis'), and 'Takasago'. New horticultural forms developed by Mr. Asari show promise of being successful garden plants for colder zones.

For a cherry, the opposite of hardiness is tolerance of warm and humid, or even warm and arid, climates without a winter season of rest. In South America, Japanese immigrants have grown flowering cherries for a century. In the warmer regions of Argentina or Paraguay, a cherry such as *Prunus* ×*yedoensis* does not have a proper winter rest and thus does not produce a flower show worth mentioning. 'Fukurokuju', 'Kanzan', 'Shogetsu', and 'Ukon', however, perform better. Breeding experiments with the almost-subtropic bell-flowered cherry (*P. campanulata*) are underway. The goal is to obtain a cherry that, without winter rest, keeps its leaves almost throughout the year and comes into bloom with the onset of the rainy season. The incredible genetic possibilities of the Japanese cherries promise in the future an even wider region suitable for planting garden cherries (see Anichi Sakura Tomo no Kai 1990).

Light, Air, and Moisture Requirements

Japanese flowering cherries are healthy plants as a rule. Centuries of gardening experience have sorted out the useless forms, and many cherries have a reputation as classic garden plants in Japan and elsewhere. When cherries fail in the West, there are two possible causes. First, grafting a plant on a too-vigorous stock leads to quick marketability but also quickly exhausted plants. Thus greedy nursery professionals bear some responsibility for spoiling their market. Second, plants fail when they are sited in the wrong soil or location. Sun, air, an open soil, cold winters, and much water in summer are the keys to healthy growth in flowering cherries.

Sun is required for all flowering cherries. The site should be airy, so that leaves and branches can dry quickly after rain. Squeezed between other plantings, cherries will suffer from molds such as *Monilia* or other diseases, and their life span will be shortened. A gentle slope facing south or southwest is ideal.

Flowering cherries are not very demanding about the soil in which they grow, but it should be fresh, airy, and moderately rich. In their native habitats, cherries grow in soils that are acidic, but they perform equally well on slightly alkaline soils, as in England. Aeration is important as cherries wither when the soil is compacted by machines or too many walking feet. Experience in Japan shows that cherries start withering after their soil becomes firmly trodden upon by too many tourists enjoying the flowers, or when the surrounding area is paved with watertight concrete or asphalt. Air and fresh water for the roots are important. The modernization of antique cut-stone drains with PVC piping has caused the loss of older cherries. The best soil is friable, fast draining, and well aerated. In places with heavy loams or sticky clay soils, it is best to plant a cherry in a raised bed, as any planting hole will act as a watertight container. Under such conditions an incurable root-rot in winter unexpectedly kills a cherry in spring bloom without any other obvious sign of disease above the ground.

Cherries in Japan receive an average of 2000 mm of precipitation per year, so in dry regions one should not forget that they are happy with plenty of water. Summer rain, especially early in the season, benefits the healthy growth of any cherry. When spring and early summer are dry, special attention must be given to a newly planted cherry. Spraying the entire tree with water should help it through a period of drought.

Cherries are rather shallow rooting, so to help a young tree establish itself, no grass or plants should be grown around the trunk. A mulched circle of at least a meter in diameter is advised for young trees; it not only retains the natural soil moisture, but also benefits the balance of organic life. When a cherry is in the full vigor of its life, it can be competitive. The tree crown does not give heavy shade, and the roots allow for lawn grass to come up to the stem. Any plant with a deeper rooting system, however, will suffer. In the usually narrow city gardens in Japan cherries are rarely planted because they make any other planting impossible. It is a common saying among Tokyo gardeners—always eager to stuff as many plants and garden knickknacks as possible in a narrow plot—that "only a fool plants a cherry."

Pruning

Pruning should be done rarely. Because cherries have a loose and open tree shape, cutting a branch often results in an unbalanced crown, which presents an ugly sight. Some cherries, such as 'Fugenzo', 'Mikuruma-gaeshi', or 'Ukon', profit from a pruning when young. Most cherries make a regular crown, but if something goes wrong in the early years, pruning to correct the problem is possible only if one has an idea of the eventual shape of the fully grown tree. Thus, in the cultivar descriptions, the tree shape is always given and should help in setting up a natural habit.

Once a balanced tree frame has been formed, cherries require no pruning for many years. Occasionally a crossed or crooked branch needs to be removed, and ambitious, watery shoots are controlled by pinching them in early summer. When older, some cherries have bare, hanging branches with foliage and blossoms only at the tip end. In this situation it is advisable to prune back the outer, flowering branches for a more beautiful tree shape. 'Pink Perfection' and 'Ukon' are examples of cherries needing this kind of pruning.

Pruning is done best early in the flowering season. Spring and summer growth will help heal the wounds quickly, and budding branches can be used for indoor arrangements. Pruning in autumn or winter should be avoided because germs, such as the spores of the silver leaf fungus, are actively transported at this time and infections occur easily. This threat is more serious in regions with damp and humid winters, such as western Europe, than in Japan where the weather is dry and crisp at this time of the year.

It is advisable to treat accidental wounds in winter carefully by cutting back irregular parts of the wood and bark to a smooth surface of sound wood. On the smoothly pared surface, a fungus antiseptic should be applied. Coal-tar or sealers should not be used; a layer of it hinders the natural covering of the wound with new bark.

Vegetative and Sexual Propagation

Cherries can be grown from seed, which is the simplest method of propagation. Mature seeds are collected from trees, preferably with juicy flesh still covering the stone. The cherries are washed and wiped clean but not dried. The stones are laid in moist sand that can be stored in a cool room or, better, in a sand-filled hollow in a cool place of the garden. Then in early spring the stones can be laid out in rows and grown under plastic tunnels. Such seed produces plants that are genetically unique and different from the parents.

Sexual propagation (that is, sowing seed) is interesting for experiments in search of new forms, and it is fully acceptable when propagating species, but in propagating garden forms we do not want the special qualities of the cultivar to be lost. Garden cherries are therefore propagated vegetatively from a part of the parent plant using specialized techniques that require a skilled hand. Such techniques as budding or grafting are usually done by professional growers, but amateur growers may want to try propagating a particular cultivar, perhaps a rare one not for sale, or may want to propagate on a particular rootstock. Anyone planning to buy a grafted cherry needs to understand the advantages or problems of the various rootstock types first. Therefore the following sections on propagation address the professional but should be of use also for the serious amateur cherry grower.

Cherries can be propagated vegetatively by cuttings, or on rootstock by budding or grafting. The latter way is most commonly practiced in the nursery. The techniques of budding and grafting cherries are basically the same as for fruit trees, and they are only discussed here in a broad sense.

Rootstock

Flowering cherries are grafted on various rootstocks. We will first discuss the methods used in Japan for centuries before turning to Western techniques. No "modern" stock is used in Japan. The Oshima cherry (*Prunus serrulata* var. *speciosa*), grown from seed selected from designated wild stands, is most commonly used as stock. 'Mazakura' (synonym *Prunus lannesiana*

真
櫻

66

Figure 31. 'Mazakura', as shown by Manabu Miyoshi, who reported a pink and a white form. This cherry is used as a cutting-propagated rootstock and supposedly is a parent for nursery forms such as 'Ariake', 'Washi-no-o', and so forth. From Miyoshi (1921b, no. 66, f. *multipetala*).

'Multiplex'), a cultivar of varied origin, is also used. One of its parents is the Chinese *P. pseudo-cerasus.* The triploid 'Mazakura' produces aerial roots and is easily propagated from cuttings. Most garden cherries and all forms of *P. ×yedoensis* are propagated on either of these stocks.

Prunus ×subhirtella from seed is used in Japan as stock onto which are grafted its cultivars 'Jugatsu-zakura' or 'Autumnalis', the weeping forms of *P. pendula,* and forms related to the Fuji cherry (*P. incisa*). Finally, forms related to the Japanese mountain cherry (*P. serrulata* var. *spontanea*) are set on seed-grown stock of their parent species.

Cultivars are always grafted low on the stock, which only serves as a temporary nurse plant: plants are deeply planted until the propagated cultivar has made its roots. Garden cherries are grown always on their own roots in Japan; for studying tree shapes and growth characteristics unaffected by rootstock influence, one has to visit the collections in their home country.

In America and Europe the wild European cherry, the mazzard or gean, *Prunus avium* Linnaeus, is a perfectly hardy, easily propagated stock for grafting most garden cherries. It gives the grafted cultivar a tree of regular shape with a growth that is more vigorous than the cultivar could show on its own roots (see Arends 1990). Sometimes *P. avium* stock is grown from seed selected for forestry purposes; it might even be available from individually selected virus-free seed-parent trees. In this case the seed was selected for growth and production, and cherries grafted onto trees from this seed of *P. avium* seem to be pumped up to an almost unnatural vigor that soon exhausts the tree. This might be desirable for commercial reasons because it quickly gives a salable tree: even an instant standard cherry is obtained when the cultivar is grafted on an established stem. An older 'Kanzan', however, when grafted on a forest-production mazzard stem, looks like a sturdy column that holds a group of slender branches as in a fist. Such a tree image, as we would see in a kindergartner's drawings, might have its appeal to the post-modernist, but it is not very cherrylike, and a slower growing tree that yields a more natural shape is preferred.

Weeping cherry cultivars of *Prunus pendula* can be trained on their own stem with some patience, but grafting on established stems is advised when growing large numbers of plants. Good stems must be selected from among the seed-grown young trees.

In the strictest sense, stock grown from seed does not give a uniform nursery product as each plant has its unique characteristics. When a uniform set of trees is required, for instance, for a formal roadside planting, cultivar trees should be raised on stock from selected seed or, better, on vegetatively propagated stock. For the latter method two types of stock are commonly used in the West.

In East Malling, England, a virus-free stock was developed known as 'Malling 12/1', or 'MF12/1'. It is vegetatively propagated by earthing up, which involves covering it with soil, thus inducing side shoots to take root. 'MF12/1' gives a less extreme but still quite vigorous growth. This stock is known for its deep and spreading anchorage roots that set the tree firmly in the ground. It makes a straight, practically unbranched stem. A weak point of this stock is its sensitivity to a root bacterium, *Agrobacterium tumefaciens,* which causes a cancerlike, swelling disease that finally obstructs the transport function of the roots. The occurrence of this bacterium is limited though to certain soils.

A second English stock is *Prunus* 'Colt', procured from a cross between *P. avium* and the Chinese cherry, *P. pseudo-cerasus*. This virus-free stock is propagated by earthing up and forms a firm root system. In the field it is recognized by its mass of leaves and the many aerial roots seen on the stem. Buds grafted on this stock strike in remarkably high percentages, but a doubtful hardiness has been reported from regions with more severe winters. 'Colt' is a trademarked, protected nursery product.

Both 'MF12/1' and 'Colt' are best used as rootstocks on which buds are grafted close to the ground. Any difference in growth of thickness between cultivar and stock will hardly show on such low-grafted trees. No reports are known to us of an incompatibility between stock of *Prunus avium,* 'MF12/1', or 'Colt' and any cultivars of *P. serrulata*.

To grow a field of garden cherries for the trade, it is advisable to start with virus-free stock and virus-free cultivar material. For the commercial nursery it is of utmost importance to keep the nursery virus-free. Therefore the soil should be healthy or even sanitized and must be free from nematodes such as *Xiphinema* and *Longidorus,* which have proved to transmit virus diseases.

Budding, Chip-Budding, and Grafting

The methods of setting a cultivar on a rootstock are in a more precise sense treated in the following paragraphs. Budding of cherries is only done in Europe; chip-budding and grafting are practiced worldwide.

Budding

In budding, the mature bud of a cultivar is inserted in the stem of the stock. The stock should not be older than two years so that the bark is still supple to facilitate handling. The stock should have a diameter between 5 and 10 mm at the place where the bud will be inserted. Bud and stock need to have entered their growth stage for successful budding. In the growing season this will be in July or August. Whether the time is right depends also on the weather; a dry spell just after a few days of rain promises much more success with budding than a period of drought. Thus, rather than looking at the calendar, one should see if the bark of the stock easily parts from the wood. Starting too early means that the bud is not developed enough and thus is too weak to start up again on the stock. Starting too late means that the sap in the stock has slowed down again. The time for budding is limited, and it really is a technique for conscientious gardeners who are sensitive to the growing characteristics of their plants.

One-year-old or two-year-old saplings planted out in the field in spring are far enough along in their growth to be used for stock. Just above the ground, a T-incision is made in the bark as deep as the wood, with the "leg" of the T pointing downwards. Again, starting too early or too late in the season means that the bark will be parted from the wood only with difficulty. It is better to postpone the budding work.

To propagate a cultivar, one must select a well-developed leaf bud on a healthy shoot of the current season's growth. First the leaf at the bud is cut off, leaving a short part of the leaf stalk. Then the bud is cut from the twig with a little chip of bark and wood. The wood behind the bud should peel away easily. Viewed from behind, the hollow shield of bark shows a green eye of the bud, about the size of a pinhead. This little pinhead will develop into a complete new tree of the cultivar from which it was taken.

The little shield of bark with bud and stalk is—right side up—slipped under the bark peel of the T-incision of the stock. The incision is firmly wrapped with a rubber strip. If the operation has been carried out successfully, the bud will attach itself to the rootstock in about a week. This can be checked by carefully touching the remaining part of the leaf stalk at the inserted bud. If it falls off, exposing a little callus layer, the bud has struck.

The following winter the stock is pruned about 2 cm above the growing bud; the bud should develop normally from May onwards and produce a sprout. A skillful gardener can train the shoot into a whip 1.5 m long in the same growing season. Budding requires top-class gardeners, but in a season without problems it is the most productive method.

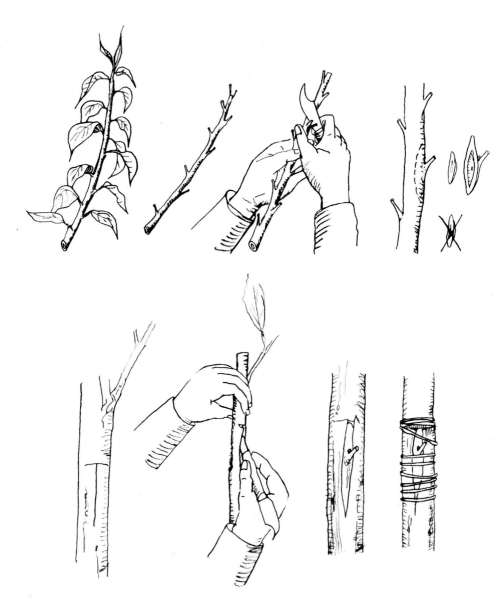

Figure 32. Budding.

Chip-budding

Chip-budding differs from budding only in a few details; it can be carried out later in the season as long as the sap is still running. Therefore, when buds are not developed enough for budding, it is possible to wait a little and to chip-bud. Chip-budding can be carried out from July to early September.

In chip-budding, a bud is prepared, as for budding except that the chip of wood behind the bark and the bud is not peeled off. The knife must be sharp enough to cut a straight chip; chips that are bent in cutting are worthless. As with budding, the leaf at the bud is cut off leaving a short piece of the stalk.

The stock for chip-budding is prepared differently than for budding. Instead of making an incision in the rootstock, one makes a slice as if another chip was being prepared. This slice, however, is not removed from

Figure 33. A successful chip-budding. Photo by Arie Peterse, 28 April 1996, Yūki Experimental Station of the Flower Association of Japan, Ibaraki Prefecture.

the rootstock. Only the upper half is cut away; the lower end of the imaginary chip is left on the stem. The prepared chip with the bud, from the cultivar to be propagated, is inserted, right side up, under the lower half of the slice that remains attached to the rootstock. The chip-bud is firmly tied to the stock with a plastic strip. The bud is completely covered so that it is impossible for the chip-bud to dry out. In Japan, however, the bud is left to stick out of the plastic, which may be less problematic because the weather is mild and humid at the time of propagation in this country.

After four to six weeks the chip has grown to the stock and the plastic should be carefully removed. Late in the following winter the stock is pruned about 10 cm above the chip-bud, leaving some buds of the stock plant above it. In late spring, after the stock and bud are growing, the stock is pruned away another time just above the cultivar sprout.

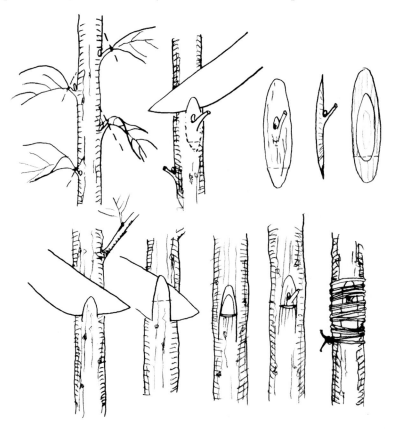

Figure 34. Chip-budding.

Grafting

In grafting, a twig from a cultivar is set on the rootstock. Such a twig is called a scion. Good scions are cuttings of 5 to 10 cm long from a one-season-old twig that is about pencil-thick. Each scion should have two or three well-developed leaf buds. For good results, the stock should be more advanced in growth than the scion. Therefore scions are collected early in December or January and kept dormant in clean, damp sand in a cold spot outdoors. They can also be kept in a cold-storage room, in which case they should be stored in plastic bags at about −2°C until the time of grafting.

Any grafting must be done in winter when trees are at rest and the sap is not running. It is therefore not necessary that the stock be standing in

Figure 35. A scion in which the bud scales have begun to show growth. Short scions give good results under the generous growing conditions in Japan. Photo by Arie Peterse, 28 April 1996, Yūki Experimental Station of the Flower Association of Japan, Ibaraki Prefecture.

the field: grafting can be done indoors on uprooted stock saplings. Indoors does not mean in a centrally heated room; care should be taken that rootstock and grafting material do not dry out. For working indoors, splice-grafting has proved to give the best results; it is a method of grafting a scion on a stock of almost equal diameter. Stock and scion are cut obliquely under the same angle and are tied together so that they fit precisely. The rind and cambium of both should be in tight and perfect contact with each other. After tying, the junction is covered with grafting wax. Work can be done from January to spring when growth starts. If it is still too cold or wet outside to plant, the prepared rootstock can be kept in the cold-storage room; otherwise it might be potted up and set under plastic tunnels. These plants can be set out in the field after June until the following winter.

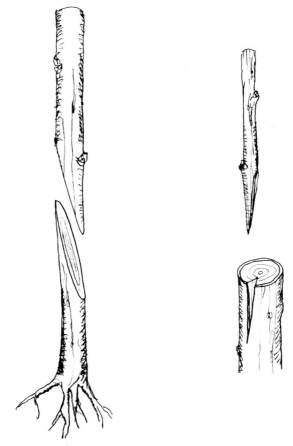

Figure 36. Splice-grafting (left) and triangle cleft-grafting (right).

Grafting outdoors in the field gives good results with triangle cleft-grafting. In this method the rootstock needs to be thicker than the scion. The stock is cut off 10 cm or so above the ground, leaving a smooth cutting surface. If necessary the end is pared smooth with a sharp knife. At the edge, a triangular sector of rind, cambium, and wood is cut out with two incising cuts. In this wedge-shaped cleft, the scion—tapered off by two slicing cuts—should fit precisely. The rind of the scion and of the stock should meet nicely. After the two are tied firmly together, the grafting must be covered with wax.

All grafting and budding methods require dexterity and a sharp knife. Buds and cambium are easily damaged; drying out must be forestalled by smooth and quick working. The cambium of stock and cultivar material should make contact.

Striking Cherries from Cuttings

Certain cherries have been propagated by cuttings in Japan for many years or even centuries. 'Mazakura' has always been widely produced by cuttings as a rootstock plant. Other cherries that show a tendency to produce aerial roots, such as *Prunus ×yedoensis,* also easily take root when a cutting is inserted in soil. Good results are also seen with cuttings of small-flowered cherries, such as *P. pendula, P. ×subhirtella,* and the Fuji cherry (*P. incisa*). Cuttings are made in summer or late in winter.

Winter cuttings in Japan are made in March or early April using well-developed one-season-old twigs with leaf buds. Thin twigs or a sprig with flower buds have a slower growth and should not be used for cuttings. The selected twigs are cut in parts that each have three buds. These parts, right side up, are set in clean water for about three hours. After this the wet end is wiped dry, another 0.5 cm or so is cut off, and the freshly cut lower end is dipped quickly in a growth-hormone powder. The cutting is then set in a well-drained mixture of friable loam and kept moist.

Summer cuttings in Japan are taken from well-developed leafy twigs in June. Again twigs that have flowered are useless. The upper part and the lower part of the twig are pruned off, leaving the middle part with four leaves of which the two lower ones are clipped away. The lower end of the cutting is set in clean water for three hours and, following the same handling as with the winter cuttings, dipped in a growth-hormone powder.

The cuttings are set slanted in a medium-grain friable loam and covered with a shade. If the two remaining leaves are large, half of each blade is cut away. The Japanese mountain cherry (*Prunus serrulata* var. *spontanea*) is said to strike rather easily from summer cuttings, at least easier than from winter cuttings.

Some European nurseries are experimenting with summer cuttings of 'Ama-no-gawa' and 'Kanzan' taken in mid-June. Cuttings 10 cm long, from the top of the twigs or from the middle, are dipped in a growth-hormone powder and set in a mixture of one part sand and four parts peat mold. Cuttings are raised at 25°C under glass and artificial mist, then hardened after having taken root. This method requires knowledge and resources. A major difficulty is getting the young plants through their first winter. So far there is not much experience with this method in Western countries, and it is still unknown how cherries on their own roots behave in the long term. Anchorage seems to be a problem as roots tend to develop mostly on one side of the plant. The less vigorous growth is seen as a weak point by the average grower who is used to trees on vigorous stock.

Many cherries, even horticultural varieties such as 'Taizan-fukun', are easily propagated from side shoots that develop from superficial roots or from a point low on the trunk. If this is the case, the tree can be cut back to a stump that is then covered with a soil mixture suitable for cuttings. In this mound, a group of rooting shoots, called a stool, can be developed. A stool can be exploited for procuring layers for many, many years. Care should be taken that molds, viruses, or other diseases are not given an opportunity to develop.

CHAPTER 3

Observing and Classifying Cherries

To take full advantage of the best that Japanese flowering cherries have to offer, it is necessary to be able to recognize each cultivar. Only then is it possible to choose, purchase, and grow the most desired one. For the collector and the nursery professional, it is even more important to be sure of the name of the tree at hand. Identification is done most adequately on living trees, and in particular on living flowers. It is, after all, because of the flowers that flowering cherries were selected, so it is there that one finds the more distinctive botanic details.

The most easily recognized part of the flowers is the petal. The color and shape of the flower from bud to fading are also important. The structure of the inflorescence, the foliage that unfolds before, after, or with the blossom, and the fruits are useful in identifying cherry cultivars. The sepals and calyx are particularly useful details because they are constant under differing growing conditions. Other distinguishing points are flowering time, whether late or early flowering, and tree shape. Finally, we will discuss the characteristics of bare twigs and buds in winter.

The descriptive details might in some cases be quite minute or even trifling, but the descriptions show that these details are often justified because of considerable differences in the practical use or the more aesthetic meaning of the plant. Details that are most characteristic and not variable are marked with an exclamation mark in parentheses (!) to facilitate quick identification of the plant. No conclusive identification is made without studying the flowers. Spring is a busy season for the cherry enthusiast!

Petals

Cherry flowers have from five to more than three hundred petals and can be divided into four groups based on the number of petals. Single-flowered cherries have five petals, though often with one to three extra. Semi-double-flowered cherries have ten to twenty petals, while double-flowered cherries have twenty-five to fifty petals. (The Japanese *yae* means "double" and is often added to names of double cherries, referred to as *yae-zakura*.) Cherries with more than one hundred petals are called chrysanthemum-flowered (*kiku-zakura* or *kiku-zaki-zakura* in Japanese). This group is discussed in more detail in a later section.

Rather than counting the number of petals per flower, we use terms such as "single" or "semi-double" to describe the general appearance of all the flowers on a tree. There is, however, the problem of variability. The cultivar 'Taoyame', for example, may have five petals per flower on one specimen and fifteen petals per flower on another specimen. The more petals per flower, the greater the potential variation. Thus chrysanthemum-flowered cherries are quite variable. One specimen may have as few as sixty petals, but the same cultivar, when grown in more favorable circumstances or when an old tree, may have one hundred petals.

Another factor affecting the number of petals is soil fertility. On lean soils the number of petals tends to be lower. Furthermore, flowers opening at the end of a tree's flowering period usually have fewer petals than the earlier ones. It is therefore wise to allow for variation in the number of petals when comparing descriptions.

Many cultivars have petaloids. Petaloids are stamens that have more or less developed into petals. Usually they are not of a perfect shape, and part of a filament or anther can be seen halfway up or at the end of the petaloid. Because they are derived from stamens, petaloids appear in the heart of the flower. As their number increases, the number of stamens diminishes. In the descriptions, petaloids are noted, but generally they are counted as petals.

Petals may be oval, ovate (egg-shaped), obovate (upside-down egg-shaped), or orbicular (round). This characteristic may vary, even within one flower; the outer petals of a double or a chrysanthemum-type flower are usually wider and less elongated than the inner ones. Petals are mostly retuse (emarginated; more or less indented at the top). The petals of 'Horinji' are not emarginate but entire, whereas those of 'Yae-murasaki-zakura' are very deeply indented.

Figure 37. Petal shapes (from left to right): oval, obovate, ovate, and round, with various degrees of indentations at the top of the petal from notched to fimbriate.

Petals may have a wavy edge or be wrinkled and rumpled as in 'Hokusai' in the early stage of developing. The emargination can be multiple and deep (fimbriate) as is seen with some petals of 'Washi-no-o'.

The size of petals is given in the descriptions as length (or height) by width.

Pistils and Stamens

A fully developed pistil, called "perfect" in the descriptions, has a mature ovary with style and stigma. Most single-flowered and semi-double-flowered cherries show perfect pistils, but double-flowered and chrysanthemum-flowered types do not show these and have all kinds of variations that are rather constant and form a useful key in identification. For example, some cultivars have one to four phylloid (leaflike) pistils. Others have phylloid pistils along with a perfect one. 'Imose' has two perfect pistils, and 'Horinji' has a group of them in the heart of its flower.

The length of the pistil with stigma compared to the longest stamens proves to be useful in identification. The stigma of 'Jo-nioi' is shorter than the longest stamens, while the pistils of 'Imose' are clearly longer than the longest stamens.

Stamens themselves are useful in identification. Some show a filament that is longer than the anther, as seen with 'Kanzan' and 'Pink Perfection'. Most have the anther simply standing at the top end of the filament. Flowers of 'Daikoku,' for example, are easily distinguished from the similar flowers of 'Pink Perfection': the latter show a filament that is longer than the anther.

Flowers

Flower Color

An important aspect of the appreciation of cherry blossoms is the color of the flowers, yet it is rarely a satisfactory feature in identification. Not only is color generally difficult to describe, in cherry flowers it is quite variable—and this not only within a cultivar but even on the same tree. A spring that begins cold and rainy followed by a sudden outburst of balmy weather gives a different blossom color than a spring that gradually warms up. Rootstock has proved to influence the color of flowers.

Figure 38. 'Fugenzo' has leaflike pistils (note their serration) with a rudimentary stigma, and filaments of stamens extending above the anther. Photo by author, 17 April 1997, Uryuyama campus of the Kyōto University of Art and Design.

All cherry flowers are darker when in bud, becoming paler or lighter when they expand. White-flowered cherries show a slight pinkish hue in bud, and pink cultivars have dark pink or almost red flowers in bud. Flowers in bud show the richly colored backside of the outer petals. When the flower opens, it shows the inner petals and the inner side of the outer petals, which are much less saturated in color. In determining the color of cherry flowers, one has to be aware of this difference and make a clear distinction between the color of the flowers in bud and the color of the expanded flowers.

Color should never be determined at the end of blossoming. Some cultivars change color when their flowers wither; then the petals in the heart may, just before shedding, turn to a purple-violet. With some cherries, such as 'Fugenzo', the color of the whole flower may change from white to pink, changing the aspect of the tree completely at the end of the blossoming. Only the stamens may turn to a darker color with the withering of the petals, as is observed for instance with 'Shibayama'. Such particulars are mentioned in the descriptions, but are not practical when working with the classification key to identify an unknown cherry. It is best to examine flower color when the flowers are fully expanded and in their prime.

To avoid misunderstanding about the difference between hues such as "purplish pink" or "splendid pink," colors in the descriptions are given as numbers of the *Colour Chart,* edited by the Royal Horticultural Society (80 Vincent Square, London). The numbers appear in brackets after the color as, for instance, bronze-green (RHS 152-A) or pink (RHS 65-D). The society has grouped colors and named these groups. The Yellow-Green Group, for instance, has forty-four distinct hues, ranging from a disco yellow that almost hurts the eyes to a dark, camouflage army-green. Referring to any shade within such extremes as "yellow-green" could be misleading. Still, the *Colour Chart* and its numbers are gratefully used for precision, and colors are described in words to give readers a general understanding.

Western cherry botanists choose their colors from the Red-Purple Group of the RHS *Colour Chart* when describing the shades of pink cherry blossoms, whereas Japanese researchers tend to choose from the Red Group. Many cultivar names include the Japanese word *beni,* always translated in English as "red," although pink would be more appropriate. *Beni* in Japan of old was the red dye stuff derived from safflower (*Carthamus tinctorius*) that women used as rouge. What is therefore an elegant word in Japanese for describing the pink flowers of cherries, becomes "red" in English, corresponding to the Red Group of the RHS *Colour Chart.*

Flower Shape

The shape of a developed flower is also characteristic for a cultivar, and some basic types can be described. The flowers of 'Ichiyo', for example, spread to an open shape that can be flat as a saucer. Other flowers may be fuzzy, with petals in curls, set obliquely, or folded a little, as seen with 'Hokusai'. Still, the ovary can be seen in the heart of its flowers: a ring of petals with a nice round hole forms the corolla in flowers of this type. Petals may be wrinkled and rumpled, and crisscrossed in the heart of the flower so that the ovary is not visible from above, as illustrated by the flowers of 'Ito-kukuri', for example. If a flower has numerous petals and looks like a powder puff, it is said to be a chrysanthemum-type flower.

Figure 39. Types of cherry flowers.

The size of flowers helps to identify a cherry. Ingram (1948) and others used to spread flowers flat on a piece of paper when measuring them. In such descriptions flower diameters turn out to be a centimeter or so more than in most other sources. In the descriptions in the present volume the diameter is measured on live flowers on the tree, fully expanded without any forceful spreading of the petals.

Chrysanthemum-type Flowers

Botanists define a cherry flower with more than one hundred petals as a chrysanthemum type. This definition should not be taken too strictly, however, because chrysanthemum-flowered cherries in colder regions or less favorable circumstances tend to have fewer petals, as few as sixty to eighty. On the other hand, up to 380 petals, including the tiny threads in the heart of the flower, can be counted in well-developed flowers of 'Kenroku-en-kiku-zakura'. The number of petals increases with the age of the tree.

Chrysanthemum-type flowers are sterile as a rule and, as might be expected, show much deviating flower anatomy, which helps in classifying plants. All the flower organs may be multiplied, and even the flower as a whole may be doubled. There may be a little second flower completely furnished with sepals, petals, stamens, and pistil in the heart of a larger flower. The form is well described as a two-story flower. A week or so after the main flower has opened, the second-story flower shows itself in bud stage as a dark pink heart inside the light pink petals of the main flower. Otherwise one may note the green sepals of the second-story flower showing up distinctly in the heart of the main flower. Cutting the flower in half with a razor shows the construction of such flowers most clearly.

The calyx of chrysanthemum-flowered forms helps in classifying these cherries. It might be narrow and funnel-shaped, set on the pedicel with a smooth transition. A cross section of such a calyx shows that it is not hollow and that all flower organs are set upon it in a disorderly way. Another type of calyx is a widely flattened disk that stands on the pedicel as a distinctly separated receptacle.

All petals of the first flower can be easily plucked off the receptacle, leaving the second-story flower in the middle as seen with 'Kenroku-en-kiku-zakura' and related cultivars. The receptacle of this type has a protruding center, most easily seen in cross section.

A disk shape without protrusion is seen with other chrysanthemum

Figure 40. Detail of a two-story flower, 'Nison-in-fugenzo'. The beginning of a third-story flower can be discerned. Photo by Arie Peterse, 30 April 1996, Mishima.

types, such as 'Kiku-zakura' or Raikoji-kiku-zakura'. Later in the season the organs of the second-story flower, and if present the third-story flower, can also be plucked off. The bare receptacle with the (accessory) sepals resembles a dandelion head after its seeds are blown away. For the calyx to be useful in classifying cherries, it is best to dissect and inspect the calyxes of at least ten flowers and, if possible, once when the flowers are at their prime and a second time just before they are shed.

Miyoshi (1916) distinguished four different multipetaled garden forms of this type and grouped them under the name *Chrysanthemiflorae*. At present about twenty so-called chrysanthemum cherries are cultivated including 'Asano', 'Kiku-shidare-zakura', 'Najima-zakura', 'Taizan-fukun', and others such as those discussed above.

Flower Buds
Apart from the color of the expanded flowers or their shape, the shape of the flower buds can be a decisive key. This shape is, however, related to the number of petals and is therefore more or less a secondary characteristic. Single-flowered cultivars usually have acute buds, semi-double ones have

egg-shaped to oval buds, and double-flowered cherries have mostly conical buds. In some cases the bud shape may confirm a classification, and
some other details may give us keys.

Sepals can be tightly pressed against the bud or, in other cultivars, distinctly separated; only rarely sepals are reflexed over the calyx tube. Few
cultivars, such as 'Ichihara-tora-no-o', show part of the style and the stigma
sticking out of the bud when it is still closed. All identification characteristics of flower buds can be perceived at their best on mature buds that will
open within a week.

Fragrant Flowers, Nioi-zakura

Many Japanese flowering cherries have distinctly scented flowers. Their
cumarin-like fragrance is similar to that of crushed almonds, although the
scent of 'Ama-no-gawa' has been associated also with freesia. Fragrant cherries are popularly called *nioi-zakura* in Japan; the word *nioi*, meaning "fragrance," is often added to a cultivar name. Thus one may come across
'Goten-nioi', 'Hakusan-nioi', 'Hirano-nioi', 'Yae-nioi', and many others.

Most individuals of the Oshima cherry have fragrant flowers in their native habitats, and many *nioi-sakura* are straight selections of this cherry.
'Hosokawa-nioi' is not seen very often outside Japan, but in the West one
may come across 'Goza-no-ma-nioi', 'Jo-nioi', 'Surugadai-nioi', or 'Taki-
nioi'. All five are nicely scented and have botanic details very similar to the
Oshima cherry. 'Nioi-zakura' as a cultivar name applies to a rarely seen selection of the Japanese mountain cherry.

As a key in identifying cultivars, fragrance is not very useful since it is
quite variable and is difficult to describe. No "Odor Chart" helps us to define scents more precisely. In cold and rainy periods no fragrance can generally be perceived, except on cherries with strongly scented flowers such
as 'Ama-no-gawa' and 'Jo-nioi'. Those flowers whose fragrance is rarely perceived, only when the weather is unusually favorable, are described as having "no distinct fragrance."

Inflorescences and Flower Stalks

The way cherry flowers are attached to their stalks provides many key characteristics, and it is worthwhile to study the inflorescences in detail. The
Prunus serrulata garden forms bear their flowers in corymbs. A flowering

cherry with umbellate inflorescences is likely to be a form of *P. sargentii* or *P.* ×*yedoensis*, or a nursery hybrid, such as *P.* 'Accolade'. *Prunus pendula* or the closely related *P.* ×*subhirtella* also have umbellate inflorescences, but are readily identified by their pitcher-shaped calyx, as discussed below. The early inflorescences of the winter-flowering 'Fudan-zakura', formed before mid-April, can sometimes be umbellate, but as spring warms up, they stretch to the usual corymbs. With the corymbose inflorescences of 'Yae-murasaki-zakura', the little stalks of the flowers, the pedicels, may all spring from almost the same point on the main stalk, seemingly to form an umbel-on-a-stalk.

From the main stalk (peduncle), the subordinate stalks (pedicels) branch off. Each pedicel holds one flower. The length of the peduncle, pedicel,

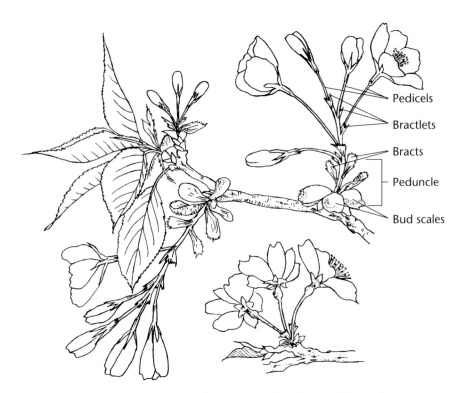

Figure 41. Two kinds of cherry inflorescence: (above) corymbose inflorescence with a main flower stalk (peduncle), on which the branching subordinate flower stalks (pedicels) are set; (below) umbellate inflorescence in which pedicels sprout from one point.

and inflorescence can be used as a key characteristic in classification. Following Ingram (1948) and Japanese sources such as the Flower Association of Japan (1982), the length of the peduncle is measured from the implantation of the inflorescence on the twig to the branching off of the first pedicel. Miyoshi (1916) measured every part of any stalk between the side-branches, numbered the parts, and gave the measure of all the parts separately. Such overly precise observation gives much superfluous information; moreover, it suggests a statistical constancy in the length of flower stalks, which is not constant at all. The length of the stalks may vary with the number of flowers per corymb, with the age and vitality of the tree, and with weather. Flower stalks are, for example, considerably longer in cooler Hokkaidō than in warmer, more southern Kyōto. The same difference is seen when comparing cherries in the Netherlands and those in southern France. Peduncles and pedicels are longer in later flowering forms. For instance, the average length of the peduncle of the early flowering 'Washi-no-o' is about 1.5 cm whereas it is about 5 cm with the late flowering 'Shogetsu'; when winter is cold and spring is late, 'Shogetsu' might have even longer peduncles. Lengths of flower stalks give us a pointer, rather than a clue; figures are certainly not absolute.

The number of flowers per inflorescence ranges from two to eight or more. Within one cultivar again one cannot speak of a constant number; there is, however, an average minimum and an average maximum.

The inflorescence sprouts from between bud scales and bracts at the twig. These leaflike organs can be green, red, or bronze-brown. The inside of these bracts in most forms of *Prunus serrulata* is pubescent (covered with hairs, which in this case are brown), while in most forms of *P. ×subhirtella* the inner side of the bracts is less pubescent than the outer side. Corymbose inflorescences have usually two more leaflike bracts higher up the peduncle, whereas smaller bractlets are found at points where pedicels branch off. The shape of bracts and bractlets varies from almost lanceolate to obovate; the top can be entire or divided in two or three ends (bifid or trifid), and the edges can be ciliate to fimbriate. Their length may vary from 6 to 12 mm and their color from yellow-green to deep, bright red. Variability of color, shape, and size is great, not only within a cultivar, but also within the inflorescences of one tree. Even within one corymb one may find considerable differences, which makes these bracts not very useful for classification purposes. Only in a rare case, such as with 'Tagui-arashi' or 'Bendono', the

Figure 42. The corymbose inflorescences of the Japanese mountain cherry (*Prunus serrulata* var. *spontanea*). Compare this Dutch plant with the Japanese plant of Figure 77 to see the effects of climate, weather, and variability on the growing characteristics of Japanese flowering cherries. Photo by Arie Peterse, 4 May 1986, Wageningen Botanic Gardens of the Agricultural University, Netherlands.

red bracts and bud scales show so obviously that they are noted in the descriptions.

Pubescence of peduncle and pedicels is typical and distinctive in *Prunus pendula* and *P.* ×*subhirtella*. Among the forms of *P. serrulata*, 'Shibayama' has little hair on the peduncle, whereas the peduncles and pedicels of 'Hiyodori-zakura', 'Taizan-fukun', and 'Takasago' are clearly pubescent.

Leaves and Stipules

Foliage unfolds in spring either before the blossom, at the same time, or after the flowers open. The appearance of the foliage in relation to the blossom is a constant characteristic for each cultivar. In time, amateur cherry enthusiasts can easily recognize the general appearance of a sprig. The flowers of 'Takasago' always open, for example, with the unfolding, typically orange-bronze foliage. Only when trees grow (very) old does the foliage tend to come out later than usual in relation to the blossom, and even a trained observer is easily confused in these situations. In colder climates, foliage of some cherries might be later.

Cherry leaves have their particularities that are of help when classifying a tree. The color is characteristic with young foliage, but the same problem arises as with the flowers. Again color differs with season, with changes in the weather, and with the rootstock. Differences in color, nonetheless, can be quite striking, and with some precautions leaf color is a useful key.

The early leaves, just at the moment when they unfold, show distinctively different colors on the inside of the leaf blade. This is the color mentioned in the descriptions of the cultivars. As many cherries unfold their leaves with the blossom, one can often examine the colors of both at the same time. Late-flowering cherries such as 'Fugenzo' already have developed leaves when flowering, and so in this case we have described the color of young foliage at the tip of a fresh shoot. Again the RHS *Colour Chart* proved helpful in defining colors exactly. They vary from yellow-green, green, or bronzelike (RHS 153-A, 152-A to 152-D, 144-A) to brown or red-brown (RHS 166-A to 166-C, 173 to 176, 199-A to 199-C). The colors are named in the descriptions to assist readers not having access to the RHS *Colour Chart.*

Freshly developed foliage in the greenish range often shows a bronze hue. Dark red-brown sprouts always expand to mature leaves that are darker green than the average but no longer red. 'Kanzan', for example, puts forth brownish shoots, and the leaves are already dark green when the flowers are in their prime. Therefore foliage color is only useful as an identification key if one has formed an idea of the full range that it may show during the developing of the leaves.

The underside of the leaf can be glaucous (whitish) as with the Japanese mountain cherry (*Prunus serrulata* var. *spontanea*) and garden forms such as 'Ichihara-tora-no-o'. It is less outspoken with such cherries as 'Raikoji-kiku-zakura' and 'Baigoji-juzukake-zakura' and always best perceived in dried and pressed leaves of a herbarium specimen.

Fine autumn colors can be found with many Japanese flowering cherries. The splendor of *Prunus sargentii* is well known and 'Sunset Boulevard' was even selected because of this. Among the forms of *P. serrulata*, 'Shirotae' shows gold-yellowish fall tints, 'Ojochin' bright orange and red, and 'Ukon' red and purple-brown. The autumn hues of 'Hokusai' vary from brownish red to orange-red.

The serrate edge of developed leaves, notched like a saw, is characteristic of Japanese cherries. This serration is best observed on well-developed leaves and is most visible on the projecting bend of the edge below the top, the "shoulder" of the leaf blade. It is there that one may note that serration can be single or double. Alpine cherries, such as *Prunus incisa* and *P. nipponica,* have a double-serrated edge that is coarsely incised.

At the time of blossoming, the foliage is barely out. This is the best time to examine the leaves for coarse or fine serration. A course serration can be easily perceived without a magnifying lens, whereas it is helpful to discern the teeth of a fine serration in unfolding sprouts. A more exact definition of the size of teeth in millimeters has not proved to be of any practical use. Teeth can terminate in long, slender bristles, as if awn-tipped. A strikingly

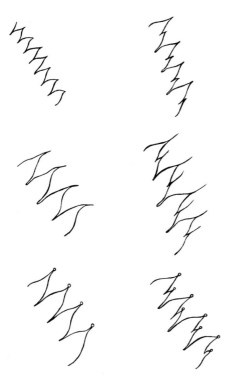

Figure 43. Single (left) and double (right) serration, both aristate (middle), and with glands (below).

extreme example is 'Shirotae'. Such serration, called aristate, is an identification aid. Teeth, or bristles, can also have a small gland at the top, which usually can be seen only with a magnifying lens. Most garden forms show a few such glands on the lower half of the leaf blade, but sometimes they are set on the tip of every tooth, up to the top of the leaf. The glands can be white, light pink, or red. It is characteristic of such cherries as 'Choshu-hizakura', 'Najima-zakura', and 'Yae-murasaki-zakura' that all teeth have dark red glands. This has to be ascertained on the young leaves that have only just unfolded; the glands disappear quickly with the expanding of the leaves.

The size of the mature (fully developed) leaf is not an identification aid because it is too variable. Moreover, in the flowering season when we are busy studying the flowers, hardly any developed leaves are found. Leaf size is therefore not discussed in the descriptions of the cultivars. Generally, the

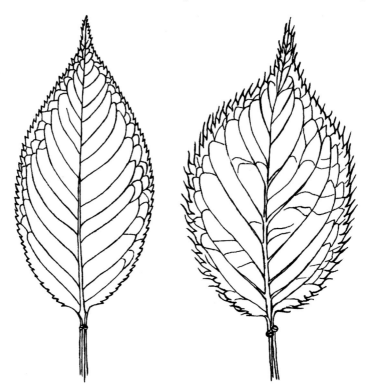

Figure 44. Fine, single serration (left) such as seen with leaves of the Japanese mountain cherry (*Prunus serrulata* var. *spontanea*), and bristled (aristate) serration (right) as seen with leaves of many *Prunus serrulata* cultivars.

leaves of bonsai selections of *Prunus incisa* are 2 to 3 cm long. Among the forms of *P. serrulata,* the rather small leaves of 'Mikuruma-gaeshi' are about 10 cm long and 5 cm wide; larger leaves, such as those of 'Tai-haku', can be 17 cm long and 8 cm wide. Within a cultivar, leaf size may vary several centimeters. Therefore, even in summer when the leaves are completely developed, measuring them is still quite useless for classification.

Although many garden forms show a wide variety in the shape of their leaves, even on one branch, many constant characteristics can be observed. The leaf tip of many cherries, for instance, may be acuminate (tapering to a point), or even caudate (like a tail), as with most cultivars of *Prunus serrulata.* Many leaves of 'Ojochin', however, lack a tip and are obtuse. The occurrence of such ovate leaves helps identify some difficult forms of *P. serrulata.* 'Kiku-shidare-zakura' has a distinctly acute leaf tip, but it is not caudate.

Figure 45. Well-developed stipules at the leaves of a rank sucker of 'Tai-Haku'. Single and divided stipules may be found, and glands at the tip of teeth are larger than normal because of the abnormal growth.

Another fairly constant characteristic is the shape of the leaf base. Usually it is obtuse, but it can also be cuneate (wedge-shaped), which is extreme with the obovate leaf blade of 'Taoyame'.

Leaf blade and leaf stalk are pubescent in garden forms that have pubescent flower stalks, such as 'Taizan-fukun' and 'Takasago'. Leaf stalks of the spring cherries *Prunus* ×*subhirtella* and *P. pendula,* and of *P. incisa* are pubescent.

The length of the petiole, the leaf stalk, offers little help for classification. The same must be said about the veining of the leaf.

Up to four nectar-secreting glands (nectaries) may be found on the leaf stalk or on the edge of the leaf at its base. If these glands are active, a drop of sugary liquid stands on the gland. Usually these glands are red, but on the leaves of one cherry the variation is so great, that this detail is usually not taken up in the descriptions. *Prunus incisa* has typical nectaries on short stalks, resembling the stalked eyes of a snail.

Cherry leaves have small leaflike appendages, the stipules on the base of the leaf stalk. The tree sheds the stipules shortly after the foliage unfolds. These leafy organs can be linear and undivided, or approximately divided in two or more forklike extensions. The extent of this bifurcation is typical and a rather constant character for each cultivar. It helps in identification. Some attention must be paid though to the place of the stipules observed. The leaves of a sprout at the tip of a flowering twig show the most typical stipules, while a rank sucker without flowers has abnormally developed stipules that cannot be used in classification. Like the serrated leaves of some cultivars, the stipules also may have glands on the tips.

Often ants can be seen on the young shoots of cherries. They are busy collecting honey from the nectaries on the leaf stalks, but also picking and carrying away the glands of the stipules and of the serrated edges of the leaves. One ant may handle thirty, fifty, or even eighty glands and nectaries in ten minutes. The advantage for the cherry tree is clear: the ants, as true landowners, protect their cherry fields from plant lice and all kinds of bugs.

Sepals

Sepals are most useful for classification. They are, within a cultivar, constant in shape and size. Age or vitality of the tree does not seem to have much influence, which provides us with an important key characteristic.

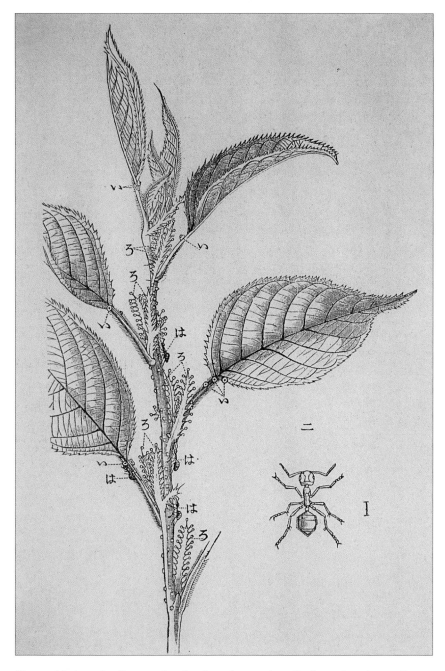

Figure 46. Ants feeding on the glands and nectaries of a flowering cherry. From a botany textbook, secondary school (Itō 1906).

Generally speaking, there are three types of sepals. Elongated or lanceolate sepals, as found with 'Jo-nioi' for example, are three times as long as wide. Elongated and triangular sepals are about two times as long as they are wide; this type is most common and found with flowers of 'Shirotae' and the like. Triangular sepals are less than two times as long as wide, as found with 'Taizan-fukun' or *Prunus incisa.*

The size of sepals can help in identification. For accurate measuring, it is necessary to cut away the calyx with a sharp razor-blade just below the sepals. After the petals are plucked off, the separated ring of sepals must be laid on a white piece of paper after which measuring is easily done with a transparent ruler. Few garden forms have sepals that narrow again at the base. This is most pronounced with the sepals of 'Hokusai', which have a blunt top. Although 'Hokusai' is one of the many double, pink cultivars, it is always quickly recognized because of its typical sepals. 'Horinji' and 'Taoyame' have dark purple-red sepals that are, moreover, in the case of 'Taoyame', reflexed over the calyx tube.

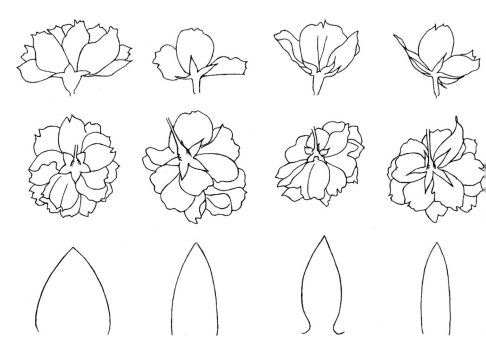

Figure 47. Sepals can be broad and triangular to narrow-lanceolate.

The serration of the sepals is an important classification key and is often easily noticed on buds just before they open. 'Pink Perfection' has serrated sepals that readily distinguish it from the similar but nonserrated 'Daikoku'. 'Fugenzo' has a distinct serration halfway up the sepals, but not at the base and not at the tip. *Prunus* ×*subhirtella* and *P. pendula* mix hairs and teeth at the edge of the sepal. Some garden forms do not show a clear serration, yet they cannot be described as unserrated. Such sepals have only a few teeth and again form a constant cultivar characteristic that helps in classifying cultivars such as 'Washi-no-o'. Some garden cherries, such as 'Kiku-shidare-zakura' and most other chrysanthemum-flowered forms, show accessory sepals; among the five main sepals are five or more smaller, extra sepals.

Calyx

Like the sepals, the calyx is a very reliable characteristic for identifying cherries. Its shape may vary among *Prunus serrulata* cultivars from broad and disk-shaped (as in 'Kiku-zakura'), or a more narrow funnel-shape (as in 'Fugenzo'), to a tightly campanulate calyx (as in 'Jo-nioi'). More or less campanulate or funnel-shaped calyxes are found between the extremes. Forms of *P. pendula* or the closely related *P.* ×*subhirtella* have an urceolate (pitcher-shaped) calyx, which has a globular base with a narrow cylindrical mouth, widening again at the edge with its five sepals and petals. The urceolate calyx of these cherries is pubescent. The calyx of *P. incisa* is funnel-shaped and can be so long that it becomes quite tubular.

All single-flowered and some semi-double-flowered cultivars have a thickening at the downward end of the calyx where the ovary is attached. This swelling is often lacking in the double-flowered cherries because the ovary is hardly developed; instead of normal pistils there are sometimes leaflike carpels. The swelling makes for a distinct transition from calyx to pedicel, which is a useful classification feature to separate cultivars that show such a swelling from those that lack a swelling and thus do not have a distinct transition between pedicel and calyx. Where the calyx narrows to the pedicel, the surface can be rumpled, as happens with the flowers of 'Pink Perfection'.

The calyx of most *Prunus serrulata* cultivars is glabrous and green with a slight purplish hue. The calyx of 'Takasago' is pubescent like the spring cherries *P.* ×*subhirtella* and *P. pendula*. The size of the calyx is given in the

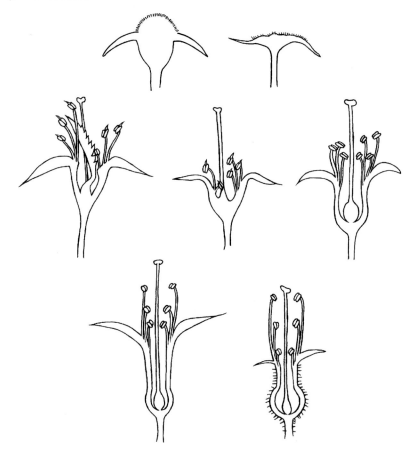

Figure 48. Calyx shapes (from top to bottom): disk-shaped, funnel-shaped, campanulate, and urceolate.

descriptions as the length by the width. It varies from 2 × 5 mm of 'Fugen-zo' to 9 × 4 mm of 'Shirotae'. To measure the calyx, it is necessary to cut it lengthwise with a very sharp knife and measure with a transparent ruler. The calyx of most chrysanthemum-flowered forms is whole, not hollow.

Fruits

Cherries are fertile plants as a rule. Hybrids and, in favorable seasons, even triploid cultivars such as 'Ariake' bear fruits. Cherry fruits form an interesting challenge for experiments and the breeding of new forms, but for classification purposes they are not very useful. In fact, identification of cherries occurs in the flowering season, so that the fruits appear long after classification is completed. Furthermore, the fruits do not stay on the tree very long, as birds are quick to discover them. Therefore, not much importance is given to the fruits in the descriptions of the cultivars. One may find ovate, little cherries that are almost black (as in 'Tagui-arashi'), purplish-black, small, and round cherries (as in 'Jo-nioi'), and even twin-fruits in 'Imose', which bears two fruits at the end of a stalk.

Time of Flowering

Time of flowering is another key in identifying cherry cultivars. One must, however, have experience and insight in the data on flowering, since changes in weather can result in earlier or later flowering by several weeks. What is constant, though, is the successive order in which the botanic forms and cultivars put forth their blossoms.

Spring as a season can be short and condensed or can be spread more evenly with gradual rising temperatures for many weeks or months. Therefore one needs to have an idea of the characteristics of spring in the region where one is observing cherries. Japan's short and explosive spring generally has only three weeks between the average early and the average late cherry blossoms of the garden cultivars. In the moderate climate of Britain or the Netherlands, spring can last six weeks or more. The length of the cherry season may also differ from year to year. After a severe winter that lasts longer than usual, early flowering cherries such as 'Shirotae' can be two weeks later than in other years. Late-flowering cherries, such as 'Fugenzo', catch up and flower on time even though spring has set in later than usual. On the whole the cherry season is two weeks shorter than normal in this case. What does not change is the relative order in which the cultivars burst into bloom.

After winter, when 'Fudan-zakura' blooms, the season begins with *Prunus pendula* f. *ascendens*, followed by *P. serrulata* var. *speciosa* and *P.* ×*yedoensis,* which both bloom before *P. serrulata* var. *spontanea*. Then the first garden cherries come into bloom with such cultivars as 'Bendono', 'Ariake', 'Tagui-arashi', 'Washi-no-o', and 'Tai-haku'. The latter, 'Tai-haku', is a good marker on the scale of flowering times as it will always and everywhere flower earlier than 'Fukurokuju' or 'Hokusai', which are representative of the later-flowering cultivars. This later group of cherries includes *P. serrulata* var. *pubescens* and the garden forms 'Edo-zakura', 'Hakusan-hata-zakura',

'Ito-kukuri', 'Kiku-shidare-zakura', 'Pink Perfection', 'Taizan-fukun', and 'Yokihi'. This group blooms a week or two before 'Kanzan', which is a marker for the later-flowering garden cherries 'Gyoiko', 'Kirin', 'Taki-nioi', and 'Taoyame'. The peak of the season is over with the flowers of 'Fugenzo', which appear a week or at least a couple of days later. The recurrent bloom of these late cherries can be seen with the blossoms of 'Shogetsu' or 'Shimidsu-zakura' and with most chrysanthemum-flowered forms such as 'Kiku-zakura'. In autumn one can expect the blossom of 'Jugatsu-zakura'.

Thus one may select several easily recognized standard cultivars and set up a calendar, filling in the flowering times of the other cherries as they are observed. Such insight into the order of flowering gives a helpful key in classification. By comparing the descriptions, one may see whether an unidentified cherry blooms earlier or later than the identified cultivar. Thus one has another characteristic that forms a key in classification.

In the descriptions an average flowering time of a moderate climate as found in western Europe is given. There one may expect the first garden cherries to blossom in the second week of April and the last, 'Fugenzo', in early June. The flowering seasons are given as an average for the temperate zone, only occasionally is the season given for Tokyo, in which case it is explicitly identified as such.

Most cherries keep their flowers longer than is generally believed. There may be two or three weeks between the first bloom and the first shedding of the petals; the double flowers remain longer than the single ones. Cherries that keep their flowers long include 'Fukurokuju', 'Shogetsu', 'Takasago', and 'Ukon'. *Prunus* ×*yedoensis* is short-lived with only sixteen days between the first flower opening and the last petal shed. *Prunus serrulata* var. *pubescens*, 'Surugadai-nioi', and 'Nara-no-yae-zakura' also have relatively short flowering seasons.

Tree Shape

Tree shape is useful for identifying cherries. Five types of tree shapes can be discerned: (1) fastigiate growth (erect, narrow crown), as in 'Ama-no-gawa'; (2) a broad ovate shape, as in 'Fudan-zakura'; (3) a funnel shape, as in 'Kanzan' and 'Hokusai', becoming very broad in 'Ichiyo', 'Edo-zakura', *Prunus pendula* f. *ascendens,* and *P.* ×*yedoensis;* (4) an umbrella shape (very broad with a flattened crown, thick and almost horizontal limbs), as in

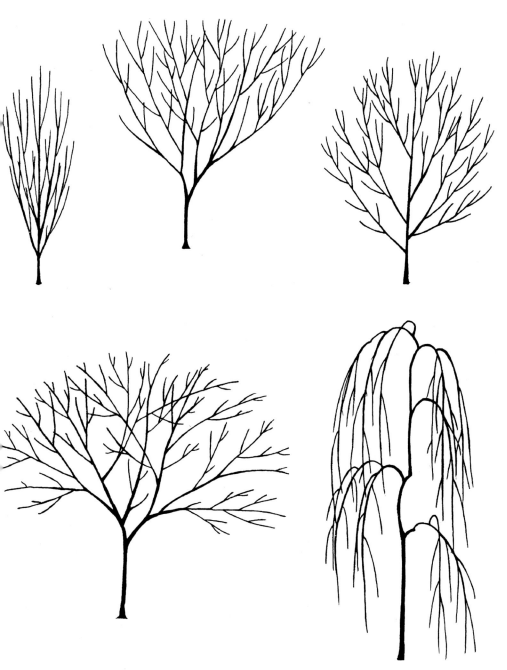

Figure 49. Tree shapes of Japanese flowering cherries (from top to bottom, left to right): fastigiate, vaselike, broad ovate, umbrella-like, and weeping.

'Shirotae' and very old specimens of *P. pendula* f. *ascendens* or *P.×yedoensis;* and (5) a weeping shape, as in 'Kiku-shidare-zakura' and the weeping forms of *P. pendula.*

Rank and young plants generally grow more erect, whereas trees with growth defects or a dwindling vitality tend to become broader or even let their branches hang a little. A free-standing tree will grow broader than one that is squeezed between other trees. Damage from wind, traffic, or pruning may have its influence as does rootstock. 'Fugenzo' may show a broad and flattened crown when grafted on a standard of *Prunus avium,* whereas it only makes a low stem with usually two heavy, ascending, and forked limbs when it stands on its own roots. Vigorous growth can cause a powerful stock to produce long limbs between the bifurcations, resulting in a more open tree form. Therefore, apart from 'Ama-no-gawa' with its fastigiate growth and the weeping forms, one must make some allowance for tree shape in the descriptions that follow.

The maximum size is typical in mature trees. 'Yae-murasaki-zakura' obviously forms a smaller tree than 'Kanzan'. The full size is usually given in the descriptions in chapters 4 and 5.

Buds and Twigs in Winter

The twigs formed in spring and early summer show variation in color after the leaves have dropped in autumn. The color of these one-year-old twigs is difficult to describe, but the upper side, turned towards the sunlight, is often more red-brown or brownish, whereas the underside of most forms of *Prunus serrulata* is more beige or goldish. The branches of 'Kanzan' are dark brown on all sides. Uncommon are the young branches of 'Ichiyo' that are chestnut-brown above and beige to almost orange below. The twigs of 'Jo-nioi' are shiny gray to pale-brown, betraying this cultivar's close relation to the Oshima cherry (*Prunus serrulata* var. *speciosa*).

Thickness and stiffness of twigs are characteristic for some cherries. For example, the twigs of 'Taizan-fukun' are thin and supple, whereas those of 'Fukurokuju' or 'Kanzan' are thick and stiff. Young trees in the full vigor of their growth, however, do not show this very obviously. An older 'Ichihara-tora-no-o' is easily recognized in winter because of the many thick, short spurs that are spaced regularly over the upper side of the thick branches; some chrysanthemum-flowered cherries have the same branching.

Twigs of *Prunus×subhirtella* and related cherries can be thin and supple with short, thin flower spurs ending in an acuminate bud. Buds may have some pubescence, as is true for *P. pendula* var. *ascendens*.

The end bud of a winter twig is more tapered as a rule. It gives a leaf sprout and blossom. The flower buds of garden cultivars are more rounded and found lower on the twig. These are larger and thicker than their counterparts in the botanic species, and show much variability. The flower buds of 'Ojochin' are large and oval to almost round. Those of 'Shirotae' are long and pointed, about 9 × 3 mm. 'Ichiyo' has short and oval buds, 7 × 4 mm, with an acuminate tip. 'Fudan-zakura' is easily recognized in winter, because the buds are pushing already in December, showing the flowers peeping between the scales; the buds are short, round, and blunt, about 5 × 4 mm. 'Ukon' has thick and oval winter buds that are 8 × 4 mm with an acuminate tip.

In winter, therefore, several identifying characteristics can be observed in cherries. These winter characteristics are found in cherries that are already easily distinguished in spring by their flowers. Information on winter details is, therefore, superfluous and not given in the descriptions in chap-

Figure 50. Twigs of four flowering cherries in winter (in pairs from left to right, with the left image of each pair showing the upper side of the twig and the right showing the underside of the twig): Japanese mountain cherry (*Prunus serrulata* var. *spontanea*), Oshima cherry (*Prunus serrulata* var. *speciosa*, round buds), 'Fugenzo' (two end buds), and 'Somei-yoshino' (*Prunus×yedoensis*). All twigs are of moderate vigor. The Oshima cherry and Oshima hybrid 'Somei-yoshino' show a clear difference in coloring of upper and under side. Photo by author, 2 February 1997, Uryuyama campus of the Kyōto University of Art and Design.

ters 4 and 5. Careful observation of flowering cherries forms the basis for a successful classification as proposed in the key that follows.

Classification Key

This classification key is not exhaustive. It focuses on Japanese flowering cherries of the *Prunus serrulata* group and some closely related cherries commonly found in Western countries. A few rarer forms, but only easily recognized ones, are also mentioned in the key. All the cherries in the key have, as a rule, corymbose inflorescences, acuminate leaves (most have an acute or even aristate serration), large and thick flower buds, narrow sepals that usually do not reflex over the calyx tube, and often large single or double flowers.

If the cherry to be classified does not have corymbs, that is, if the pedicels of its flowers are not borne on a stalk (peduncle) but appear from the bud on the twig in an umbel, it is more likely to be a form of *Prunus sargentii, P.* ×*yedoensis,* or something similar to *P.* 'Accolade'. If the flowers in an umbel have a pitcher-shaped calyx, and if the pedicels are pubescent, the cherry is likely to be a form of *P. pendula* or *P.* ×*subhirtella.* Cherries with umbellate inflorescences are not covered in this key.

The differences between garden cultivars are often slight and can vary according to site or even weather. One way to avoid some problems has been to define more than one characteristic per step and to allow for a choice among three options at some points. After determining the classification of a plant by using the key, one always needs to verify other botanic details with the description of that cultivar in the text.

Key

4. Flower diameter small, ca. 2.5–4.0 cm 5

    Flower diameter medium-sized, ca. 4.0–4.8 cm 8

    Flower diameter large, ca. 4.8–6.0 cm 12

5. Flowers in autumn, midwinter, or very early spring before the
cherry season 6

    Flowers in spring 7

6. Flowers early in the season, often with frozen, half-opened flower
buds; peduncle shorter than 1 cm; young foliage bronze-brown;
flower diameter 3.0–3.7 cm . . . . 'Fudan-zakura'

7. Petiole pubescent; young foliage green or bronze-green; peduncle
longer than 1.5 cm; flower diameter 2.5–3.0 cm, late flowering
. . . . *Prunus serrulata* var. *pubescens*

    Young foliage red to brown-red; sepals not serrated; flower diameter
2.5–3.5 cm. . . . . *Prunus serrulata* var. *spontanea*

    Young foliage bronze-green to green; sepals lanceolate, with a few
teeth, or serrated; flower diameter 3.5–4.0 cm . . . .
. . . . *Prunus serrulata* var. *speciosa*

8. No flowers with petaloids. 9

    Flowers have petaloids or some flowers show few petaloids. 10

9. Young foliage brown to bronze-brown; richly blossoming; blossom
fragrant . . . . 'Taki-nioi'

    Young foliage bronze-green to green; sepals lanceolate, with a few
teeth, or serrated; flower diameter 3.5–4.0 cm . . . .
. . . . *Prunus serrulata* var. *speciosa*

10. Blossom strongly fragrant, petals 12–16 mm wide; heart of flower
does not turn red at end of flowering; vase-shaped tree with
flattened crown . . . . 'Jo-nioi'

    Blossom occasionally fragrant, sparingly pubescent on petiole,
peduncle, pedicel, or calyx; heart of flower turns red at end of
flowering. . . . . 'Shibayama'

    Not like that, blossom not or only slightly fragrant 11

11. Blossom with no distinct fragrance; broad, fastigiate tree shape;
petals 16–19 mm wide . . . . 'Hakusan-hata-zakura'

    Blossom not distinctly fragrant, petals with irregular wrinkles and
often fimbriate at the top end. . . . . 'Washi-no-o'

12. Young foliage bronze-green; mature leaves often lack the caudate tip;
flower diameter 5.0–5.5 cm; quite a few flowers with more than

5 petals . . . . 'Ojochin'
Young foliage brownish; leaves usually with an acuminate tip;
flower diameter 5.5–6.0 cm; almost no flowers with more than
5 petals. . . . . 'Tai-haku'

13. Petiole pubescent; young foliage green or bronze-green; peduncle
 longer than 1.5 cm; flower diameter 2.5–3.0 cm . . . .
 . . . . *Prunus serrulata* var. *pubescens*
 Petiole glabrous 14

14. Flower diameter medium-sized, less than ca. 4.7 cm. 15
 Flower diameter large, more than ca. 4.7 cm 16

15. Flowers rather early; 2–3 flowers per corymb; vigorous growth;
 petals ca. 18 × 15 mm . . . . 'Bendono'
 Flowers early or in the middle of the cherry season; rather slow
 growing; petals ca. 18 × 13 mm . . . . 'Tagui-arashi'
 Flowers early or in the middle of the cherry season; rather slow
 growing; blossom fragrant, petals ca. 19 × 16 mm . . . . 'Arashiyama'
 Flowers in the middle of the cherry season; 3–4 flowers per corymb,
 remarkably pink, frequently with extra petals; rather slow growing;
 petals ca. 20 × 17 mm. 'Choshu-hizakura'

16. Mature leaves mostly with caudate tip; corymb less than 5 cm long;
 petals very smooth; blossoms on spurs . . . . 'Mikuruma-gaeshi'
 Mature leaves often lacking caudate tip; corymb often more than
 5 cm long; petals a little folded with undulations at the edge; no
 blossoms on spurs . . . . 'Ojochin'

17. Flowers cream-yellowish or yellowish green . . . . 'Ukon'
 Flowers white or pink. 18

18. Tree shape narrow and erect, corymbs erect. . . . . 'Ama-no-gawa'
 Tree vase-shaped or broadly vase-shaped, corymbs horizontal or
 nodding 19

19. Pedicel, calyx, and sepals remarkably purplish red; leaf base cuneate;
 mature leaves ovate. . . . . 'Taoyame'
 Not like that. 20

20. Mature leaves often lacking caudate tip; many flowers with only
 5 petals; pedicel not particularly sturdy or thin . . . . 'Ojochin'
 Mature leaves with caudate tip; many flowers with more than
 5 petals; flowers shell-pink and somewhat bell-shaped or cup-shaped;
 pedicel thin . . . . 'Shujaku'

Mature leaves with caudate tip; many flowers with more than
5 petals; petals sturdy and with undulations; pedicel sturdy 21

21. Flowers fragrant; stigma lower than stamens; sepals clearly serrated;
fully opened flowers often with a pinkish shade . . . .
. . . . 'Ariake' or 'Senriko'
Flowers fragrant; flower diameter more than 5 cm; tree broadly
spreading; sepals occasionally with a few teeth; fully opened flowers
pure white and hanging. . . . . 'Shirotae'
Flowers somewhat fragrant; flower diameter 4.0–4.5 cm; style with
stigma as long as the stamens; sepals occasionally with a few teeth;
fully opened flowers white; petals with irregular undulations and
fringes at the tip. . . . . 'Washi-no-o'

22. Mature leaves with velvety pubescence. . . . . 'Takasago'
Not like that. 23

23. Tree shape narrow and erect, corymbs standing upwards . . . .
. . . . 'Ama-no-gawa'
Not like that. 24

24. Flowers cream-yellowish or yellowish green . . . . 'Ukon'
Flowers white or pink. 25

25. Pedicel, calyx, and sepals remarkably purplish red or red-brown . . 26
Not like that. 27

26. Flowers usually with one pistil; 5–15 petals slightly emarginate
at the top; sepals occasionally with a few teeth; leaves obovate;
vigorous growth . . . . 'Taoyame'
Flowers occasionally with accessory pistils; 14–15 petals entire at
the top; sepals unserrated; leaves narrow and oval; weak growth
. . . . 'Horinji' (rare)

27. All (or almost all) flowers with one perfect pistil. 28
More than half the flowers with either two perfect pistils, or one
or two (partly) phylloid pistils (open at least 10 flowers to check
this) 37

28. Flower diameter large, more than ca. 4.8 cm 29
Flower diameter medium-sized, ca. 3.5–4.8 cm 33

29. Flowers with 10–14 petals, cup-shaped, white with slight pinkish
shade. . . . . 'Botan-zakura'
Flowers with 10–13 petals or less, somewhat or quite fragrant,
saucer-shaped, white when fully opened. 21

Many or all flowers with more than 13 petals, not (or hardly)
fragrant, pink or light pink when fully opened 30
30. Petals not particularly wrinkled; flower cup-shaped, light pink
(or white with slight pinkish shade) . . . . 'Botan-zakura'
Petals wrinkled; style and stigma as long as or longer than stamens
. . . . 31
31. Few orbicular mature leaves, lacking caudate tip; flowers turn to
deep pink before fading; calyx broadly funnel-shaped. . . . .
. . . . 'Sumizome' (Ingram)
No orbicular mature leaves; vigorous growth 32
32. Sepals narrower at the base, tops blunt; calyx bell-shaped to funnel-
shaped. . . . . 'Hokusai'
Sepals lanceolate and acute; calyx bell-shaped to funnel-shaped
. . . . 'Fukurokuju'
Sepals lanceolate and acute, occasionally serrated; calyx broadly
bell-shaped. . . . . 'Yae-akebono'
33. Underside of mature leaves glaucous; flowers white or only slightly
pink-shaded. . . . . 'Ichihara-tora-no-o' or 'Albo Plena' (rare)
Underside of mature leaves not glaucous 34
34. Flower diameter ca. 3.5–4.0 cm; some flowers with only 5 petals;
sepals entire; flowers shell-pink and somewhat bell-shaped or cup-
shaped; pedicel thin. . . . . 'Shujaku'
Flower diameter 4.0–4.5 cm; flowers somewhat fragrant; sepals
occasionally with a few teeth; flowers white when fully opened;
petals with irregular undulations and fringes at the tip . . . .
. . . . 'Washi-no-o'
Young foliage light bronze-green to brown; flowers light pink to
pink. 35
35. Petals ca. 17–21 mm wide (or wider) 30
Petals ca. 10–17 mm wide 36
36. Petals ca. 10–13 mm wide, deeply notched at the top; flowers a
soft purplish pink; young foliage coppery red to dark green . . . .
. . . . 'Yae-murasaki-zakura'
Petals ca. 13–17 mm wide, slightly emarginate at the top; flowers
light pink; young foliage light bronze-green; peduncle rather short;
pistil perfect . . . . 'Edo-zakura'
Petals ca. 13–17 mm wide, slightly emarginate at the top; often few

undeveloped petals halfway to the opening of the calyx; flowers light pink, 5 or more per corymb; young foliage light bronze-green; peduncle rather short; style somewhat phylloid at the base. . . . 'Ito-kukuri'

37. More than half the flowers with two perfect pistils (style never phylloid in flowers with only one style) (open at least 10 flowers to check this) . . . . 'Imose'
More than half the flowers with one or two pistils that are (at least at the base) phylloid (open at least 10 flowers to check this). 38

38. Flower buds in their prime ovate with pink stripes on the outward side of the outer petals; expanded flowers fuzzy; the phylloid part of the style hidden in the calyx and usually not visible without tearing the flower apart. 39
Flower buds in their prime cylindrical or tapered without clear pink stripes; flowers expanding to an open saucer-shape; the phylloid part of the mostly two styles clearly visible, protruding from the calyx. . . . . 'Ichiyo'

39. Flower diameter 4.0–4.5 cm; some undeveloped petals remain halfway in the calyx of many flowers; flowers 5 or more per corymb . . . . 'Ito-kukuri'
Flower diameter 4.8–5.3 cm; no petals remain halfway in the calyx . . . . 'Okiku-zakura'

40. Petiole pubescent . . . . 'Hoki-zakura' or 'Taizan-fukun'
Petiole glabrous 41

41. Flower diameter less than 4 cm; one perfect pistil; underside of mature leaves glaucous. . . 'Ichihara-tora-no-o' or 'Albo Plena' (rare)
Not like that. 42

42. More than half the flowers with two perfect pistils (style never phylloid in flowers with only one style) (open at least 10 flowers to check this) . . . . 'Imose'
Not like that. 43

43. More than half the flowers with only one pistil that is phylloid at the lower end (open at least 10 flowers to check this) 38
More than half the flowers with at least two phylloid pistils (open at least 10 flowers to check this). 44

44. Inflorescence long, pendulous; pedicel thin; fully opened flowers white with pleated petals . . . . 'Shogetsu'
Not like that. 45

45. Fully opened flowers almost white . . . . 'Ichiyo'
    Flowers in their prime almost white, but fading to rather dark
    pink; large sepals distinctly serrated halfway, but not at the top
    and base . . . . 'Fugenzo'
    Flowers in their prime clearly pink, not fading to a darker pink . . . .
    46
46. Two phylloid pistils per flower, rarely three, never four (open at
    least 10 flowers to check this) . . . . 'Kanzan'
    Four phylloid pistils in some flowers (open at least 10 flowers to
    check this) 47
47. Stamen filament extends above the anther; sepals serrated (check
    the flower buds in their prime); thin, twiggy branches hanging
    down at the outer side of the tree . . . . 'Pink Perfection'
    Anther stands at the top end of the filament; sepals not serrated;
    no thin, hanging branches . . . . 'Daikoku'
48. Tree shape weeping. . . . . 'Kiku-shidare-zakura'
    Tree shape erect 49
49. Petiole pubescent; peduncle and pedicel short; thin twigs in
    broomlike tree shape . . . . 'Taizan-fukun'
    Pedicel pubescent; peduncle and pedicel long. . . . .
    . . . . 'Hiyodori-zakura' (rare)
    Not like that. 50
50. Stamens in half-developed flowers visible as a yellow ring; calyx a
    hollow receptacle . . . . 'Najima-zakura' (rare)
    Not like that. 51
51. Inflorescence mostly a peduncled umbel, often with abortive flower
    on peduncle; not all flowers in umbel equally well developed; calyx
    a protruding receptacle . . . . 'Kenroku-en-kiku-zakura'
    Inflorescence a corymb. 52
52. Flower diameter ca. 3.5 cm; rather early flowering; peduncle less
    than 2 cm long; calyx widely funnel-shaped . . . . 'Asano'
    Flower diameter ca. 4 cm; rather late flowering; peduncle 2–5 cm
    long; calyx funnel-shaped; floriferous . . . . 'Baigoji-juzukake-zakura'
    Flower diameter ca. 4 cm; late flowering; peduncle longer than
    2 cm; calyx disk-shaped with hole or depression in the middle. . . . .
    . . . . 'Kiku-zakura'

CHAPTER 4

Japanese Wild Cherries

Prunus campanulata, Bell-flowered Cherry

The bell-flowered cherry is called *kan-hi-zakura* ("cold scarlet cherry") in Japan for its very early flowering and deep red blossom, which is most striking and for its color reminiscent of a flowering peach. In Tokyo, where this southern cherry is still hardy, it flowers among the earliest cherries in cold mid-March, whence the *kan* ("cold") in its name. *Hi* refers to the brilliant scarlet of robes worn exclusively by certain aristocratic ranks in ancient China and Japan. An obsolete name is *hi-kan-zakura,* which could lead to confusion with *higan-zakura,* a name used for spring cherries. One also may find the name *Ganjitsu-zakura* ("New Year's Day cherry"), but this name applies also to a form of *P. serrulata* that formerly was exported as 'Gwanjitsu' or 'Gwanjitsu-zakura'. In these cases the confusion is only in the names as the bell-flowered cherry is easily identified by its peculiar flowers.

This cherry is almost a subtropical plant and is cultivated throughout southern Japan up to Tokyo. It is found in the wild on the southern Ryukyu Islands, although it has been suggested that it was imported from Taiwan, where it is native in mountains at altitudes from 500 to 2000 m. It is also indigenous to Fujian, Guangdong, and Guangxi Provinces in China. It is related to the cherries of the Himalayas and has some characteristics that distinguish it clearly from other Japanese cherries. Its thick calyx contains much nectar, which may drip from the tree when the weather has favored its production. Although most cherries shed their petals after flowering, this one does not. After flowering, its almost tubular whorl of petals falls with stamens and calyx from the style and ovary.

Prunus campanulata Maximowicz

Bell-flowered cherry, kan-hi-zakura

Synonyms: Formosan cherry, hikan-zakura, Taiwan cherry

Description: Tree rather small, with spreading, usually rather blackish branches. Young foliage greenish, appearing after the flowering. Serration double and single, with acute tips. Mature leaves often show the main vein at the back with a reddish shade, similar to the reddish petiole. Umbels carry three to four (or more) flowers. Peduncles short, about 5 mm. Pedicels 7–15 mm long. Flower diameter 1 cm when tightly campanulate, or up to 3.5 cm when petals bend out; flowers nodding(!), sometimes bleak pink, or pink, but usually deep purplish red(!), without distinct fragrance. Petals five, oval to ovate, bifid, about 1 cm long. There is one pistil, perfect. The calyx is campanulate and deep red, usually deeper than the petals, glabrous(!). Sepals triangular, not serrated, the same color as the calyx,

Figure 51. The bell-flowered cherry (*Prunus campanulata*). Photo by author, 20 March 1996, Tokyo.

glabrous. Flowering season is early to mid March in Tokyo. *Prunus campanulata* has a diploid set of chromosomes (2n = 16).

Prunus incisa, Fuji Cherry

The Fuji cherry is distributed on the slopes of Mount Fuji that, geologically speaking, belong to the same region in which the Oshima cherry (*Prunus serrulata* var. *speciosa*) is distributed. It is known and described in Japan under *mame-zakura* ("midget cherry"). It forms thickets on the lean, young volcanic soils close to the top of Mount Fuji. It is known as *Fuji-zakura* ("Fuji cherry") or *Hakone-zakura* ("Hakone cherry") because the plant is found on slopes and mountain sides in the national parks of Fuji and Hakone.

Prunus incisa is healthy and reproduces under the severe conditions of a young volcanic area where plants such as *Weigela coraeensis* and *Hydrangea macrophylla* also grow. It is also a strong and healthy plant in the garden. It forms a large spreading shrub with an elegant show of little, nodding white flowers. It has up to three small, white or slightly pinkish flowers in an umbel that appear just before the foliage. The leaves have a striking, incised, and double serration that makes for easy identification with the stalked nectaries at the leaf base. The flowers show a typical reddening of the center at the end of flowering. *Prunus incisa* was imported to England in 1910.

A wild tree was discovered in 1962 with flowers that had up to four hundred petals; it is now propagated as 'Fuji-kiku-zakura'. A variety found in mountain forests in and around the Kinki region is 'Kinki-mame-zakura' (synonym *Prunus incisa* var. *kinkiensis* (Koidzumi) Ohwi). It has a different ecology and comes up here and there among the numerous other species of broad-leaved trees of the Kinki forests. It has a long, tubular calyx and the same leaves, typical for the species, though incisions are more regular. In the wild young plants start to flower when they are only knee-high; the domestication of this diploid variety as a bonsai plant has a long history, similar to that of *P. incisa* itself. For centuries these cherries have been present in nurseries as pollen parents. Garden forms such as 'Kumagai-zakura' or 'Shibayama' show obvious influence. Indeed, *P. incisa* is quite variable and many forms are found in the wild; it is always fertile and easily fruiting, readily crossed with most other cherries. It is used in nursery experiments and many recent nursery products exist. *Prunus incisa* is vital in its regeneration and easily propagated from cuttings for which it is favored for dwarfing as a bonsai tree.

Figure 52. Abundant beauty of the Fuji cherry *(Prunus incisa)*. Photo by Arie Peterse, 2 May 1986, Hemelrijk, Belgium.

Prunus incisa Thunberg ex Murray
Fuji cherry

Less current synonyms: Fuji-zakura, mame-zakura, Hakone-zakura

Description: Large shrub to 3 m, sometimes to 5 m (or even 7 m), with spreading, not too heavy branches that divide in many branchlets, making an umbrella-shaped crown. Young leaves green to bronze (RHS 199-B), starting to sprout at flowering. Mature leaves 2–5 × 1.5–3.0 cm wide (small for a flowering cherry), with caudate tips, no distinct glands, pubescence on both sides of the leaves, most outspoken on the underside. Serration of mature leaves double and acute, with typical incisions(!). Petiole pubescent. Nectaries on short stalks at the leaf base(!). Stipules short. Umbellate inflorescence, with one to three flowers. Peduncles absent or very short, pedicel short, 1.0–1.5 cm, pubescent. Flowers light pink in bud

Figure 53. Leaves of *Prunus incisa* var. *kinkiensis* in fall color, showing the incised and double serration typical of the species. Photo by author, 17 November 1996, Hiei-zan.

(RHS 65-D), expanding to an open, flat shape; white or with a light pink shade. Flowers nodding(!), 2.0–2.5 cm in diameter. Petals five, emarginate, obovate, about 1 × 0.8 cm. There is one pistil, about 1.2 cm long, perfect. Calyx funnel-shaped or tubular, 0.4–0.9 cm long, glabrous or some sparing hairs, distinct, red shade. Sepals are broad and triangular, with a red shade. Fruits maturing to black. Flowering season is early April in Tokyo. *Prunus incisa* has a diploid set of chromosomes (2n = 16).

Fuyu-zakura (synonyms *Prunus parvifolia* Koehne 'Parvifolia', 'Koba-zakura') is an autumn-flowering cherry. It is understood as a hybrid of *P. incisa* and a form of *P. serrulata*. The white (RHS 55-D), single flowers are larger than those of the autumn cherry 'Jugatsu-zakura' and are found in

Figure 54. *Prunus incisa* var. *kinkiensis* trained as bonsai. Photo by author, 28 March 1996, Kyōto Botanic Garden.

greater number throughout winter. The tree is more floriferous in spring but supposedly less hardy. *Fuyu* means "winter."

Hime-midori-zakura (synonym *Prunus incisa* 'Hime-midori') is a bonsai selection of 'Midori-zakura' with slightly smaller leaves and flowers, many more little twigs, and many red-purple fruitlets 6–7 mm in diameter. *Hime* (pronounced "hee-meh") means "princess" and translates as "pretty little" in this case.

Komame-zakura (synonyms *Prunus incisa* 'Micrantha', 'Hime-fuji-zakura') has the smallest flowers (about 1 cm in diameter) of any cultivar of *P. incisa*.

Figure 55. The erect form of 'Spire' (Hillier 1937); its calyx and sepals betray its affiliation to the Fuji cherry *(Prunus incisa)*, as does the reddening heart of the flower at the end of flowering. Photo by author, 13 April 1997, Yūki Experimental Station of the Flower Association of Japan, Ibaraki Prefecture.

Calyx and sepals are reddish; the stigma sticks out of the developing buds. 'Komame-zakura' is easily propagated by cuttings and used for bonsai.

Midori-zakura (synonyms *Prunus incisa* Makino 'Yamadei', 'Ryoku-gaku-zakura') was discovered near Mount Fuji by a teacher, Mr. Jirō Takazawa, from the Gotenba Agricultural School in Shizuoka Prefecture in 1916. The principal of the school, Mr. Hanjirō Yamade, sent material to the great botanist Tomitarō Makino, who described it as *ryoku-gaku-zakura* ("green-calyxed cherry"). This form resembles the species but does not have any red shade in its buds or flowers, or towards the end of blossoming. The calyx and sepals are perfectly light green, whence the folk name 'Midori-zakura', meaning "light green cherry" (the word *midori* is reserved for a light grass-

Figure 56. 'Midori-zakura'. Photo by author, 12 April 1997, Tama Forest Science Garden, Tokyo.

green). Years later, other cherries of this type were discovered around Mount Amagi (after which 'Amagi-yoshino' was named) and southwestern Kantō region. Some of these came in circulation as nursery material so that perhaps not every 'Midori-zakura' is a *Prunus incisa* 'Yamadei'. Some botanic details that distinguish this cultivar from the parent are yellow-green young foliage; broader, more lozengelike, mature leaves; green pedicels; calyx 5 mm long, tubular, glabrous, and light green; and green sepals. Flowers do not open fully, but are somewhat campanulate; elliptic petals are about 12 mm long, pure white. Fruits about 9 mm diameter, dark red.

Okame was presented by Collingwood Ingram in 1947 as a hybrid between *P. incisa* and *P. campanulata*. It is known as Okame cherry and makes

Figure 57. 'Okame'. Photo by Arie Peterse, 16 April 1985, Wageningen Botanic Gardens of the Agricultural University, Netherlands.

a floriferous shrub of about 3(–5) m high with single, long-calyxed flowers of a rather deep pink (RHS 63-C). It is useful for the small garden and is propagated by cuttings. Grafting on *P. avium* is less successful.

Oshidori-zakura (synonym *Prunus incisa* Thunberg ex Murray 'Oshidori') is a valuable, small garden tree with light pink, double flowers. It was discovered in a farmer's garden at Gotenba in Shizuoka Prefecture. *Oshidori* means "mandarin ducks." The ducks have a reputation for matrimonial loyalty in the Far East, and the name was given to this cherry because of the two pistils that are found as a loyal pair in many of its flowers. 'Oshidori' is similar to the parent species except for the following. Its crown is more cup-shaped. It has few hairs on young twigs of shoots. Young leaves are yellow-green, sprouting at the time of flowering. The petiole is pubes-

Figure 58. 'Oshidori-zakura'. Photo by author, 13 April 1997, Yūki Experimental Station of the Flower Association of Japan, Ibaraki Prefecture.

Figure 59. Distribution of *Prunus incisa* and *P. incisa* var. *kinkiensis*. Adapted from the Flower Association of Japan (1982). ● = *P. incisa*. ○ = *P. incisa* var. *kinkiensis*.

cent, with nectaries mostly on its upper end and not at the leaf base. A corymbose inflorescence bears one or two dangling flowers; the peduncles are 5–10 mm long, the rather thin pedicels are long, up to 4 cm(!). Both flower stalks are somewhat pubescent. Flowers in bud pink (RHS 53-D), expanding to a lighter pink (RHS 55-D) with a diameter of 3.0–3.5 cm. A flower has twenty to fifty elliptic petals, about one hundred stamens, and two (but as few as one or as many as five) pistils(!). Calyx funnel-shaped, with a distinct swelling that is thicker than the average *Prunus incisa,* with some sparing hairs and a red shade. Flowering season is from early to mid April in Tokyo. Many of the botanic details suggest that this cherry is a hybrid rather than a selection of the species.

Pendula Alba (synonym *Prunus incisa* 'Pendula Alba') is a white weeping form. It has single flowers and shows autumn colors.

Umineko is a hybrid between *P. incisa* and *P. serrulata* var. *speciosa* (Ingram 1948). It is an erect, small tree, a little wider than 'Ama-no-gawa'. It resembles 'Snow Goose', which has the same parents. *Umineko* means "sea gull."

Prunus nipponica, Japanese Alpine Cherry

Japanese alpine cherry is called *takane-zakura* ("cherry from the lofty peaks") or *mine-zakura* ("peak cherry") in Japanese, confirming the English common name. Indeed, on the main island of Honshū, this cherry is found in mountains at altitudes above 1500 m. Farther north it is found in a wide region on mountains and in plains of Hokkaidō and Sakhalin. Like *Prunus incisa*, it grows on mountains that are higher in altitude than the hills on which grow the mountain cherries proper, such as *P. serrulata* var. *spontanea* and *P. sargentii*. Small pinkish flowers are set on pubescent pedicels with two or three per umbel. Like the other Japanese cherries, this one shows great variability and has some regional forms. Its influence on garden cultivars is unimportant.

   Both *Prunus incisa* and *P. nipponica* have double serrated leaves with regular incisions; they resemble each other in some other respects, so that the two are often grouped together in systematic classifications. *Prunus nipponica* tolerates heavy snowfall and makes new leader branches from side shoots that stand up with a bend from the stem. This characteristic of-

Figure 60. *Prunus nipponica* var. *kurilensis* 'Ruby' grafted on *P. avium.* Photo by Arie Peterse, 29 April 1986.

ten results in peculiar curves and crooks, which can be found also in garden plants that do not suffer from snow. The polished chestnut-bronze bast of older branches, shining as in *P. serrula,* is most typical and makes for easy identification. This cherry was brought to Europe in 1915.

Prunus nipponica Matsumura
Japanese alpine cherry
Less current synonyms: mine-zakura, takane-zakura

Description: Large shrub to 3 m, spreading, with an ovate or broad vase-shaped crown. Bast of older branches shiny chestnut-brown with horizontal gray lines that have a corky center(!). Young foliage greenish brown to red-brown (RHS 178-B), unfolding with the blossom. Serration double, with glandular acute teeth and regular incisions(!). Mature leaves, with caudate tip, often with few hairs on upperside, usually hairless on underside. Umbellate inflorescence, with two to three flowers. Peduncles 2–5 mm long. Pedicels thin, glabrous, 1.0–2.5 cm long. Flowers in bud usually slightly pink; completely opened flowers are white. Flower diameter 1.5–3.0 cm. Flowers expand to a rather flat plane, or remain somewhat campanulate, flowers not hanging down. Petals five, few are emarginate at the top, elliptic or obovate, 12–13 × 9–11 mm. There is one glabrous pistil, perfect, as long as or longer than the longest stamens. The glabrous calyx is campanulate, with a distinct transition from pedicel to calyx, with a red shade. Sepals are elongated and triangular, 4–5 mm long, glabrous, unserrated, with a reddish hue. Flowering season is early May in Tokyo.

Collingwood Ingram was chosen by Ingram in 1979 as the most beautiful cherry in a set of 'Kursar' seedlings at the Arboretum Kalmthout, Belgium. The dark pink petals (10 × 12 mm) show an even darker pink at the edges and tip. *Prunus* 'Collingwood Ingram' has an erect tree shape (Van Trier 1990).

Kurile cherry (synonyms *Prunus nipponica* var. *kurilensis* (Miyabe) Wilson, *P.* ×*kurilensis,* chi-shima-zakura) is a variety of *P. nipponica* that grows in even colder regions, the Kuriles, Sakhalin, and mountainous Hokkaidō and Honshū. It was described in detail by Kingo Miyabe in 1890. In the West it often is presented as a hybrid, which it is not. According to *Kokon-yōran-kō* (Yashiro 1821–1841), it has been cultivated in Japan since at least the early

Figure 61. A profusely flowering specimen of the Kurile cherry *(Prunus nippon-ica* var. *kurilensis)* from seed. Photo by Arie Peterse, Boskoop, Netherlands.

nineteenth century. In its native habitat, it sends its branches from a procumbent stem, adapting to the heavy snowfall. Botanic details that separate it from its parent are minor: it has no glands on the tips of the leaf serration, its leaves have more hairs, its petiole and pedicel are also pubescent, its calyx is shorter, and its sepals are serrated. Although it flowers briefly, it flowers very early and this has inspired various nursery products such as 'February Pink' (Great Britain), 'Brillant' (Germany, 1977) or 'Spring Joy' (Netherlands, 1958).

Figure 62. A dark-pink flowered form of the Kurile cherry *(Prunus nipponica var. kurilensis)*. Photo by Arie Peterse, 19 April 1987, Wageningen Botanic Gardens of the Agricultural University, Netherlands.

Figure 63. Distribution of *Prunus nipponica*. Adapted from the Flower Association of Japan (1982). ● = *P. nipponica*.

Kursar was made by Collingwood Ingram as a cross of *Prunus nipponica* var. *kurilensis* with *P. campanulata*. Mistakenly he thought that the other parent was *P. sargentii* for which reason he named his hybrid "Kur-Sar." It is a very hardy garden plant growing to about 5 m high and broad. The young foliage is bronze-green, and the bright-pink (RHS 62-B) early blossom appears in mid-March in Tokyo. *Prunus* 'Kursar' is rather easily propagated from summer cuttings.

Rosy Veil is a splendid selection dated 1988 from 'Kursar' seed raised at the Arboretum Kalmthout, Belgium. It is a low, large shrub with spreading branches full of bright, pink flowers. The inflorescences are small umbels with up to five flowers (Van Trier 1990).

Prunus pendula, Weeping Spring Cherry

Weeping cherries have been cultivated in Japan for many centuries and were named *ito-zakura* ("thread-cherry"), a name that appears in poems since the twelfth century. The name was taken over by Philipp Franz von Siebold, who introduced this species to Europe in 1862 as *Prunus itosakura*. It was offered for export under various names such as *P. subhirtella ascendens pen-*

Figure 64. A white-flowered selection of the weeping spring cherry *(Prunus pendula),* known locally as 'Sakigake.' Photo by author, 1 April 1997, Hirano Shrine, Kyōto.

dula (Wada 1937). Maximowicz properly described it as *P. pendula*. Later, it was understood to be a form of the ascending and later-described *P. pendula* f. *ascendens*. The weeping, spontaneous form was described anew for esoteric taxonomic reasons as *P. spachiana* f. *spachiana*. Indeed it is a wild form, and there is no generally accepted clonal cultivar. Details of the flowers differ from specimen to specimen, but these pose no practical problem as all the specimens are nice and well flowered, although never so nice and deep pink as the more narrowly defined 'Beni-shidare' discussed below.

The thin branches weep because of their fast growth and supple character, indeed like threads, and not because of differences in growth speed between the upper and lower sides of a spreading branch. Once developed the branches make a firm wood and become stiff (Kawasaki 1994, after Teruko Nakamura). Good gardeners make use of this characteristic by tying up a leader branch to train it as the stem of the tree. Weeping branches on older trees are pruned on upward buds making for a widely cascading tree, in Japan often supported by many stilts. A less time-consuming approach in the nursery involves grafting this cherry on an established stem; however, this practice results in a less beautiful tree shape as no branches grow higher than the place of grafting. The Japanese common name *shidare-zakura* means simply "weeping cherry" and could be confused with other weeping cherries.

Prunus pendula Maximowicz
Ito-zakura
Synonyms: *Prunus itosakura* Siebold, *P. pendula* Makino, *P. pendula* Maximowicz 'Pendula', *P. spachiana* Kitamura f. *spachiana*, *P. subhirtella* var. *pendula* (Maximowicz) Tanaka, *P. subhirtella* Miquel 'Pendula'
Less current synonyms: weeping spring cherry, shidare-zakura

Description: Tree large, to 8 m high or more when trained, with drooping branchlets. Young leaves not out at the time of flowering, or sparingly here and there a light green sprout (more sprouts together with some blossoms in young trees). Twigs of young shoots pubescent. Serration of mature leaves double mixed with single; with small acute tips, without glands; the underside is pubescent especially on the central vein. Petiole pubescent. Stipules about 10 mm. Umbellate inflorescence, with three to four flowers. Peduncles very short or absent, pedicel 1–3 cm, pubescent, with a red shade. Flowers pinkish, turning to almost white towards the end of flowering, but variable. Flower diameter 2–3 cm. Petals five, about 1 cm long, width a little narrower, emarginate at the tip, but quite variable in size and shape. There is one pistil, perfect, the lower end of the style shows hairs. The small calyx is urceolate, as a globular pitcher with a distinctly narrower mouth; the lower, bulby half is pubescent, the upper half has fewer hairs; the calyx has a red hue. Sepals are triangular and pubescent on the outside, and have a few teeth and hairs at the edge. Flowering season is late March in Tokyo. *Prunus pendula* has a diploid set of chromosomes (2n = 16).

Beni-shidare (synonyms *Prunus pendula* Maximowicz 'Rosea', *P.* ×*subhirtella* Miquel 'Pendula Rubra') has a long history as a cherry name and is reserved for a rather deep pink form of *P. pendula*. Like its parent, this cherry has no strictly defined status, although Japanese nurseries make a clear difference between the two. Some variation is seen in trees of 'Beni-shidare' in collections, and a deep pink form from Tama, Tokyo, formed the basis of the following description. It forms a large tree to 8 m or more with branchlets drooping almost straight down. Young leaves green-bronze, but not out at the time of flowering. Twigs of young shoots pubescent. Serration of mature leaves single, with rather small acute tips, without glands; the underside is pubescent above all on the central vein, petiole pubescent. Stipules short. Umbellate inflorescence, with three to four flowers. Peduncles very short or absent, pedicel 1–3 cm, pubescent, with a red shade. Flowers deep pink in bud, turning to perfect pink towards the end of flowering, but variable. Flower diameter 2–3 cm, expanding to an open cup shape. Petals five, about 1 cm long, width narrower, emarginate at the tip that is often deeper in color, but petals quite variable in size and shape. There is one pistil, perfect, the lower end of the style shows hairs. The small calyx is urceolate, as a globular pitcher with a distinctly narrower mouth; pubescent; distinctly red. Sepals are triangular, serrated, and pubescent on the outside. Flowering season is late March in Tokyo.

Yae-beni-shidare (synonyms *Prunus pendula* 'Pleno-rosea', *P.* ×*subhirtella* var. *pendula* f. *plena rosea*) is also called yae-shidare-higan, double weeping rosebud cherry, pendula plena rosea, Sendai spring cherry, Sendai-ito-zakura, and Endo-zakura. *Yae-beni-shidare* means "double-red weeping," and indeed this is a double, deep-pink-flowered weeping cherry. It was a rare specimen on the grounds of the imperial palace in Kyōto. In the early seventeenth century small plants were brought to northern Japan by the daimyo

Figure 65. 'Beni-shidare'. Photo by author, 6 April 1997, Kyōto Botanic Garden.

Masamune Date (1567–1636), who is remembered for having sponsored Christianity until it became prohibited. The daimyo cultivated this cherry in the gardens of his castle at Sendai; in Kyōto it was forgotten. In 1895, about three centuries later, at the founding of Kyōto's Heian Shrine, the mayor of Sendai, Mr. Endō, presented seventy young trees for its garden, and splendid specimens made the garden of the Heian Shrine famous. The cherry was offered for export in the 1930s as *P. subhirtella ascendens pendula* Sendaica (Wada 1937). Collingwood Ingram imported it into England in 1928 and named it *P. subhirtella* var. *pendula* f. *plena rosea* and Sendai spring cherry, or Sendai-ito-sakura. Among the weeping and ascending cherries of *P. pendula,* this one has the deepest pink flowers. It is not as vigorous growing as the others, and it flowers later in great abundance. It is easily identified by its red pitcher-shaped calyx with equally red flower buds that show the yellow stigma on the outer end of the style for many days before the flowers open(!). It forms a tree to 5(–7) m, with weeping branches, becoming as broad as high. Young leaves bronze-green, but not out at the time of flowering. Twigs of young shoots pubescent. Serration of mature leaves double, mixed with single, with rather small acute tips, without glands; the upperside has hairs on the central vein, the underside is more pubescent above all on the central vein; petiole pubescent. Stipules short. Umbellate inflorescence, with three to four flowers. Peduncles absent, pedicel 1–3 cm, pubescent, with a red shade. Flowers deep, dark pink in bud when the yellow stigma at the end of the style can be seen sticking out. Flowers expanding to an open rather flat shape, not as dark pink as when in bud, 1.7–2.5 cm in diameter. Petals ten to twenty, elliptic or obovate, about 1 cm × 1.5–1.8 cm, twisted, emarginate at the tip. There is one pistil (sometimes two), perfect, partly pubescent, about 1 cm long, much longer than the stamens. The small calyx is urceolate, as a globular pitcher, with a rather narrow mouth, about 8–5 mm × 6–4 mm, some pubescence, distinctly red. The small sepals are triangular and pubescent on the outside, and have tiny teeth and hairs at the edge. Flowering season is from early to mid April in Tokyo.

Prunus pendula f. *ascendens,* Edo-higan

Prunus pendula f. *ascendens* is native in the remote forests of broad-leaved trees in Japan's mountainous landscape. It is found all over the islands of Honshū, Shikoku, and Kyūshū in Japan, and farther on the Korean penin-

Figure 66. Typical buds and downy pedicels of 'Yae-beni-shidare'. Photo by author, 3 April 1996, Hirano Shrine, Kyōto.

sula, with very similar cherries in central China and Taiwan as well. It is called Edo-higan or Edo-higan-zakura in Japan, which means "the equinox cherry from Edo," and was exported as *higan-zakura* at the beginning of the twentieth century. It is one of the earliest cherries to flower, and it was grown often in the gardens of Edo, the old name for Tokyo. It was not known in ancient Japan as a wild or "mountain" cherry.

In the remote countryside one comes across the folk name *uba-higan,* or *uba-zakura,* which means "old woman's cherry." One explanation is that the bare leafless twigs on which the flowers are set resemble the toothless mouth of an old woman. An ancient folk practice forms the real explanation of the name: in poor regions of agricultural northern Japan, old, weak and "worthless" women were carried to remote mountains in times of bad harvests and famine, leaving their fate to the gods, and saving a mouth to fill in the village. *Prunus pendula* f. *ascendens* lives to an old age. Some famous trees are reportedly three to four hundred years old and by legend even a thousand or more. It is not surprising that the trees with their black and heavy limbs holding up an umbrella-shaped crown of flowers inspired legends and lore. The phantasmal trees reminded people of the female ancestors who were left behind and were called *uba-zakura.* Many old trees are now designated as natural monuments.

The species shows variability in flower color and in tree form. Weeping forms are found in the wild as well as ascending forms. From the weeping form the species was described by the Russian botanist Carl Johann Maximowicz (1827–1891) in 1893 as *Prunus pendula,* before the more common, ascending form. The species crosses freely with *P. apetala, P. incisa, P. sargentii, P. serrulata* var. *pubescens,* and *P. serrulata* var. *spontanea* wherever regions of distribution overlap.

Prunus ×yedoensis is a hybrid of the Edo-higan cherry (*P. pendula* f. *ascendens*) and the Oshima cherry (*P. serrulata* var. *speciosa*). *Prunus ×subhirtella* is a hybrid of the Edo-higan cherry (*P. pendula* f. *ascendens*) and the Fuji cherry (*P. incisa*). The weeping and the ascending *P. pendula* were classic garden plants in nurseries and collections. Though not yet completely clarified, the influence of *P. pendula* f. *ascendens* on forms of *P. serrulata* must be reckoned with. For example, although pubescence of leaf blade or stalk in some of these garden forms seems to point to *P. serrulata* var. *pubescens,* it might also be due to an influence of *P. pendula* f. *ascendens.*

The pitcher-shaped, pubescent calyx is characteristic of this cherry as well as the slight pubescence on the underside of the mature leaf. Before the leaves appear, the blossoms are out, with pinkish or white small flowers. The typical bark of an old stem shows fissures lengthwise. It takes many years before a tree begins to flower in more abundance, something that makes its marketing difficult for the garden center.

Prunus pendula f. *ascendens* (Makino) Ohwi
Edo-higan
Synonyms: *Prunus itosakura* var. *ascendens* Makino, *P. aequinoctialis* Miyoshi, *P. subhirtella* var. *ascendens* (Makino) Tanaka
Less current synonyms: spring cherry, equinox cherry, higan-zakura, uba-zakura, azuma-higan, uba-higan
Description: Tree large, with an erect trunk, branches spreading upwards to 12 m or more, rarely to 20 m, long lived. Young leaves not out at the time of flowering, or sparingly here and there a light green sprout (more sprouts together with few blossoms in young trees). Twigs of young shoots pubescent. Serration of mature leaves double, with rather small acute tips, without glands; the underside shows hairs on the central vein. Petiole pubescent. Stipules about 10 mm. Umbellate inflorescence, with three to five flowers. Peduncles very short or absent, pedicel 2.0–2.5 cm, pubescent, with a distinct red shade. Flower in bud pinkish, turning to almost white towards the end of flowering (RHS 56-C). Flower diameter 1.5–2.0 cm. Petals five, obovate, 9–15 × 7–11 mm, emarginate at the tip. There is one pistil, perfect, about 12 mm long; it is about as long as, or sometimes longer than, the longest stamens. The small calyx is urceolate, as a wide, globular pitcher with a distinctly narrower mouth(!); it is less pubescent than the pedicel but has a deeper red hue. Sepals are elongated, triangular, and a little pubescent, and have a few teeth and hairs at the edge. Flowering season is late March in Tokyo. *Prunus pendula* f. *ascendens* has a diploid set of chromosomes (2n = 16).

Beni Higan Sakura (synonym *Prunus subhirtella* var. *rosea* (Miyoshi) Ingram) is a pink selection discussed by Ingram (1948). At present it is not found in collections or in nursery catalogs. Shrubs or small trees sold now as the rosebud cherry or *P. subhirtella* 'Rosea' seem to be a form of the triploid *P.* ×*subhirtella* rather than Collingwood Ingram's 'Beni-higan-sakura', but some questions remain.

Pandora is a hybrid between *Prunus* 'Beni Higan Sakura' (described above) and *P.* ×*yedoensis* (described below). The floribund 'Pandora' was raised by Messrs. Waterer Sons and Crisp in England before 1939. It is used as a roadside tree in open ground; its vase shape is not too broad and its flowers are light pink (RHS 69-B). By now some strains of this popular cherry circulate; the less favorable ones show heavy branching.

Rebecca was raised as a selection from 'Pandora' seedlings in the Arboretum Kalmthout, Belgium. Its pale pink, almost white flowers show a striking contrast with the coppery red unfolding foliage. Tree shape is rounded (Van Trier 1990).

Shiro Higan Sakura is a white selection discussed by Ingram (1948). At present it is not found in collections or in nursery catalogs.

The Bride is another promising selection of 'Pandora' seedlings at the Arboretum Kalmthout, Belgium; it has large petals (14 × 17 mm) in its flat,

Figure 67. 'Pandora'. Photo by Arie Peterse, Kesteren, Netherlands.

Figure 68. Distribution of *Prunus pendula* f. *ascendens.* Adapted from the Flower Association of Japan (1982).

open flowers and gives a spectacular floral show on a small, broad tree (Van Trier 1990).

Prunus sargentii

Prunus sargentii is found in northern Japan, in mountainous regions to very high altitudes. Leaves and flowers are similar to but larger than those of the Japanese mountain cherry, whence the folk name *ō-yama-zakura* ("big mountain cherry"). It differs from the Japanese mountain cherry in its umbellate inflorescences that rarely or never stand on a peduncle. The bud scales and young sprouts are sticky, which is characteristic for this species. The blossom is pinker than that of the Japanese mountain cherry, but varies in color, shape, and size. Leaf serration is larger and coarser. The species shows nice autumn hues. Weeping specimens have been reported from wild stands, and a columnar-shaped selection is in cultivation.

The Japanese mountain cherry (*Prunus serrulata* var. *spontanea*) is related to *P. sargentii,* and in classifications they are grouped with *P. serrulata* var. *pubescens.* The American plantsman Charles Sprague Sargent collected in Japan in 1892 and published his *Forest Flora of Japan* in 1894. Alfred Rehder described Sargent's cherry as *P. sargentii* in 1908, but there is a good case for calling it *P. serrulata* var. *sachalinensis* as well.

Man's civilized occupation of northern Japan, where *Prunus sargentii* grows in the wild, is rather recent, and it is said that this cherry's genetic influence on the old garden cultivars is unimportant. Nonetheless, the flowers of wild specimens may show such a striking deep pink that the tree must have attracted the attention of traveling gardeners in olden days, and maybe it has been of more influence than believed. It makes a beautiful tree on a standing stem. Forms have been selected for use as roadside trees, such as the columnar 'Rancho' (Scanlon 1961); other selections, such as 'Sunset Boulevard', have a splendid autumn color as well.

Prunus sargentii Rehder
Synonyms: *Prunus serrulata* var. *sachalinensis* (Fr. Schmidt) Wilson,
    ō-yama-zakura, North Japanese hill cherry
Description: Tree large, broad-ovate, to 18 m high or more. Bast of younger branches somewhat shiny dark red or purple-brown. Young foliage reddish brown (RHS 178-B). Bud scales and young sprouts sticky(!). Serration

Figure 69. The umbellate inflorescences of *Prunus sargentii*. Photo by Arie Peterse, 19 April 1987, Netherlands.

Figure 70. Foliage of *Prunus sargentii*, showing the glaucous underside. Photo by author, 5 August 1997, Obihiro, Japan.

single and double, with irregular triangular teeth with tiny glands, and with caudate-acuminate tips. Mature leaves 8–15 × 4–8 cm, with distinctly whitish underside(!). Stipules large, to 3 cm, and much divided. Umbels with two to three flowers that are out with the foliage sprouts. Bud scales at umbels also sticky(!). Pedicels 13–20 mm long, glabrous (sometimes with hairs), with a red shade. Flower buds elongated, satured pink (RHS 54-C). Flower diameter 3.5–4.0 cm. Flowers with no distinct fragrance. Petals five, ovate, 15–19 × 12–14 mm. There is one pistil, perfect. The calyx is narrow and campanulate, about 5.5 mm long, glabrous, purple-red. Sepals are narrow and elongated, not serrated. Fruits purple-black, sour. Flowering season is mid-April in Tokyo. *Prunus sargentii* has a diploid set of chromosomes (2n = 16). The species is more variable than this description suggests. In Japan it may have some flowers in autumn as well.

Accolade is an English hybrid between *Prunus sargentii* and a form of *P. ×subhirtella,* released from the Knap Hill Nurseries in 1952. The pink (RHS 62-C) semi-double flowers have about twelve petals and stand in umbels. In the climate of western Europe, this cultivar is a favorite park tree, and if grafted and trained on an erect stem, it is also useful as roadside tree. Propagation by summer cuttings has proved successful.

Juddii was procured in 1914 at the Arnold Arboretum, Jamaica Plain, Massachusetts, by Edgar Anderson. *Prunus ×juddii* is a hybrid between *Prunus sargentii* and *P. ×yedoensis.*

Prunus serrulata var. *pubescens*

The center of distribution of *Prunus serrulata* var. *pubescens* is the Korean peninsula, but it is also found in northeastern and eastern China, the old Manchuria, and throughout Japan, excluding Kyūshū and the islands south of it. Typical of *P. serrulata* var. *pubescens* are the hairs found on its flower stalks, petiole, and often the underside of the leaf. The young foliage is not deep red-brown as is that of the Japanese mountain cherry (*P. serrulata* var. *spontanea*), and the mature leaves have a rather course serration.

    Prunus serrulata var. *pubescens* is called *kasumi-zakura* ("mist cherry") in Japan, as the trees may cover a mountainside with a spring mist of tiny, white flowers. Another name is *ke-yama-zakura* ("hairy mountain cherry").

Figure 71. 'Accolade' is a hybrid between *Prunus sargentii* and a form of *P.* ×*subhirtella*. Photo by Arie Peterse, Wageningen Botanic Gardens of the Agricultural University, Netherlands.

Usually the backside of the leaf is not whitish, as is in the Japanese mountain cherry (*P. serrulata* var. *spontanea*), but the two resemble each other in many details.

Whenever *Prunus serrulata* var. *pubescens* grows with *P. sargentii* or *P. serrulata* var. *spontanea,* hybridizations occur. Though not as variable as *P. serrulata* var. *spontanea, P. serrulata* var. *pubescens* shows many differing forms that are reported mostly in Japanese articles by Takenoshin Nakai (1882–1952).

A wild stand of double-flowered *Prunus serrulata* var. *pubescens* was reported from Yono in Mie Prefecture. A selection with an excellent, erect tree shape is known as 'Yono-no-yae-zakura' (synonym *P. leveilleana* Koehne 'Nara-zakura' in Kokuritsu Idengaku Kenkyujo 1995, p. 58). The com-

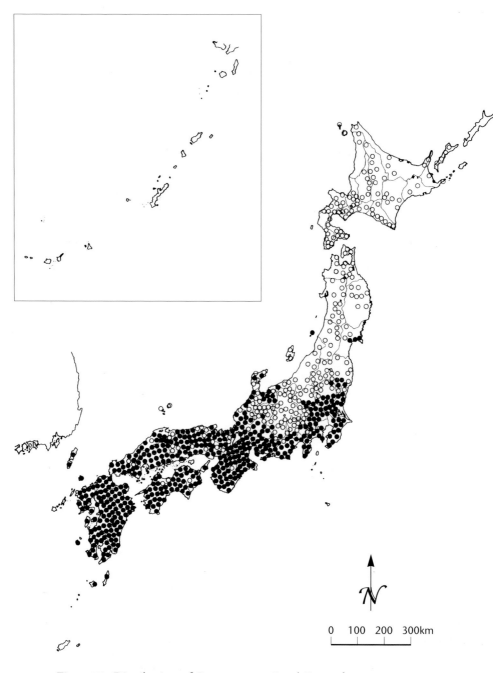

0　　100　200　300km

Figure 72. Distribution of *Prunus sargentii* and *P. serrulata* var. *spontanea*. Adapted from the Flower Association of Japan (1982). ○ = *P. sargentii*. ● = *P. serrulata* var. *spontanea*.

monly seen form is a very similar 'Nara-no-yae-zakura' (synonym *P. vere-cunda* 'Antiqua' in Kawasaki 1994, p. 204). This historical garden form originated from the Chisoku-in Temple in Nara and was offered for export as *P. serrulata antiqua* 'Nara-yaezakura' (Wada 1937).

Collingwood Ingram tells of the enormous crowds that came to view the blossom of *Prunus serrulata* var. *pubescens* in Shotoku-en Park (the Japanese pronunciation of the original Korean), now known as Changdeog Park in Seoul, Korea. Since 1877 Changdeog Palace was home to the Korean royal family. In 1905 Korea became a Japanese protectorate and five years later was fully annexed. On 1 November 1909 the palace grounds were opened by the Japanese colonial government as a museum and zoological-botanical garden. Most Koreans viewed this as an offensive desecration of the palace grounds. The "enthusiasm" of the masses of Koreans

Figure 73. The Korean mountain cherry (*Prunus serrulata* var. *pubescens*). Note the pubescent pedicels. Photo by author, 29 April 1996, Tama Forest Science Garden, Tokyo.

that Ingram says were celebrating the cherries must have had its political undertones. The cherries in the grounds might even have been Japanese imports. In 1945 Korea became independent. Today in Korea the coming spring is celebrated with picnic and partying, and the flowering trees that delight the partying public include cherries (*buttkott*) as well as *Forsythia*, *Spirea*, and others.

Although the Arnold Arboretum had raised plants of *Prunus serrulata* var. *pubescens* from Chinese seeds already in 1907, Ingram received seeds from Changdeog Park in 1929. Among these Korean seedlings, Ingram had in England one plant that showed a brilliantly red autumn hue. It is likely that this seedling formed the origin of the cultivar 'Autumn Glory'. The young leaves of 'Autumn Glory' are a light bronze-green. The flowers are about 2.5–3.0 cm, which is average for the parent species as well.

The diploid *Prunus serrulata* var. *pubescens* has been used by the cherry breeder Mr. Masatoshi Asari to create new forms in the Matsumae region of Hokkaidō. Influence on other garden cherries can be assumed.

Prunus serrulata var. *pubescens* (Nakai) Wilson

Kasumi-zakura, ke-yama-zakura, Korean mountain cherry
Synonyms: *Prunus jamasakura* var. *verecunda* Koidzumi, *P. leveilleana*
      Koehne, *P. mutabilis* Miyoshi, *P. verecunda* (Koidzumi) Koehne,
      P. verecunda var. *compta* (Koidzumi) Nakai
Description: Tree broader and more umbrella-shaped than the more ascending Japanese mountain cherry (*Prunus serrulata* var. *spontanea*). Young foliage greenish, sometimes with bronze shades. Mature leaves more coarsely serrated than leaves of *P. serrulata* var. *spontanea* and somewhat resembling the serration of leaves of the Oshima cherry (*P. serrulata* var. *speciosa*). Hardly any awns on the leaves. Leaf underside and stem are pubescent. Compact corymb, with four to six flowers. Flowering season is early May, quite late when compared with the average *P. serrulata* var. *spontanea*.

Prunus serrulata var. *speciosa*, Oshima Cherry

The Oshima cherry is an insular form closely related to the mountain cherries *Prunus sargentii*, *P. serrulata* var. *pubescens*, and *P. serrulata* var. *spontanea*. It is named after Ō-shima Island in the Sagami Bay near Tokyo that forms the center of its area of distribution. It is indigenous on Ō-shima

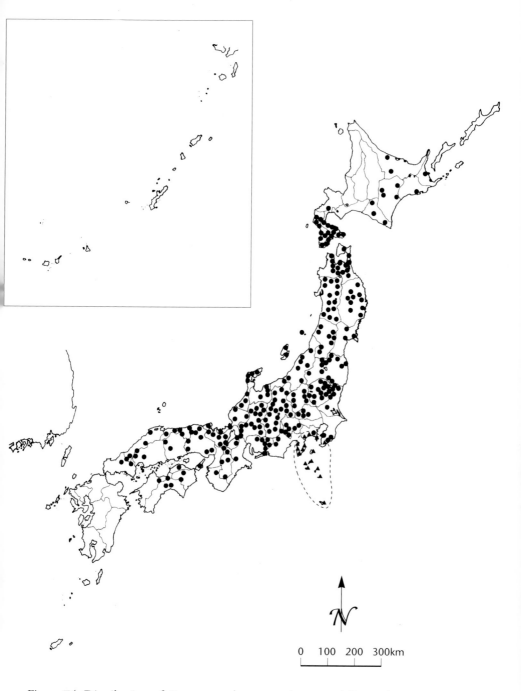

Figure 74. Distribution of *Prunus serrulata* var. *pubescens* and *P. serrulata* var. *speciosa*. Adapted from the Flower Association of Japan (1982). ● = *P. serrulata* var. *pubescens*. ▲ = *P. serrulata* var. *speciosa*.

and on all the other neighboring Izu Islands, and on the southern Izu Peninsula and the coastal region of the Boso Peninsula (see Figure 74). Both peninsulas lie opposite the Izu Islands. According to one theory, the Oshima cherry was brought to the mainland long ago by charcoal burners. The area has active volcanoes, some below sea level, and new islands appear from time to time. Here the Oshima cherry is perfectly adapted to the young and active, volcanic geology of the region, matching a great variability to an easy germination of the seeds. The wide variability found in the wild covers largely the botanical details that set the identity of most garden forms classified as *Prunus serrulata*. The typical Oshima cherry has bristled leaves with aristate serration, and its flowers resemble those of the Japanese mountain cherry (*P. serrulata* var. *spontanea*).

The Oshima cherry differs from the Japanese mountain cherry in the green color of its young foliage with, at most, only a shade of bronze, the heavier, spreading main branches, the large and coarse leaves with their fresh, green underside, and the slightly larger flowers with serrated sepals. The slender bristles at the tips of the serration of the leaves are also typical.

The Oshima cherry was important in originating many of the garden forms; fragrant cultivars such as 'Jo-nioi' and 'Taki-nioi' are undiluted selections of it. 'Ichiyo' shows a great influence of the Oshima cherry, and 'Ariake' and 'Shirotae' must be close relatives. The Oshima cherry has been used by Japanese gardeners for centuries as stock for grafting garden trees. The stock was always cultivated from seed, so that its variability also was present in many nurseries. The Oshima cherry was present in nurseries as a pollen parent in many parts of the country in spite of its limited area of natural distribution.

Double-flowered trees are found on Ō-shima Island in the wild as well as trees with pinkish flowers or with bronze, young foliage, rather than the usual green. A profusely blooming, double, pink selection is in cultivation as 'Yae-beni-oshima'. Its flowers are smaller than those of other cultivars of *Prunus serrulata* and appear after the foliage has partly unfolded. 'Yae-beni-oshima' is a good tree for a park or a wider roadside planting, but is less competitive in the garden-center commerce.

In its homeland the Oshima cherry is considered to have a strong resistance towards salty winds and air pollution. It must be remembered, however, that the area of its natural distribution has a mild climate with an annual rainfall of well over 2000 mm.

The Oshima cherry is not only loved for its flowers, but also appreciated in Japan for its edible leaves, which are used to make a rice cake called *sakura-mochi*. A bite-size morsel of soft, sweet cake made of sticky rice and red beans is wrapped in a fresh, young but fully grown leaf that has been lightly salted, pressed and, after a week or so of steeping, quickly rinsed and wiped dry. The treatment sets free the almondy fragrance of the cumarin in the leaf that, together with the salt, balances the sweetness of the

Figure 75. The flat, open flowers of the Oshima cherry *(Prunus serrulata* var. *speciosa)* on long pedicels with lanceolate, serrated sepals. Photo by author, 9 April 1996, Kyōto Botanic Garden.

Figure 76. Full-grown tree of the Oshima cherry *(Prunus serrulata* var. *speciosa).*
Photo by Arie Peterse, 6 May 1985, Wageningen Botanic Gardens of the Agricultural University, Netherlands.

rice cake. The leaves are quite large and keep their color more or less during the treatment—two reasons that have made this cherry a favorite of
Japanese pastry makers and have led to another folk name, *mochi-zakura*
("rice-cake cherry").

Prunus serrulata var. *speciosa* (Koidzumi) Koehne

Oshima cherry, Oshima-zakura, mochi-zakura

Synonyms: *Prunus jamasakura* var. *speciosa* Koidzumi, *P. lannesiana* f.
  albida (Makino) Wilson, *P. lannesiana* var. *speciosa* (Koidzumi)
  Makino, *P. kiusiana* Koidzumi, *P. mutabilis* f. *speciosa* Miyoshi,
  P. serrulata var. *serrulata* f. *albida* Makino

Description: Tree umbrella-shaped, open, with heavy spreading branches,
to 12 m high or more. Bast of one-year-old twigs shiny gray to pale brown.
Young foliage green or with a bronze-green shade. Serration single, sometimes double, with awn-tipped teeth. Immature leaves sometimes show a
few hairs on the central vein. Mature leaves 8–13 × 5–8 cm. Flowers in
loose corymbs, rarely in umbels. Peduncles about 1 cm long; pedicels
0.9–2.4 cm, glabrous (sometimes with hairs). Flower buds elongated with

a faint pink shade. Flower diameter 3.5–4.0(–5.5) cm. Flowers occasionally fragrant. Petals five. There is one pistil, perfect. The calyx is narrow and campanulate, about 5.5 mm long. Sepals are elongated and serrated (sometimes entire). Fruits purple-black, sour. Flowering season is late April. *Prunus serrulata* var. *speciosa* has a diploid set of chromosomes (2n = 16). The species is more variable than this description suggests.

Prunus serrulata var. *spontanea,* Japanese Mountain Cherry

Prunus serrulata var. *spontanea* is known in its homeland as *yama-zakura* ("mountain cherry"). *Yama* stands for the landscape of steep foothills between the coastal plain of Japan and the more alpine mountains of several thousand meters in central Japan (see Figure 72). This tree is not alpine; it is one of the trees typical of the secondary forests on the hilly *yama* of southern and western Japan. Most remarkable is the bright red, young foliage that appears with the pinkish buds that expand to white flowers. The spring show of contrasting white and red is magnificent and without equal among other flowering cherries in Japan.

Specimens may differ in shape of the tree, in the color of the young foliage, and in the color of the flowers, which can be pink as well. Unique specimens can be found among wild seedlings: trees may have fragrant flowers, pubescent pedicels, or flowers with double the number of petals. In its exhaustive study on flowering cherries, the Flower Association of Japan (1982) described no less than twenty-seven cultivated forms, some of which have double flowers. Miyoshi (1916) distinguished, named, and described more than a hundred forms. On the other side of the Japan Sea, Korea has its set of classic selections. None of these selections is in cultivation in the West.

The Japanese mountain cherry is rarely seen in Europe or North America, because gardeners tend to overlook botanic species when planting a foreign and exotic tree. Yet, this cherry cannot be praised enough: it is healthy, vigorous, and profusely blooming—something even more spectacular when its size is considered. Its small, single flowers contrast charmingly with the red-brown young foliage that heralds the warmer days of spring. Mature leaves show a fine, acute, and single serration, and a glaucous underside. The bracts and bractlets are usually conspicuous red at the height of blossoming. Compared to other flowering cherries, this one is long lived. Collingwood Ingram regretted that his "oft repeated praise of this cherry would appear to have fallen on deaf ears." It certainly is a pity that this cherry is not seen more often. It is difficult to grow on *Prunus avium* stock, but selections are easily raised on rootstock grown from the very fertile seeds of the species. A Chinese mountain cherry, *P. serrulata* var. *hupehensis,* was described by Collingwood Ingram in 1948.

Prunus serrulata var. *spontanea* (Maximowicz) Wilson

Japanese mountain cherry, yama-zakura, Japanese hill cherry
Synonyms: *Prunus jamasakura* Siebold ex Koidzumi, *P. jamasakura*
     Siebold, *P. mutabilis* Miyoshi
Description: Tree large, 12–15 m high or more, with a broad-ovate crown held by ascending limbs. Young foliage red-brown (RHS 166-A) to bronze-green (RHS 152-A) or even fresh green, unfolding with the blossom. Serration single, often with a few glands at the base. Mature leaves whitish green on the underside (!). Stipules deeply bifurcated, 5–15 mm long and usually narrow. Bracts and bractlets usually bright red. Corymbose inflorescence, with two to five flowers (rarely umbellate). Peduncles

Figure 77. Blossom and young foliage of a splendid specimen of the Japanese mountain cherry *(Prunus serrulata* var. *spontanea).* Photo by Kense Kuitert, 1 April 1997, Uryuyama campus of the Kyōto University of Art and Design.

Figure 78. Twig and leaves of the Japanese mountain cherry *(Prunus serrulata* var. *spontanea)*. Note the whitish underside. Photo by author, 1 June 1996, Uryuyama campus of the Kyōto University of Art and Design.

1–6 cm long. Pedicels 2–4 cm long. Flowers in bud usually slightly pink; completely opened flowers are white. Flower diameter 2–3 cm. Flowers open to a flat plane; the petals sometimes do not touch each other when the flower is fully expanded. Petals five, emarginate at the top, elliptic, 10–15 × 5–10 mm. There is one pistil, perfect; just a little shorter than the stamens. The calyx is narrow and campanulate, 5 × 2 mm, with no distinct transition from pedicel to calyx, usually green colored. Sepals are elongated, 7 × 2 mm, unserrated, with a slight purple hue. Winter buds are acute. Flowering season is late April. The species is more variable than this description suggests.

Tsukushi-zakura (synonym *Prunus jamasakura* var. *chikusiensis* (Koidzumi) Ohwi) has thick twigs, large, pure white flowers, and fresh, light green, young foliage that is a little sticky. This cherry is found here and there along the coasts of the southern islands and mid Honshū, the main island of Japan, where it occurs together with the species. It supposedly is a parent of some of the garden cherries that originated in western Japan and the

Kyōto region (Flower Association of Japan, 1982). This variety should be named *Prunus serrulata* var. *chikusiensis* (Koidzumi) Ohwi.

Prunus ×subhirtella

Prunus ×subhirtella Miquel (synonyms *P. ×subhirtella* 'Subhirtella', 'Ko-higan-zakura') is believed to be a cultivated hybrid between the Fuji cherry (*P. incisa*) and the Edo-higan cherry (*P. pendula* f. *ascendens*). Rather recently, wild cherry trees matching the description of *P. ×subhirtella* were discovered on Boso and Izu peninsulas, but research has not yet been conclusive. In Japan this cherry is called *ko-higan-zakura: ko* means "small" and refers to the tree's size, which is about 4 m high, and *higan* is the Japanese word for spring equinox, the time when this cherry flowers in Japan. The other equinox cherry, *P. pendula* f. *ascendens,* makes a much larger tree and is called Edo-higan. In the West, large shrubs known as higan cherry or spring cherry are usually the triploid 'Ko-higan-zakura' though. It was cultivated in Japan as higan-zakura and exported to the West under this name, so that confusion with the diploid *P. pendula* f. *ascendens,* also known as higan-zakura, may have occurred. What is sold as rosebud cherry is probably a deeper pink form of 'Ko-higan-zakura'. The more narrowly defined *P. ×subhirtella* 'Subhirtella' grows to 5 m at the most and presents, with its slender twigs full of flowers in early spring—still cold—a fragile kind of gorgeousness, quite different from the sturdy appearance of majestic trees of *P. pendula* f. *ascendens.* This is the most distinguishing difference between the two; other botanic details differ only slightly. The single flowers of *P. ×subhirtella* 'Subhirtella' are somewhat campanulate and have a pitcher-shaped calyx on pubescent pedicels. Each umbellate inflorescence bears two or three flowers. The calyx of *P. pendula* f. *ascendens* is more globular at the base, whereas the mouth of the calyx of *P. ×subhirtella* 'Subhirtella' is longer and more tubular. Leaves of the former are larger, more narrow, and finely serrated. The latter has more ovate, rather coarsely serrated leaves. The pink clouds of a local form of 'Ko-higan-zakura' on the old castle grounds in the town of Takatō in Nagano Prefecture are famous in Japan. *Prunus ×subhirtella* has a triploid set of chromosomes (2n = 24).

Jugatsu-zakura (synonyms 'Autumnalis', *Prunus ×subhirtella* Miquel 'Autumnalis', autumn cherry, autumn-flowering higan cherry) flowers in autumn. Its Japanese name, *jugatsu-zakura,* means "cherry of the tenth month" or "October cherry." Indeed it seems to profit from Japan's "October spring," a fall warm spell that occurs quite commonly. In other parts of the world, this cherry quickly reacts to a few warm days in fall, but it flowers sparingly, and comes in bloom one more time, and to be honest, most floriferously in spring. Another folk name for this cherry is *o-eshiki-zakura* after the O-eshiki, a Buddhist service held on the 13th of October, the anniversary of the death of Nichiren, founder of a sect of Buddhism. 'Jugatsu-zakura' is illustrated and described in the encyclopedia *Kokon-yōran-kō* (Yashiro 1821–1841). It is an old garden form, and the name 'Jugatsu-zakura' has priority over the later invented Latin name. The Takagi nursery offered it in 1904, and it was imported in England around this time. In the 1930s it was seen in the catalogs as *Prunus subhirtella ascendens pendula autumnalis* (Wada 1937). The tree is small to 5 m, sometimes more, broad

Figure 79. Even in midwinter, *Prunus ×subhirtella* 'Jugatsu-zakura' may surprise us with a few hesitating flowers. Photo by author, 5 December 1996, Tama Forest Science Garden, Tokyo.

and open in form, with rather thin branches. Young leaves are pale bronze to bronze-green (RHS 173-C), in spring sprouting just after flowering. Twigs of young shoots pubescent. Serration of mature leaves double, with rather small acute tips, with glands; some hairs on both sides of the leaves; petiole pubescent. Stipules short. Umbellate inflorescence, with one to three flowers. Peduncles very short, pedicel short, 1.0–1.5 cm, but longer with spring flowers, some pubescence. Flowers pink in bud, expanding to an open, flat shape, of a lighter pink (RHS 63-D) or almost white. Flower diameter in autumn about 1.5–2.0 cm, in spring 2.0–2.5 cm. Petals ten to twenty, elliptic or obovate, about 1.0 × 0.8 cm. There is one pistil, perfect, partly pubescent, about 1.3 cm long. Calyx urceolate, but not extremely globular at the base nor extremely narrow at the mouth, with some hairs, red. Sepals are triangular and pubescent on the outside, and are serrated. Flowering season is in autumn, about October with rather small flowers and again in early April in Tokyo with more and larger flowers(!). *Prunus* ×*subhirtella* 'Jugatsu-zakura' has a triploid set of chromosomes (2n = 24). A more intensely colored form of 'Jugatsu-zakura' is 'Autumnalis Rosea' (synonym *Prunus* ×*subhirtella* Miquel 'Autumnalis Rosea'). It has buds of a deeper pink (RHS 63-C), and its flowers expand to pink (RHS 65-D).

Koshi-no-higan (synonyms 'Koshi-no-higan-zakura', *Prunus pendula* var. *koshiensis* Ohwi) is found in a wild stand designated as a natural monument in Jōhana-chō, Toyama Prefecture, and appears to be a hybrid of *P. pendula* var. *ascendens* and either *P. sargentii*, *P. incisa*, or *P. serrulata* var. *pubescens*. It is also given as *P.* ×*koshiensis*. Trees do not produce much fruit, and young plants develop from roots some distance from the parent. This cherry is seen in cultivation here and there in Japan and merits our attention. It is an early flowering form with elegant, somewhat bell-shaped flowers. This cherry has a triploid set of chromosomes (2n = 24).

Omoigawa (synonym *Prunus* ×*subhirtella* Kubota 'Omoigawa') is named after the Omoigawa River in Oyama, Tochigi Prefecture, where it sprouted from a seed of 'Autumnalis'. It was found, described (1971), and raised by Mr. Hideo Kubota of the Nikkō Botanical Gardens. This small umbrella-shaped tree has many floriferous twigs set on spreading branches. Buds are dark pink (RHS 63-C) among the light pink (RHS 69-A) flowers. It is a favorite, hardy garden plant, quickly becoming popular in Europe.

Figure 80. 'Koshi-no-higan' is an early flowering and most elegant triploid spring cherry still hardly known outside Japan. Photo by the author, 30 March 1997, Kyōto Botanic Garden.

Prunus ×*yedoensis,* Somei-yoshino

The history of *Prunus* ×*yedoensis* is closely related to the history of the modern nation of Japan as explained in "The Nation's Flower" in chapter 1. As the national flower, it was planted throughout the country and is found now in many other parts of the world. It was exported under the name Yoshino cherry in the early twentieth century and might still be found under this name in the West. This might lead to confusion with cherries from Yoshino, that is to say, the Japanese mountain cherry (*P. serrulata* var. *spontanea*). In fact, the advice to refrain from the name Yoshino is almost a century old.

Breeding experiments by Y. Takenaka using the Oshima cherry (*Prunus serrulata* var. *speciosa*) and the Edo-higan cherry (*P. pendula* f. *ascendens*) resulted in cherries closely resembling *P.* ×*yedoensis*. This led Takenaka to conclude and publish in the 1960s that 'Somei-yoshino' originated as a hybrid of the two. The regions of distribution of both parents overlap at

Figure 81. *Prunus* ×*yedoensis* is a short, spreading tree on the lean soils of Kyōto. On the loam soils of Tokyo it can become twice as high and broad. Photo by author, 8 April 1997, Hirano Shrine, Kyōto.

Figure 82. An old, broadly spreading *Prunus* ×*yedoensis*. Photo by Arie Peterse, 20 April 1985, Kesteren, Netherlands.

the Izu Peninsula especially on and around Mount Amagi. Details on the origin of *P.* ×*yedoensis* keep challenging researchers. Takashi Kaneko (1992), for example, concluded from chromosome research that the Edo-higan cherry (*P. pendula* f. *ascendens*) was the seed parent and the Oshima cherry (*P. serrulata* var. *speciosa*), the pollen parent. The late Shōzō Kōnomori (1985), owner of a flower shop at the entrance of the Somei Cemetery in Tokyo, pointed to the cherry nursery Ōkō-en and its owner Gonbei Kawashima, who most probably released *P.* ×*yedoensis.*.

Prunus ×*yedoensis* is a clonal cultivar and can be understood as a *satozakura* form (Ingram 1948). It is a successful nursery plant, easily propagated from cuttings and quickly growing to a marketable size on its own stem. Compared to the Japanese mountain cherry (*P. serrulata* var. *spontanea*) or the Edo-higan cherry (*P. pendula* f. *ascendens*), it is short-lived; an

Figure 83. *Prunus × yedoensis*. Drawing by Miss C. J. M. Bäcker, 13 April 1964, Laboratory of Plant Taxonomy, Wageningen Botanic Gardens of the Agricultural University, Netherlands.

eighty-year-old tree is exceptionally old. Usually before that time the tree starts to fall apart: the stem becomes twisted with fissures that show adventive roots growing in decaying parts of the trunk. Young shoots and flower buds may come up from adventive buds, even in old, mossy parts of the bark. Though very strong in the cityscape, where it can survive gasoline fumes with asphalt coming up to its trunk (at least if provided with a deep, good soil), it is not very disease resistant in Japan, where witches'-broom can cause serious problems.

Prunus ×*yedoensis* is one of the cherries that flower before the leaves appear, giving a spectacular effect in mass planting.

Prunus ×*yedoensis* Matsumura
Somei-yoshino
Synonyms: *Prunus paracerasus* Koehne, *P.* ×*yedoensis* Matsumura 'Yedoensis'
Less current synonyms: Tokyo cherry (not Yoshino, not Yoshino cherry,
    not *Prunus yoshino*)
Description: Tree umbrella-shaped, to 10 m high or more, with ascending branches and few spreading horizontally low on the stem. Twigs of young sprouts showing hairs that disappear during the year. Young foliage green or with a slight bronze-green shade, appearing after the flowering(!). Serration double, sometimes single, with acute tips. Mature leaves show some pubescence on the underside, 7–11 × 4–6 cm. Petiole pubescent. Umbels carry three to four flowers. Bracts at the outer side with many tiny hairs. Peduncles short(!). Pedicels 2.0–2.5 cm long. Flowers in bud a light shade of pink (RHS 56-B), expanded flowers are almost white (RHS 155-D). Flower diameter 3.0–3.5 cm. Flowers have no distinct fragrance. Petals five, oval to ovate, 1.6–1.9 × 1.2–1.6 cm. There is one pistil, perfect, lower part of style shows few hairs. The calyx is narrow and urceolate or pitcher-shaped, with only a slightly narrower mouth. Sepals are ovate to elongated, triangular, serrated, with a reddish hue. Fruits black, bitter, sweet. Flowering season is the first week of April in Tokyo. *Prunus* ×*yedoensis* has a diploid set of chromosomes (2n = 16).

Akebono is a popular American cultivar (Clarke, California, 1925) with soft-pink, semi-double flowers that appear in a neat and regular covering around the branches; it forms a small tree or large shrub if it stands on its own roots. It is named 'Amerika' in Japan.

Amagi-yoshino was found by Y. Takenaka in 1959 among hybrids from his experiments to identify the parents of 'Somei-yoshino'. He named it after Mount Amagi, where hybridization between the Oshima cherry (*Prunus serrulata* var. *speciosa*) and the Edo-higan cherry (*P. pendula* f. *ascendens)* is often seen in the wild. This valuable discovery has large, white petals, 2 cm or more, and blooms early and profusely.

Ivensii started as a weeping seedling of *Prunus ×yedoensis* found by Hillier before 1929. It is an attractive dome-shaped shrub that flowers rather briefly but very floriferously on older plants. Some clonal selections exist.

Sendai-shidare (Ohwi, 1973) is sometimes sold as "Shidare Yoshino," which it somewhat resembles from a distance. 'Sendai-shidare', however, is

Figure 84. 'Amagi-yoshino', a hybrid showing strong influence of its seed parent, the Oshima cherry *(Prunus serrulata* var. *speciosa),* such as twig color, flower, calyx, and sepals. The lesser influence of its pollen parent, the Edo-higan cherry *(Prunus pendula* f. *ascendens),* also shows, such as almost umbellate inflorescences, and some pubescence on calyx and pedicels. Photo by author, 30 March 1997, Kyōto Botanic Garden.

quickly identified by its long, slender, campanulate calyx, and tapered flower buds, quite different from any form of *Prunus* ×*yedoensis*. Mature leaves suggest *P. serrulata*. It has no relation with 'Sendai-ito-zakura', a name for the 'Yae-beni-shidare' form of *P. pendula*.

Shidare-yoshino is not clearly defined as a nursery product. Weeping mutants appear now and then among large-scale plantings of *Prunus* ×*yedoensis* and some are taken in cultivation, usually as 'Shidare-yoshino', 'Weeping Yoshino Cherry', or something like that. Most forms show an irregular or straggling tree shape, often with bare branches that have blossoms only at the end. For weeping cherries, one of the forms of *P. pendula* is usually a better choice.

CHAPTER 5

Japanese Garden Cherries

The cherries described in this chapter are old garden forms that often have been cultivated since the feudal Edo period and thus can be traced in nursery catalogs or garden books of the period. Nonetheless, most of them lack a clear hybrid or selection history, and we cannot be sure about their parents. These garden cherries are known loosely in Japan as *sato-zakura*.

Looking closely at the *sato-zakura*, one may make an educated guess about parental influence and even put the garden cherries into groups, as Kawasaki (1994) has endeavored. Fragrant and single-flowered garden cherries, such as 'Jo-nioi', 'Surugadai-nioi', and 'Taki-nioi', are without doubt selections from the wild Oshima cherry. More than likely the double 'Goza-no-ma-nioi' and 'Hosokawa-nioi' also belong to this group. Many other double-flowered cherries, such as 'Fugenzo' or 'Ichiyo', show botanic details such as leaf shape and serration that are similar to the Oshima cherry and must be close relatives. Other single-flowered forms, often with red bracts and bractlets, seem to be selections of the Japanese mountain cherry; these include 'Arashiyama', 'Bendono', 'Koshio-yama', and 'Tagui-arashi'. 'Choshu-hizakura', 'Horinji', 'Murasaki-zakura', and 'Taoyame' come close to this supposed parent. Many chrysanthemum-flowered forms must be related to the Japanese mountain cherry. Their reddish young sprouts and their serrated mature leaves with a whitish underside betray a connection with this supposed parent.

Japanese sources group all the garden cherries usually under the Oshima cherry, *Prunus lannesiana*, a name authored by Carrière in 1872; no living tree nor herbarium exists, but the description could cover the Oshima cherry. This is the only reason why *P. lannesiana* can be used.

On the other hand, because of the convincing herbarium and living specimens that back it up, the name *Prunus serrulata* is valid according to the internationally accepted rules.

The garden forms 'Ama-no-gawa' to 'Yokihi' are discussed below in alphabetical order as if they were cultivars of *Prunus serrulata*. Other opinions are mentioned in the text. To indicate the lack of a conclusive plant history, each cherry is described without a species name. The old Japanese

Figure 85. *Prunus serrulata* 'Albo Plena'. Photo by Arie Peterse, 16 May 1986, Zetten, Netherlands.

names have priority; they are valid and should be used. Latin cultivar names were invented later and are listed as synonyms. Names that should not be used because they create confusion are placed in parentheses.

Prunus serrulata 'Albo Plena'

Prunus serrulata Lindley is not the name of a wild species, but traces back to a plant introduced to Engand in the early nineteenth century (see "A Botanist's Discussion" in chapter 1). It is a double-flowered garden form to which the cultivar name 'Albo Plena' was added by Camillo Schneider in 1906. Thereafter it became known in Europe as *P. serrulata* Lindley 'Albo Plena' Schneider. Manabu Miyoshi recognized *P. serrulata* in 1916 as the type for most *sato-zakura* cherries.

Prunus serrulata 'Albo Plena' is found in the Royal Botanic Gardens, Kew; the Arboretum Kalmthout, Belgium; and the Rombergpark, Dortmund, Germany. No 'Albo Plena' is in cultivation in Japan. It should be remembered, however, that Carrière reported two forms: the gorgeous one that he depicted is 'Ichihara-tora-no-o', and his less gorgeous form, this 'Albo Plena'.

The shape of 'Albo Plena' is broadly spreading; the thick branches barely ramify and are full of short spurs. This typical branching is seen also high up in the crown of old specimens of the Japanese mountain cherry and is apparently a matter of slow-growth physiology. Similar branching is found with several chrysanthemum-flowered forms that have a slow growth because of the much-energy-absorbing blossom. A large-flowered, single form, 'Mikuruma-gaeshi', has the same spurs on limbs.

'Albo Plena' has glabrous-shiny, dark green leaves with fine-aristate teeth and a strikingly whitish underside similar to that of the Japanese mountain cherry. 'Albo Plena' is described here from a tree in Kalmthout.

Prunus serrulata Lindley 'Albo Plena'

Description: Tree broad, with almost horizontally extending, barely ramifying branches with short twigs and spurs. Young foliage green. Serration single with short-aristate teeth, 0.5 mm, with small dark red glands up to the tip of the leaf. Underside of the mature leaves is markedly whitish(!). Stipules medium to deeply bifurcated, quickly shedding, 7–10 mm long. Corymbose inflorescence, with four to five flowers. Peduncles 2.0–2.5 cm long. Pedicels 2–3 cm long. Flower in bud sometimes with a faint shade of pink, becoming pure white when completely opened. Flower 3.5–4.0 cm in diameter, opening to a rather flat plane. Petals eighteen to twenty-one, with one to five petaloids, ovate, often slightly emarginate at the top, 18–19 × 11–14 mm. There is one pistil, perfect, 12–14 mm long, much longer than the stamens(!). Filament of the stamen extending above the yellow anther. The calyx is broad and vase-shaped, 4 × 5 mm, with a faint purple tinge; there is no distinct transition from pedicel to calyx. Sepals triangular, 6.5–7.0 × 3.0–3.5 mm, unserrated, with a faint purple tinge. Flowering season is late—second to third week of May, flowers appearing with the leaves. (Compare this description with the one of 'Ichihara-tora-no-o'.)

'Ama-no-gawa'

'Ama-no-gawa' ("heaven's river") is the Japanese word for the galaxy, which in Japan is viewed as a river rather than a way as in Milky Way. *Ama* is an old word for the abode of the gods. According to a myth, the tears of the goddess Amaterasu dropped in the ocean and turned into firm land. This event marked the creation of the Land of the Rising Sun.

The cultivar 'Ama-no-gawa' was first recorded in 1886 in a list of cherries planted along the Arakawa River near Tokyo. It is easily recognized by its fastigiate growth and was described in 1916 by Miyoshi as *Prunus serrulata* f. *erecta* and by Wilson as *P. lannesiana* f. *erecta*. It blossoms profusely with semi-double, light pink flowers set closely to the erect branches; a sweet fragrance, described by some as resembling freesia, surrounds the flowering tree. The fastigiate character extends to the inflorescence, which resemble a group of little flowers standing upright at the side of the branches. The erect flowers are typical for 'Ama-no-gawa' and distinguish it from other, less successful fastigiate forms of flowering cherries.

When 'Ama-no-gawa' grows older, its branches tend to sag, the tree loses its typical stiff-erect shape, and tree identification is a little harder. The column shape might seem rigid to the naturalist, but has proved useful in many garden schemes. Trees in Japan are less floribund and weaker than their European counterparts.

'Ama-no-gawa' is very compatible with *Prunus avium* stock. Healthy, hardy, easily propagated, and useful for the small private garden, 'Ama-no-gawa', not surprisingly, has become a very popular flowering cherry in the

Figure 86. 'Ama-no-gawa' has a fastigiate shape. Photo by Arie Peterse, 1997, Kesteren, Netherlands.

Figure 87. 'Ama-no-gawa' has erect corymbs. Photo by Arie Peterse, 1997, Kesteren, Netherlands.

West. Healthy trees can easily be kept small to accommodate a narrow place in the garden; they can be rejuvenated every five years or so by cutting back in early summer some old branches at a low point, cut surfaces to be treated with an antiseptic. In propagation, it should be grafted low on the stock. In this way full advantage is taken from the natural character of 'Ama-no-gawa' as a fountain of flowers, indeed a galaxy against the sky at twilight in early spring.

Prunus 'Ama-no-gawa'
Less current synonym: 'Erecta'
   Description: Tree cone-shaped, with fastigiate growth(!), to 5 m high and 1.5 m wide. Young leaves at the time of flowering slightly bronzed light green to green. Serration single and double, without glands. Stipules about 10 mm. Corymbose inflorescence, with four to five flowers, more or less upright(!). Peduncles 2–4 cm long. Pedicels 2.5–4.5 cm long. Flower in bud pink, turning to a light shade of pink when fully developed and to almost white at the end of flowering, with a purplish pink heart just before shedding. Flower about 4.5 cm in diameter, opening to a saucer shape with an open center, strong and agreeable sweet fragrance(!). Petals six to fifteen of which five are perfect and the rest more or less petaloid, 19–21 × 14–17 mm, slightly emarginate at the top. There is one pistil (rarely 2), perfect, 11 mm long, about as long as or sometimes longer than the longest stamens. The calyx is campanulate, has a slight red hue, is about 8 × 3 mm, with a distinct transition from calyx to pedicel. Sepals are oblong, somewhat narrower at the base, 7–8 × 4.0–4.5 mm, often with a few teeth at the tip. Flowering season is late April. 'Ama-no-gawa' has a diploid set of chromosomes (2n = 16).

Tanabata is an erect, less floriferous cherry with white flowers. The name is derived from the star Vega (weaving woman) who, according to a very old Chinese legend, married the star Altair on the seventh day of the seventh month. The name also is applied to a Japanese festival celebrated on 7 July.

'Arashiyama'

Arashiyama is the name of a scenic place east of Kyōto that has been famous for its cherries since the late twelfth century when Japanese mountain cherries were brought from Yoshino and planted on the estates of aristocrats. It is likely that there were no cherries at Arashiyama before this time and that particularly nice cherries were brought there. A "selection-pressure" by gardeners of these ancient days has brought 'Arashiyama' and 'Tagui-arashi' to the foreground. The Japanese mountain cherry and 'Tagui-arashi' are diploids, and supposedly so is 'Arashiyama', although it has not yet been checked.

'Arashiyama' appears in an 1823 description of the cherries at the Hirano Shrine (a Shinto temple in Kyōto) and since then in other collection lists in Japan. Wilson saw it at Arakawa and gave a short description under *Prunus lannesiana* f. *ranzan*. "Ran-zan" is a different reading for the Chinese characters that can also be read as Arashi-yama. In the 1930s this cultivar was offered for export to the West by Japanese nurseries. Japanese sources list it as *P. lannesiana* 'Arashiyama'.

'Arashiyama' is a spreading medium-sized tree with a lovely show of slightly fragrant, single flowers mixed early in the season with bright-pink flower buds. The aristate serration of the leaves made Ohwi (1965) suggest an influence of the Oshima cherry, but Hayashi (1995) thought the flowers to be perfectly in line with the Japanese mountain cherry, which at least must be responsible for the bright red bracts and bractlets. Two other valuable flowering cherries, 'Bendono' and 'Tagui-arashi', also show such a similarity to the Japanese mountain cherry; the three must be undiluted selections of it. All three have remarkably red bracts and bractlets that, depending on the weather and the season, may be so bright as to effect the aspect of the whole tree in bloom. 'Arashiyama' is preferred for its few more petals in fragrant flowers.

Prunus 'Arashiyama'

Less current synonym: Ranzan

Description: Tree spreading, to 6 m high, rather vigorous growth. Young foliage red-brown (RHS 175-C), serration single with bristles(!). Stipules much divided. Bracts and bractlets red. Corymbose inflorescence, with two to three or even four flowers. Peduncles 1.0–1.5 cm long. Pedicels 2.5–3.5 cm long; flower stalks with a reddish shade. Flower in bud dark pink (RHS 62-A), becoming white with a pinkish edge when completely opened. Flower about 4 cm in diameter, opening to a flat plane, with a slight fragrance. Petals five, often with two to three or even five extra petaloids, round, 19 × 16 mm, usually slightly emarginate at the top, occasionally entire.

Figure 88. 'Arashiyama'. Photo by author, 15 April 1995, Hirano Shrine, Kyōto.

There is one pistil, perfect, about 15 mm long, as long as the stamens. The calyx is campanulate (to funnel-shaped), about 6 × 3 mm, green with a reddish shade; there is a distinct transition from pedicel to calyx. Sepals are elongated and triangular, slightly narrowing again at the base, about 8 × 2 mm, often with a few teeth; reddish shade. Many fruits. Flowering season is mid-April.

'Ariake'

The Japanese word *ariake* referred in ancient days to the rare sight of an early morning sunrise while a full moon was still visible. On such a morning the color of the moon changes, with the fading of the reddish twilight, from pinkish to pure white after the sun has risen over the horizon. In modern Japanese *ariake* simply means "daybreak," but the older meaning associates poetically with the color change that flowers of 'Ariake' undergo during expanding and with their open "moonlike" shape.

'Ariake' has been known in Japan for at least three centuries; it appeared as far back as 1681 in the horticultural treatise *Kadan-kōmoku* (Flower bed catalog). It appears in lists of collections ever since and was exported by Japanese nurseries at the beginning of the twentieth century. The continuous string of records makes it likely that we are dealing with the same cherry 'Ariake' now as the one of 1681. It is a good garden plant likely to have survived centuries of garden criticism. Miyoshi described it in 1916 as *Prunus serrulata* f. *candida*. In Japan one finds it as *P. lannesiana* 'Candida'.

The buds of 'Ariake' have a slight pinkish hue, which still lingers—like the daybreak moon—when opening. When expanded completely, however, the petals turn to an almost pure white. This daybreak-moon coloring is seen with other cherries also and is not typical only of 'Ariake'.

Most flowers are single, but some have more petals and might be even called semi-double. The petals give a waxy, sturdy impression and have wrinkled undulations in the surface. This is typical of cherries that are considered to be related to 'Mazakura', a common rootstock in Japan (Kawasaki 1994).

Fully developed flowers may be 5.5 cm in diameter; those with only five petals resemble blackberry flowers or white, single-flowered roses. The inflorescences are robust with sturdy peduncles that resemble those of 'Shirotae'. The latter though, has a more spreading, almost level tree shape, and

Figure 89. 'Ariake' has a rather narrow tree shape when young. Photo by Arie Peterse, 1997, Opheusden, Netherlands.

Figure 90. 'Ariake', sprout, calyx, sepals, and flowers (note petaloid). Photo by author, 8 April 1997, Hirano Shrine, Kyōto.

its flowers and buds are pure white. On the point of fragrance, 'Ariake' does not fall short of 'Shirotae'. On better soils its broad ascending growth is so vigorous that it has been recommended for less sheltered, colder places. 'Ariake' is a beautiful and healthy cherry with flowers borne in great profusion; it certainly deserves to be propagated and planted more often.

Prunus 'Ariake'

Less current synonyms: Ariyake, 'Candida', Kanto-ariake

Description: Tree funnel-shaped, broader at a later age, to 7 m high. Young leaves light bronze-green (RHS 152-C). Serration usually single with markedly elongated, fine awns that occasionally have white or slightly pinkish small glands(!); an occasional leaf lacks the caudate tip. Stipules 19–23 mm long. Corymbose inflorescence, with four to seven (usually six) flowers. Peduncles long, 3–4 cm. Pedicels 2.0–3.5 cm long. Flower in bud a light shade of pink, showing a slight pinkish hue when freshly opened, and turning pure white (RHS 155-C) when completely opened. Flower 5.0–5.5 cm in diameter, spreading to a flat saucer shape, strongly scented(!). Petals 5 plus

有明櫻

三熊思孝之所寫生 弘子々再摸

Figure 91. 'Ariake' in a woodblock print that catches the ephemeral beauty of the flowers rather than their botanic details. From Takeda (1902–1907), adapted from Mikuma Katen.

one to two petaloids (a few flowers may have up to seven petaloids), oval-orbicular, waxy, showing some undulations, 24–27 × 11– 19 mm, sometimes slightly emarginate or crenate at the top. There is one pistil, perfect, about 12 mm long, clearly shorter than the stamens (distinctly different from 'Shirotae' with pistil and stamens about equally long). The calyx is campanulate, 8 × 4 mm, with a faint purple tinge; there is a distinct transition from pedicel to calyx. Sepals long, ovate, triangular 9–10 × 3.5– 4.0 mm, entire, with a faint purple tinge. Flowering season is about four days earlier than 'Shirotae', from mid-April to early May. 'Ariake' has a triploid set of chromosomes (2n = 24). The 'Ariake' in cultivation in the Netherlands has serrated sepals.

Omuro-ariake is found at Ninna-ji Temple in Kyōto, alongside 'Yae-omuro-ariake'. Neither of these two cherries are directly related to 'Ariake'. They have a respectable local history. For centuries they have been propagated from layer-stools in the temple's garden. 'Omuro-ariake' has a few more petals than 'Ariake', forms a spreading tree, and vaguely suggests a flush of the Fuji cherry with its triangular sepals and a heart of the flower turning red after its prime. To avoid confusion, 'Ariake' is called 'Kanto-ariake' in the Kyōto area.

Senriko resembles 'Ariake' in the smallest detail. It is difficult, if not impossible, to keep the two apart. For practical reasons they may be considered identical, but if a difference should be found, 'Ariake' might have a little more pink in its young flowers, and 'Senriko' might show a few green hairs or tiny notches on its sepals. *Sen-ri-kō* translates as "thousand-miles-fragrance," promising with some literary imagination a fragrance to be discerned from a distance of one thousand miles. 'Senriko' has a triploid set of chromosomes (2n = 24).

'Asano'

Ingram excited his readers by telling how he discovered this beautiful chrysanthemum-flowered cherry in 1926 "in a little wayside garden, standing head and shoulders above a wooden fence" in the village of Kami-Yoshida in present-day Yamanashi Prefecture. A locally famous and one-legged veteran of the Russo-Japanese war sent some scions to Ingram in England the following winter. Ingram only saw the cherry one more time in a Shinto shrine in Kyōto.

Ingram described this cherry as *Prunus serrulata* 'Geraldinae' in 1929 and named it 'Asano' to commemorate a hero, the warrior Naganori Asano (1665–1701). This Asano was the lord of the domain Akō and will always be remembered because of his remarkable suicide. When visiting the shogun's castle in Edo, he happened to meet his eternal rival Kira Yoshinaka. Yoshinaka began insulting Asano in such a way that the latter could no longer contain himself and drew his sword. Immediately he was arrested by the shogun's police officers, because drawing swords within the castle compound was a capital offense. In spite of extensive pleading, Asano was without any mercy ordered to obey the rules and to commit *seppuku,* that is, to kill himself by ripping up his abdomen. He did as he was ordered since this was an honorable way of death for a warrior in feudal times. Not long after the funeral, forty-seven men, Asano's retainers, murdered Yoshinaka in revenge. The forty-seven were also punished and commanded to kill themselves by seppuku. They obeyed, as loyal followers, and were buried with their master. Any Japanese of the Edo period knew the history of Asano's retainers and profoundly felt that Asano and his men stood rightfully in defense of the humane, in contrast to the formalities of justice associated with the central government in Edo. Despite the heroism attached to it, 'Asano' is felt by Japanese cherry specialists to be a weird name for a cherry. Ingram's sympathy for the one-legged veteran in Kami-Yoshida perhaps inspired this martial name. Ingram was, after all, a retired navy captain.

'Asano' has small flowers with up to a hundred narrow petals. The flowers resemble the little powder puffs of the chrysanthemum-flowered 'Kiku-shidare-zakura', and the leaves of the two are also similar. 'Kiku-shidare-zakura', however, is a weeping tree, and 'Asano' has a rather narrow and erect shape. Moreover 'Asano' flowers one or two weeks earlier. This cultivar's erect shape, abundant blossoms, and deep pink persistent flowers make it worthy of a place in the small garden. In spite of these qualities and Ingram's appraisal of it as being one of his best introductions, 'Asano' is rarely grown. A disadvantage might be that its growth is not very vigorous, and Ingram reported some problems with witches'-broom. It is not known to be in cultivation in Japan, but if it stood in a Shinto shrine in Kyōto, as Ingram reported, it cannot have escaped the attention of that city's cherry lovers. 'Asano' must be related to 'Taizan-fukun'.

Figure 92. 'Asano' typically has pointed petals. Photo by Arie Peterse, 4 May 1986.

Prunus 'Asano'

Synonym: 'Geraldinae'

Description: Tree rather narrow funnel-shaped, to 6 m high. Young leaves bronze-green to dark green (RHS 152-A, 146-A). Serration single with glands. Stipules 13–18 mm long. Corymbose inflorescence, with two to six flowers each. Peduncles short, 0.1–1 cm long. Pedicels 2–3 cm long. Flower in bud deep pink (RHS 65-B). Flower about 3.5 cm in diameter, with a spherical shape. Petals seventy to eighty, elliptical, 12–14 × 7 mm, slightly emarginate at the top. Pistil usually one, sometimes two or absent, perfect, 4–9 mm long, hidden among the petals. The calyx is widely funnel-shaped, 3 × 4 mm, with a gradual transition from pedicel to calyx. Sepals triangular, 2.5 × 5 mm, accessory calyx with 5 little sepals, unserrated, slightly purple. Flowering season is from late April to early May.

Figure 93. 'Asano' grafted on *Prunus avium*. Photo by Arie Peterse, 1996, Opheusden, Netherlands.

Figure 94. 'Asano'. Drawing by Miss C. J. M. Bäcker, 22 April 1965, Laboratory of Plant Taxonomy, Wageningen Botanic Gardens of the Agricultural University, Netherlands.

'Baigoji-juzukake-zakura'

The origin of this chrysanthemum-flowered cultivar is a tree designated as a natural monument in Baigo-ji Temple at Kojima, close to the village of Kyōgase, about twenty kilometers east of the city of Niigata. *Juzukake* means "hanging the beads," referring to the beads (*juzu*) of a Buddhist rosary. The name was taken from an old legend about Saint Shinran (1173–1263), who, when he was to leave the area in 1211 after a period of exile, passed a cherry on the side of the road. Hanging his rosary on one of the branches, the saint said, "If my teachings are true, the flowers on this tree will appear as beads." His prayers and sincere intentions were rewarded, leaving us with a valuable garden plant. This story is attached to trees of this garden form that are found in several places in the area.

Figure 95. 'Baigoji-juzukake-zakura'. Note the glaucous backside of the leaf and the pale pink color of the many, rather small flowers. Photo by author, 24 April 1997, Kyōto Botanic Garden.

Miyoshi described this cherry in 1922 as *Prunus serrulata* f. *floribunda*. Jefferson (1984) gives 'Floribunda' as a cultivar name. In Japan one finds it as *P. lannesiana* 'Juzukakezakura'. Its relation to the Japanese mountain cherry is evident in the reddish, young foliage and the somewhat whitish underside of the leaves.

Among the chrysanthemum forms, 'Baigoji-juzukake-zakura' flowers a little earlier. Its peduncles and pedicels can be quite long, making for inflorescences up to 10 cm or more. Indeed the flowers may be viewed as beads dangling from the tree. The tree's compact growth and healthy appearance recommend it for the smaller garden. A disadvantage might be that the pink of the flowers is somewhat dull. Most flowers form a second-story flower in the heart that only opens a few days after the main flower has opened. A few green sepals of this second-story flower can be seen in the heart of the main one.

Prunus 'Baigoji-juzukake-zakura'

Synonym: Juzukake-zakura
Less current synonym: 'Floribunda'

Description: Tree narrow erect, small, to 5 m high. Young foliage dark green to reddish. Serration with short awns and small, red glands. Foliage is almost completely developed in the flowering season. Underside of the mature leaves somewhat whitish. Petioles on young, sprouting leaves often have three to four nectaries rather than the usual two(!). Corymbose inflorescence, with two to four flowers. Peduncles 2–5 cm long. Pedicels 4–7 cm long. Flower in bud dull purplish pink, becoming light pink (RHS 69-A) when completely opened. Flower about 3.5 cm in diameter. Petals about sixty to ninety (including the petals of the second-story flower), elliptic-oval, orbicular, or slightly emarginate at the top, about 20 × 10–15 mm. One pistil in the main flower, in the second flower it is phylloid, normal, or absent. The calyx is narrow and funnel-shaped, not hollow, with a faint purple tinge. Sepals are triangular 6–7 × 4–5 mm, unserrated, sometimes with a few sepal-like petals. Flowering season is late April (early May in Tokyo), earlier than 'Kenroku-en-kiku-zakura'.

'Bendono'

In Japanese 'Bendono' is written with Chinese characters that can also be read as 'Benden', the name by which this cultivar is known in the West. The word *Bendono* is a first name in Japan, created by adding the suffix *-dono* to the character *ben*. This suffix *-dono* or *-tono*, is derived from the old colloquial Japanese *tonosama* that meant "feudal lord." According to the encyclopedia *Kokon-yōran-kō* (Yashiro 1821–1841), it was common for the daimyo (feudal lords) to add this suffix to their children's names. Literally, *Bendono* could be translated as "Mister Ben," a name by which a servant would address a lord's son.

Ingram, when visiting the Sakura Kwai in 1926, requested grafting material of 'Bendono' to be sent to his home in England. The scions he received formed the origin of the introduction of this cherry to Europe.

In its tree shape and botanic details, 'Bendono' resembles the wild Japanese mountain cherry. It has the same kind of single, not extremely large flowers, with a reddish calyx and pedicel. The underside of the mature leaves shows a slight, whitish shade, pointing to the same parent. In fact, according to the *Kokon-yōran-kō* (Yashiro 1821–1841), 'Bendono' was found on Mount Nikkō, near Tokyo, and we may understand it as another selection of the Japanese mountain cherry such as 'Arashiyama' and 'Tagui-arashi'. It is preferred for its early flowering.

In its overall appearance 'Bendono' has an uncultivated quality that certainly must be called lovely, but the single, pale-pink flowers among the copper-brown young leaves do not make a gorgeous garden center plant, and it has never become a popular commercial cherry. The colored foliage and red bud scales and bracts inspired Miyoshi to use the Latin *rubidus* ("red") in naming it *Prunus serrulata* f. *rubida*. In Japan one finds it as *P. lannesiana* 'Rubida'. It bears many fertile little cherries, propagation from seed might explain the existence of slightly deviating forms.

'Bendono' presents in the Arboretum Kalmthout, Belgium, a beautiful light orange-red foliage in autumn. It is a very fertile cherry; the seedlings show only minor variability, which further confirms its wild origin.

Figure 96. 'Bendono'. Photo by author, 13 April 1997, Yūki Experimental Station of the Flower Association of Japan, Ibaraki Prefecture.

Prunus 'Bendono'

Less current synonyms: Benden, 'Rubida'

Description: Tree funnel-shaped, to 10 m high or more, with erect branches, vigorous growth. Young foliage red-brown, readily changing to green, serration often double with bristles and light red, small glands. Stipules slightly divided, 10–15 mm long. Bracts and bractlets bright red(!). Corymbose inflorescence, with two to three or even four flowers. Peduncles 1–2 cm long. Pedicels 2.5–4.0 cm long. Flower in bud dark pink, becoming pale pink when completely opened. Flower about 4 cm in diameter, opening to a flat plane. Petals five, only rarely a few extra petaloids, oval, 18 × 15 mm, usually slightly emarginate at the top, rather quickly shedding. There is one pistil, perfect, about 15 mm long, longer than the stamens. The calyx is campanulate, about 6(–7) × 3 mm, green with a reddish shade; there is a distinct transition from pedicel to calyx. Sepals are elongated and triangular, about 8 × 3 mm, rather narrow, unserrated. Flowering season is mid-April. 'Bendono' has a diploid set of chromosomes (2n = 16).

'Botan-zakura'

'Botan-zakura' ("tree peony cherry") suggests a cherry with large, loose, globular, and double flowers that are typical of a tree peony. The first mention of a cultivar with this name is made in a Japanese book on horticulture, *Kadan-jikin-shō* (Flower bed embroideries), dating from 1695. This source says that the pink-hued, large, double flowers are in bunches that hang a little. This name appears also in the encyclopedia *Kokon-yōran-kō* (Yashiro 1821–1841), and Miyoshi described a 'Botan-zakura' in 1916 under the name *Prunus serrulata* f. *moutan*. The old English word *moutan* was used to indicate the tree peony (*Paeonia suffruticosa*); it is in fact an old Japanese romanization of the modern *botan*. Wilson referred to this cherry as *Prunus lannesiana* f. *botan-zakura*.

Throughout the twentieth century 'Botan-zakura' was present in Japanese collections and was also exported to Western countries. It was, for instance, offered as a cherry with "large, double, rose-pink" flowers in the 1937 catalog of the Hakoneya nursery (Wada 1937). There is some doubt that the historical 'Botan-zakura' is the same one we have today; it is not seen very often, trees are few, and there might be different forms around.

Another problem is that the word *botan-zakura* is still used in certain regions of Japan for any double garden form.

Ingram (1948) described a different, mostly single-flowered "Botan-zakura." The young foliage was bronze-colored, with coarse aristate serration to the edge of the leaf. Ingram's tree was straggling. His brief description is accompanied by a photo of the plant in his garden in Kent. The picture shows a profusely blooming cherry with single flowers tightly set around erect branches that seem to belong to a young, multistemmed tree. An occasional flower has some extra petaloids. The cherry in the photo does not look like a typical 'Botan-zakura' as it was shown by Miyoshi (1921b), and later by the Flower Association of Japan (1982) and Kawasaki (1994). Apparently Ingram got some kind of "Botan-zakura" from a Japanese nursery.

The description given below is based on a few trees in the collection at Tama, Japan, conforming to recent Japanese descriptions of 'Botan-zakura' that give it as *Prunus lannesiana* 'Moutan'.

'Botan-zakura' has nodding corymbs with remarkably large, double flowers. These resemble peony flowers in shape because the inner petals stand in a loose bowl shape on the outer petals that are fully flat when expanded. Among the flowers in their prime are some that show a typical and quite interesting cup-and-saucer shape. There are ten to fifteen petals, and the flowers may measure well over 4.5 cm. The flowers are pink or rose-pink when opened, but often pinkish white or almost completely white. In that case, however, pink shades are found at the edges of the petals. 'Botan-zakura' resembles 'Shirotae', but is less vigorous in all its characteristics.

Prunus 'Botan-zakura'

Less current synonyms: Botan, 'Moutan'

Description: Tree umbrella-shaped, open frame with few branches supporting a loose crown, to 5 m high. Young foliage light green (RHS 152-A) with a bronze shade. Serration single, awn-tipped, flowers appearing with the foliage. Stipules serrated with tiny glands on awns, about 15–20 mm long, some show bifurcations. Mature leaves large, 10–14 × 6–8 cm. Pendulous corymbose inflorescence, with two to four flowers. Peduncles (0.8–)1.2–1.5 cm long. Pedicels 2.0–3.8 cm long. Flower in bud white with a shade of pink, staying white when completely opened with a faint pink shade at the margin of the petal and along the deep indentation. Flower about 4.5 cm in diameter (about 5.5 cm when flattened out),

Figure 97. 'Botan-zakura'. Photo by author, 12 April 1997, Tama Forest Science Garden, Tokyo.

slightly fragrant, opening to a loose cup shape with outer petals expanding to a flat plane; some large flowers show the typical cup-and-saucer shape(!). Petals ten to fourteen, (one to three petaloids, sometimes vexillate), orbicular with a deep indentation at the top, 22–26 × 22–28 mm. There is one pistil, perfect, shorter than the stamens. The calyx is funnel-shaped, 3–6 × 9 mm, green with a faint red tinge that extends in the veins of the sepals; there is no distinct transition from pedicel to calyx. Sepals are triangular, slightly narrowing at the base; 10–12 × 5–6 mm, unserrated. Flowering season is mid-April in Tokyo.

'Choshu-hizakura'

'Choshu-hizakura' was exported by Japanese nurseries in the early twentieth century, in a rare case under the name 'Choshu-hizakura', but usually under the name 'Hizakura'. *Hi* referred to the bright, scarlet color of the robes of aristocrats in the ancient Orient. As cherries do not have scarlet flowers, the name cannot be taken literally but should be rather understood as a poetic praise of the brilliant color of the flowers of this cherry. Miyoshi (1916), when describing this cherry as *Prunus serrulata* f. *splendens,* understood the comparison thus and applied the Latin *splendens* to 'Choshu-hizakura' with its singularly splendid pink, mostly single flowers. The blossom color is reminiscent of that of *P. sargentii.* In Japanese sources this cherry is known as *P. lannesiana* 'Chosiuhizakura'.

The cumbersome 'Choshu-hizakura' is the correct name and means "Hizakura from Chōshū," an ancient province now part of Yamaguchi Prefecture in southwestern Honshū. This name distinguishes it from other "Hizakura" cherries, a name loosely used for many centuries for cherries with deep pink flowers. Albert Wagner, for example, reported a dark-red "Hiza-

Figure 98. 'Choshu-hizakura'. Petals tend to be more round and more developed under better climatic conditions. Photo by Arie Peterse, 1997, Opheusden, Nursery Peterse, Netherlands.

kura" (without doubt *Prunus campanulata*) in 1902, sparking off a most confusing discussion as he was the only one who had seen such a southern cherry on the islands north of Okinawa. In the same year Koehne took "Hizakura" as an epithet for 'Ichiyo'. The Flower Association of Japan (1982) and Kawasaki (1994) give *P. lannesiana* Wilson 'Hizakura' as a synonym of 'Ichiyo'. To compound the confusion, Jefferson (1984) gives 'Hizakura' as a folk synonym for 'Ichiyo', and the U.S. National Arboretum, Washington, D.C., documents 'Hizakura' as synonymous with 'Ichiyo'. Some minor identity problems exist with other forms that are related to 'Choshu-hizakura' (Kawasaki 1994, p. 227).

At present "Hizakura" often indicates a relation with a form of the Taiwan cherry, *Prunus campanulata,* such as 'Yokohama-hizakura' or 'Ryukyu-kan-hizakura', but other less well-defined cherries named "Hizakura" are found. Moreover, the double-flowered 'Kanzan' may still be sold as "Hizakura." In light of all these conflicting uses of the name "Hizakura," it advisable to conform to the Japanese 'Choshu-hizakura' to help end such confusions.

'Choshu-hizakura' is a beautiful cherry. The flowers have five, occasionally up to eight or twelve, petals that are nicely shaped and of a pure and splendid pink that contrasts brilliantly with the reddish brown young leaves. This cherry resembles 'Yae-murasaki-zakura' in some respects, but has larger and single flowers and grows into a larger tree. It is a healthy grower.

Prunus 'Choshu-hizakura'

Less current synonyms: 'Chosiuhizakura', *Prunus serrulata* f. *splendens,*
   (not Hizakura)
Description: Tree narrow funnel-shaped with spreading and ascending branches, to 6.5 m high. Young foliage reddish brown, quickly changing to dark green (RHS 148-A) in the flowering season. Serration single, remarkably fine, with small red glands up to the top of the leaf. Stipules moderately divided, 7–15 mm long. Corymbose inflorescence, with three to four flowers. Peduncles 2.0–4.5 cm long. Pedicels 1.5–3.0 cm long. Flower in bud purplish pink, becoming a pure, splendid pink (RHS 68-D) with a white heart when completely opened. Flower 4.0–4.5 cm in diameter, opening to a flat plane, fragrant. Petals five, sometimes one to three or even up to seven extra, orbicular, deeply emarginate at the top, 19–20 × 15–17(–20) mm. There is one pistil (rarely one to two small pistils without ovary found in late flowers), perfect, 12–13 mm long, as long as or

slightly shorter than the longest stamens. The calyx is campanulate, 7×4 mm, with a distinct transition from pedicel to calyx. Sepals are elongated and triangular, $8 \times 3–4$ mm, unserrated, with a faint purple tinge. Occasionally a few fruits; pedicels rather sturdy. Flowering season is from late April to early May, a few days to a week before 'Kanzan'. 'Choshu-hizakura' has a diploid set of chromosomes ($2n = 16$).

'Daikoku'

'Daikoku' was, along with 'Kanzan', 'Mikuruma-gaeshi', and related cultivars, a very popular export in the early twentieth century. It is related to 'Fugenzo' and at one time was called 'Beni-fugen' or, in a different reading of the same Chinese characters, 'Ko-fugen'. This name was, according to Wilson (1916)—although he was mistaken—synonymous with 'Fugenzo', which on that account means it could not be used. At present the name 'Ko-fugen' is used by some nurseries in Japan for cherries that have no relation to this classic form. Therefore, we must be grateful that Ingram renamed the older 'Ko-fugen' as *Prunus serrulata* 'Daikoku', not only ending the existing confusion, but also preventing future confusion and misunderstandings around this excellent garden cherry.

Some other opinions can be cleared here as well. Chadbund (1972) mentions a cherry 'Kurama-yama' that, according to him, should be identical with 'Daikoku'. A tree of this type named 'Kurama', from the Wageningen Botanical Garden, was planted in the experimental collection of the Flower Association of Japan and shows no difference from 'Daikoku'. The 'Kurama' found in Western countries will be the same or a nursery clone of 'Daikoku'. The white-flowered 'Kurama-zakura', though, is a completely different cherry, a form of *Prunus ×yedoensis* (Kawasaki 1994), also known as 'Higo-yoshino'.

Daikoku is the name of one of the seven Chinese gods of fortune and happiness. Another cherry was named after the god Fukurokuju. The seven gods became intimately interwoven with popular culture in Japan. Daikoku personified good fortune and riches. He is always depicted as a fat and happy man with a typical bonnet, carrying an enormous bag on his shoulder, and sitting on a straw bale of rice. The flowers of the cherry 'Daikoku' have a somewhat opulent appearance to which Ingram likened the appearance of the god Daikoku.

Figure 99. The seven Chinese gods of fortune and happiness in their treasure ship. Daikoku is leaning on a bale of rice (right foreground), and Fukurokuju, with his prominent, bald skull, is behind him. Two cultivars were named after these gods. From the magazine *Shinsen Tōkyō saijiki* of *Fūzoku gahō*.

The double flowers of 'Daikoku' are superior in shape and color, 5.0–5.5 cm in diameter, and a pure pink, without any purplish hue. In this aspect they resemble those of 'Pink Perfection'. 'Daikoku', however, is more robust and lacks the sometimes leafless, twiggy, and hanging branches that may give 'Pink Perfection' a less desirable ragged appearance. In the open heart of the flower of 'Daikoku' one may see two to four phylloid carpels, hence the association with the flowers of 'Fugenzo'. The remarkably dark red flower buds have a blunt top, looking a little plump. This healthy and vigorous cherry is reportedly used in Australia for roadside plantings.

Prunus 'Daikoku'

Less current synonyms: (not Ko-fugen, not Beni-fugen)

Description: Tree stiff, narrow vase-shaped, more upright than 'Pink Perfection', to 7 m high. Young foliage green, slightly bronze, but not bronze-green as 'Pink Perfection'. Fully developed leaves usually have a single serration, always rather coarse and without glands. Stipules rather deeply bi-

Figure 100. 'Daikoku', flowers. Photo by Arie Peterse, 14 May 1986, Hemelrijk, Belgium.

furcated, 12–19 mm long. Corymbose inflorescence, with three to five flowers. Peduncles 2.0–3.5 cm long. Pedicels 2.0–3.5 cm long. Flower in bud pink-red, becoming light pink with a slight lilac hue when completely opened, with the outsides of the outer petals showing a dark purple-pink stripe remaining from the bud stage. Flower 4.5–5.5 cm in diameter, opening to a rather flat plane. Petals thirty-four to thirty-six (sometimes as few as twenty-eight), including petaloids, orbicular, 17–19 × 15–19 mm. Pistils two to four, phylloid, with only a few stamens. Calyx wide and urceolate to saucer-shaped, very short, 3 × 5 mm, with no distinct transition from pedicel to calyx. Sepals are elongated and triangular, 7–8 × 4–5 mm, unserrated, occasionally with an extra sepal (serration to be examined in bud stage). Flowering season is from late April to mid-May.

Figure 101. The Yokohama Nursery Company offered 'Shiro-fugen' (synonym 'Fugenzo') and 'Ko-fugen' (synonym 'Daikoku'). From *Descriptive Catalog of the Yokohama Nursery* (1926–1927).

'Edo-zakura'

Edo, or in an old romanization, *Yedo,* is the name of Japan's capital from about 1600 until the end of the nineteenth century. After the reforms of the 1860s Edo became known as Tokyo (Tō-kyō), the eastern capital, to distinguish it from the old capital Kyōto, more to the west.

'Edo-zakura' is given as 'Yedo-zakura', 'Yedo', or simply 'Edo' and should not be confused with *Prunus ×yedoensis.* It appears from the end of the seventeenth century in Japanese written sources. Miyoshi (1916) described it as *P. serrulata* f. *nobilis.* In subsequent Japanese sources it is found as *P. lannesiana* 'Nobilis'. 'Edo-zakura' was regularly offered by Japanese nurseries exporting to the West from the late nineteenth century until about the 1930s.

Several semi-double, pink-flowered garden cherries resemble 'Edo-zakura'. 'Beni-tora-no-o', offered in the past as a pink strain of 'Tora-no-o', was classified as a cultivar by Miyoshi (1916), but was considered by Ingram (1948) as being almost the same as 'Edo-zakura'; it is no longer found. Another cherry called 'Yae-beni-tora-no-o' is still in cultivation: its flowers have slightly smaller, more orbicular petals, appearing in larger numbers than those of 'Edo-zakura'. Other cultivars that resemble 'Edo-zakura' are 'Ito-kukuri', 'Okiku-zakura', or 'Yokihi'; the respective differences are slight and discussed in each description.

Among all these semi-double, pink-flowered cherries, 'Edo-zakura' is most well known. It makes a medium-sized tree with a broad, flattened crown. When unfolding, the foliage is remarkably yellowish green to bronze-green. Mature leaves are broadly elongated and have a relatively short, acuminate top. The flowers have about fifteen petals that seem arranged in three tiers, of which the outer one has a soft pink tinge, whereas the inner tier is almost completely white. The flower diameter is well over 4 cm. Compared with the other resembling cultivars, 'Edo-zakura' has rather short and

Figure 102. 'Edo-zakura'. The heart of the flower is not always as open as in this photograph. Photo by Arie Peterse, 6 May 1985, Wageningen Botanic Gardens of the Agricultural University, Netherlands.

narrow sepals. The corymb is compact, due to the short flower stalks, and it may have up to five, occasionally even six, flowers in compact clusters.

Prunus 'Edo-zakura'

Less current synonyms: Edo, Edozakura, 'Nobilis', Yedo, Yedo-zakura, Yedozakura

Description: Tree broad and vase-shaped. Young foliage light bronze-green (RHS 152-B, C). Serration single or double, with small pink-red glands. Stipules medium divided, 13–18 mm long. Corymbose inflorescence, with four to five or even six flowers. Peduncles fairly short, 0.9–2.0 cm long. Pedicels 1.5–2.5 cm long. Flower in bud pink-red, becoming very light pink (RHS 65-D) to almost white when completely opened. Flower 4.0–4.5 cm in diameter, opening fluffy, occasionally to a flat plane, always a little disorderly but never remaining with folded petals in the heart. Petals twelve to fifteen or even twenty-two, of variable shape, slightly emarginate at the top, 17–22 × 13–17 mm. Pistil one, occasionally 2, perfect (rarely phylloid), 8–9 mm long, about as long as or a little longer than the longest stamens. The calyx is campanulate, 7 × 4 mm, with a faint purple tinge; there is a distinct transition from pedicel to calyx. Sepals are elongated and triangular, 6–7 × 2.5–3 mm, unserrated, occasionally with an extra sepal. Flowering season is from late April to early May. 'Edo-zakura' has a diploid set of chromosomes (2n = 16).

'Fudan-zakura'

The name 'Fudan-zakura' is literally translated as "cherry-without-interruption" (*sakura-fu-dan*) and refers to the flowers that may appear almost continuously from November to April. The "ever-flowering" cherry inspired Miyoshi to name it *Prunus serrulata* f. *semperflorens* in 1916. Subsequent Japanese sources give it as *P. lannesiana* 'Fudanzakura'.

In regions or periods with milder winters the flowering season starts with some flowers between the autumn-colored leaves, something highly appreciated by *ikebana* flower arrangers. A 'Fudan-zakura' is named in the early nineteenth-century plant list of the garden Yokuon-en. This plant was probably propagated from a famous specimen, now legally preserved as a natural monument, in the temple compound of Kannon-ji, Shirako, Suzuka, in Mie Prefecture. This fabulous tree blooms from late November to the end of April, retaining some of its autumn-red leaves up to late March among the flowers, whereas young leaves are almost continuously sprouting. Frost may kill the flowers of any 'Fudan-zakura' in bud. After a severe winter with temperatures of −10°C or −20°C, as may occur in Europe, this cherry only starts flowering in April. Having suffered from the unsparing frost, many buds do not develop. The first flowers to appear seem to be almost sessile umbels; only towards the end of the flowering season appear the more regular corymbs. Pedicel, calyx, and sepals have a red hue. In bud, the single flowers are pink, expanding to white, with a diameter of 3.5–4.0 cm.

In the garden 'Fudan-zakura' does not give a spectacular blossom show. Nonetheless, for someone who has an eye for it, its quiet and modest flowering in the bare midwinter garden will have its charm, certainly in places with a milder climate. A spray brought indoors will, within a couple of days, develop flowers from New Year's Day to the end of March.

Ingram (1948) stated that the underside of the leaf is pubescent, but trees in the Netherlands show a light pubescence on the upperside and tightly appressed hair on the petiole. Neither the Flower Association of Japan (1982) nor Kawasaki (1994) mentions any hairs or pubescence. Sepals of the Japanese forms are clearly serrated, whereas those of the European forms are entire. The obviously varied forms in cultivation have led to diverging opinions on this cherry's parentage. Some botanists (Ohwi and Ohta 1973) have named it *Prunus leveilleana* 'Fudanzakura' as a form of *P. serrulata* var. *pubescens*. Others believe it is a hybrid between the Oshima cherry and the Japanese mountain cherry. The ornamental value of all the forms is the same, and apart from the differing details mentioned here, 'Fudan-zakura' is described as below.

Prunus 'Fudan-zakura'

Less current synonyms: 'Fudanzakura', *Prunus serrulata* f. *semperflorens*

Description: Tree large, straight-trunked, with an ovate crown, 8–10 m high. Young foliage coppery brown. Serration single, without glands. Foliage is already well developed in April, more than other forms of *Prunus serrulata* and about as well as the early forms of *P.* ×*subhirtella*. Stipules not divided, 10 × 1 mm. Early inflorescence at first sessile, later corymbose, usually with three flowers per cluster. Peduncles about 4 mm long. Pedicels 1.0–2.5 cm long, but differing with the season. Flower in bud light

Figure 103. 'Fudan-zakura', blossom. Photo by Arie Peterse, 28 April 1986, Wageningen Botanic Gardens of the Agricultural University, Netherlands.

pink, becoming white when completely opened. Flower 3–4 cm in diameter, opens to a flat plane. Petals five, ovate, emarginate at the top, 13–17 × 12–13 mm. There is one pistil, perfect, 13 mm long, longer than the stamens. The calyx is campanulate, 7 × 4 mm, with a distinct transition from pedicel to calyx. The calyx and the sepals show a darker purplish-red shade than the pedicel. Sepals are elongated and triangular, 6 × 3 mm. Flowering season is from late November (depending on the weather) to late April.

'Fugenzo'

'Fugenzo' is a historic cherry of classic beauty, a healthy and vigorous plant that has been a gardener's delight for one century in Western countries and five times as long in Japan. Five centuries means many generations, and many possible nursery clones. The 1822 catalog *Hana-no-kagami* (A paragon of flowers) shows four different types, including a red form that is even darker than the "Beni-fugen" in the same source. Several identity problems exist, as might be expected for a cherry with such a long history, and it took some study to straighten out the confusion. Our research on cherries of this type in Europe and Japan led to two conclusions: (1) 'Shirofugen' is an export name synonymous with 'Fugenzo', and (2) a related,

Figure 104. As far back as the early eighteenth century, a winter-flowering 'Wakaki-fudan-zakura' was grown as a potted plant to be brought indoors for early flowering. From Itō IV (1710).

dark pink cherry 'Beni-fugen' (or 'Kō-fugen' in a different reading of the same Chinese characters) was later renamed 'Daikoku'.

Fugenzō means "Fugen-elephant," referring to the white elephant (*zō*), which, in Buddhist paintings and sculpture, was ridden by Saint Fugen. In some representations Fugen rides on a group of elephants. The sacred elephants are usually depicted with a baggy hide and large ears hanging in loose folds. The elephant's trunk associates with the long phylloid pistils of a 'Fugenzo' flower, an explanation found in an entry dated 1480 in an old Japanese diary (*Oyudono-noueno-nikki,* 1768), and the elephant's face associates with the wavy white petals and the open flowers, as explained in other sources (*Hekizan-nichi-roku,* 1459). Other explanations take the trunks and tusks as associating with the pistils. With references dating back to the fifteenth century, this form is indeed a classic one, which must have inspired Miyoshi (1916) to name it *Prunus serrulata* f. *classica.* In Western countries it was known as 'James H. Veitch' after it was introduced at the end of the nineteenth century.

The synonymous name 'Shiro-fugen' ("white-Fugen") refers to the same Saint Fugen mentioned above. *Shiro* in the name suggests that this cherry is a whiter-flowered form of 'Fugenzo', but as early as 1916 Miyoshi noted that 'Fugenzo' was named 'Shiro-fugen' (sometimes read as 'Haku-fugen') when it was sold with the dark pink "red Fugen," known as 'Beni-fugen' or 'Ko-fugen'. In Japanese catalogs of plants offered for export to the West, 'Shiro-fugen' is always listed along with 'Ko-fugen' or 'Beni-fugen', whereas 'Fugenzo' is never offered for sale (see Figure 101).

For Miyoshi (1916) 'Ko-fugen' was a subforma of 'Fugenzo', which in turn was a synonym of 'Haku-fugen'. In Germany Späth had a 'Beni-fugen' and a 'Shiro-fugen' in his garden in 1902, and in 1910 *Gartenflora* (59: 203) discussed 'James H. Veitch' (synonym 'Fugenzo') along with 'Beni-fugen', pointing to the same idea of red and white Fugen forms. The Germans, who could easily read Miyoshi's German notes, were never misled by fancy nursery names. Russell (1934) was confused but carefully concluded that 'Shiro-fugen' was probably known in Japan under a different name. In the experimental collection of the Flower Association of Japan, 'Shiro-fugen', grown from material of the Royal Botanic Gardens, Kew, does not show any obvious difference with the Japanese 'Fugenzo' planted alongside. Russell (1934) and Ingram (1948), nonetheless, were outspoken in their praise of 'Shiro-fugen' and its identity as differing from 'Fugenzo'.

Figure 105. The Buddhist Saint Fugen appeared in this world, traveling from the Eastern Paradise on a group of white elephants. From *Fugen-enmei-bosatsu-zuzō*, Kyōō-gokoku-ji, Kyōto.

It is not clear what they were growing as "Fugenzo." Could an influence of *Prunus avium* rootstock explain some differences?

'Shiro-fugen' appears in the list of cherries at Arakawa in 1886, as well as in other specialized Japanese collections of a later date (Kawashima 1910; Ogiwara 1916). A contemporary Arakawa post card in my possession shows 'Fugenzo' titled 'Shiro-fugen'. In the Netherlands a sanitized, virus-free clone 'Shiro-fugen', distributed by the Dutch test service for nursery products (NAKB), shows a more healthy, coarse growth than the usual 'Fugenzo' also in cultivation in this country.

'Shiro-fugen' was named *Prunus serrulata* f. *albo-rosea* by Wilson in 1916, and 'Albo-rosea' is used at present in Japan as the cultivar name of 'Fugenzo'. The word *albo-rosea* ("white-pink") refers to the striking shift in color that takes place just before the shedding of the petals; the flowers may turn to such an intensely purplish pink that from a distance the tree looks almost like the 'Kanzan' cherry. This change is observed in trees known as 'Shiro-fugen' in Europe and as 'Fugenzo' in Japan.

The double flowers may reach 5 cm in diameter. In bud the flower is dark pink, expanding to a pink-hued white. When the flowers of 'Fugenzo' are in their prime, the large, purplish sepals, which are distinctly serrated along the larger part of the edges, are distinctive. The inflorescences are always hanging or nodding, because flower stalks are long and tend to be longer in cooler regions. Peduncles are about 2 cm long in mid-Japan, but up to 7 or even 10 cm in the north as reported by Kawasaki (1994), who gives 'Fugenzo' as *Prunus lannesiana* 'Albo-rosea'.

'Fugenzo' is late-flowering, as is 'Shogetsu'. When the blossom is in its prime, the young coppery foliage is already very well developed, which makes 'Fugenzo' a beautiful cherry among those that combine young coppery leaves with double, pink flowers, such as 'Kanzan'. The latter's popularity has taken over from 'Fugenzo', probably because of its easier propagation, larger flowers, and slightly earlier blossoming. 'Fugenzo' has, regrettably enough, become a rare sight in western Europe. In the United States it is one of the "best known selections" (Jefferson 1984).

After blossoming, the flowers drop with the pedicel from the tree rather than shedding petals, leaving the peduncle with its large bracts. Sometimes the flowers drop their petals first and the leaflike pistils develop into two perfect little leaves, complete with serration, that are hard to be discerned from true leaves. Only the veining is different.

'Fugenzo' always looks healthy and makes a spreading tree with a flattened crown. On a favorable soil, specimens may reach up to 15 m in about fifty years. Trees show a typical, repeated bifurcation in the branches so that in the crown they often have the habit of growing crosswise. Care should be taken to raise the young tree on a single stem; left to itself, it mostly makes a double stem that will make the tree unbalanced and susceptible to storm damage at a later age. 'Fugenzo' is easily identified by (1) the characteristically forked branching with interlocking boughs higher up in the tree, (2) its open, flat flowers that show in the heart two or three phylloid pistils with occasionally a few small, erect petals in between, and (3) the dark, purplish, and large sepals with their typical serration.

Figure 106. 'Fugenzo' flowers turn red before fading. Photo by Arie Peterse, 22 May 1986.

Figure 107. 'Fugenzo'. Photo by Arie Peterse, 28 April 1996, Yūki Experimental Station of the Flower Association of Japan, Ibaraki Prefecture.

Figure 108. 'Fugenzo', typical sepals. Photo by Arie Peterse, 28 April 1996, Yūki Experimental Station of the Flower Association of Japan, Ibaraki Prefecture.

Figure 109. 'Fugenzo' may reach 18 m tall on a deep friable loam. Photo by Arie Peterse, 30 April 1996, Mishima.

Prunus 'Fugenzo'

Synonym: Shiro-fugen

Less current synonyms: Shiro-fugen cherry, 'Albo-rosea', *Prunus serrulata* f. *classica*, 'Haku-fugen', 'James H. Veitch'

Description: Tree broad and vase-shaped with a flattened crown, 10 m high or more and 8 m wide. Young foliage coppery red (RHS 166-B), in the flowering season quickly turning to bronze-green (RHS 152-A). Serration double often with tiny red glands. Foliage is well developed in the flowering season. Among the developed leaves, one may often find some that lack the acuminate top. Stipules medium bifurcated, 15–18 mm long, quickly shed. Corymbose inflorescence, with three to five (sometimes as few as two or as many as six to seven) flowers. Peduncles 2–6 cm long. Pedicels 2–4 cm long. Flower in bud pinkish red, becoming pure pink and lighter (RHS 65-C, 73-C) in the heart when completely opened. Flower 4–5 cm in diameter, opening to a flat plane, with petals pressed close to each other, not loose as with 'Kanzan'. Petals twenty-five to thirty or even up to forty, including a few petaloids, orbicular or obovate, slightly emarginate at the top, 17–22 × 13–20 mm. Pistils two, sometimes three, phylloid, about 8 mm long, longer than stamens, occasionally a small, narrow petal stands upright in between the two carpels in the heart of the flower. The calyx is widely funnel-shaped or saucer-shaped, about 2 × 5 mm, with a distinct transition from pedicel to calyx. Sepals are elongated and triangular, about 8 × 4 mm, clearly serrated halfway, but unserrated at the base and at the tip; sepals tend to reflex over the calyx tube at the end of the flowering period. Flowering season is from late April to late May, with a few late flowers in early June. 'Fugenzo' has a diploid set of chromosomes (2n = 16).

'Fukurokuju' and 'Hokusai'

Among the many semi-double, pink-flowered cherries we find such vigorous growers as 'Fugenzo' and related forms, but large trees and big flowers are also typical of the cultivar group around 'Fukurokuju'. The pistil of flowers of 'Fukurokuju' and its forms is always perfect, the petals are wrinkled, and the flowers are big, often 5 cm in diameter. These details distinguish this cultivar group from other garden cherries.

Fukurokuju, like Daikoku, is one of the seven Chinese gods of fortune. The god Fukurokuju promises longevity and is represented as an old, laughing man with a bent stick and an improbably elongated bald skull in which to keep all the wisdom and experience of a long, long life. The cherry 'Fukurokuju' keeps its flowers for a long time; about three weeks is not rare. Nevertheless, other cherries, such as 'Fugenzo' or 'Shogetsu', are also blessed by this god of longevity, so the meaning of the name 'Fukurokuju' should not be taken too literally.

'Fukurokuju' and the related 'Yae-akebono' are mentioned in the earliest historical records of the collection at Arakawa (1886). A set of slightly older illustrations could very well be showing the same cherry that was sold as *Cerasus rosea-pleno* by European nurseries and was said to have been introduced to Europe by Philipp Franz von Siebold in 1866 (see Figure

110 and discussion of 'Fukurokuju' under "Japan's Cherries to the West" in chapter 1). Ingram received scions of 'Fukurokuju' after his visit to the Sakura Kwai in 1926.

'Fukurokuju' has its distinctive qualities in the large, open, and pink flowers, springing from sturdy, rather short twigs. The semi-double flowers in corymbs resemble those of 'Edo-zakura' and the like, but they are much larger and may expand to more than 5 cm. The petals are perfectly orbicular and have, when the flowers have just opened, a starchy kind of wrinkling that is typical. The contorted, twisted petals inspired Miyoshi in naming this cherry *Prunus serrulata* f. *contorta*. Sano IV (1961) characterized 'Fukurokuju' as having a "masculine" character because of its vigorous, healthy growth and abundant blooming.

A few cultivars bear a strong resemblance to 'Fukurokuju' and are strains or clones of it. Both Ingram (1948) and Sano IV (1961) cultivated several garden cherries that were closely related to 'Fukurokuju'. One of them was selected by Ingram in 1925 and named 'Hokusai' for the Japanese artist Katsushika Hokusai (1760–1849). Even for modern Japanese ears, it is strange to name a cherry after an artist with no apparent relation to cherries, but hardly a better name could have been chosen to make this cultivar popular in the West. Around the time this cultivar was named, the West was experiencing a second wave of *Japonaiserie* in fashion and design, and Hokusai was a well-known artist. Although he was known principally for his woodblock prints, it was said that he could paint anything under the sun.

Ingram's enthusiasm for the cherry 'Hokusai' was based on a fabulous specimen in his garden. This tree was 8 m tall with a crown about 15 m in diameter. It was grafted on *Prunus avium,* which would have helped the tree reach this size. Specimens of 'Hokusai' in the experimental station of the Flower Association of Japan are identical to 'Fukurokuju', apart from the sepals, which in 'Hokusai' are distinctly narrow at the base, and elongated and triangular in 'Fukurokuju'. In 'Hokusai' the sepals are narrower at the base, have their greatest width one-third from the base to the top, and have blunt tops; they measure 7–8 × 4.5–5.0 mm. In 'Fukurokuju' the sepals are elongated and triangular, acute, and up to about 8 mm long. 'Fukurokuju' might have a few more petals than 'Hokusai'.

'Hokusai' is, like 'Fukurokuju', hardy and vigorous. Both reach a height of up to 8 m, though 'Hokusai' may be a little more spreading than 'Fukurokuju'. The semi-double, pure pink blossoms of both can retain their

Figure 110. *"Cerasus Juliana floribus roseis"* (named *Cerasus caproniana flore roseo pleno* in *Flore des Serres*) was offered for sale at the Belgian nursery of Louis van Houtte. The cherry resembles 'Fukurokuju' very much. From *Revue Horticole,* 1875, Wageningen University Library Special Collections.

beauty for up to three weeks, at the end of which the heart of the flower takes on a purplish tinge. When the flowers have just opened, their petals have a wrinkled, rumpled appearance that is typical of the 'Fukurokuju'-related forms such as 'Yae-akebono' and 'Sumizome' (Ingram).

With the introduction of 'Kanzan', the popularity of 'Hokusai' in Europe diminished. The newcomer, with its darker, more purplish flowers, over-shadowed the older cultivar. Yet the soft pink blossom of 'Hokusai' gives the cultivar a charm of its own, and fortunately it has never been entirely forgotten. It is one of the few ornamental cherries that is able to match 'Kanzan' for vigor and abundance of blooms.

Prunus 'Fukurokuju'
Prunus 'Hokusai'

Less current synonym: *Prunus serrulata* f. *contorta*

Description: Tree vase-shaped, to 8 m high, crown 15 m wide. Color of the young foliage bronze-green (RHS 152-A, 199-A). Serration single and fine, with tiny, white glands. Foliage is not yet well developed in the flowering season. Stipules slightly divided, 16–20 mm long. Corymbose inflorescence, with three to five flowers (often with one abortive). Peduncles 1.5–3.0 cm long. Pedicels fairly short, 1.5–2.5 cm long. Flower in bud purplish pink, becoming pale pink (RHS 69-C) when completely opened. Buds slightly angular in appearance, with petals tightly crumpled in bud. Petal edges have a slightly darker color. Flower about 5 cm in diameter, opening to a flat plane, with the opening of the ovary always visible, no distinct fragrance. Petals ten to fifteen, orbicular, uniform, usually slightly emarginate at the top, 17–21 × 18–21 mm, rumpled in appearance when the flower first opens. There is one pistil, perfect, 9 mm long, as long as or slightly longer than the longest stamens. The calyx is campanulate to funnel-shaped, 6 × 4.5–5.0 mm, with a faint purple tinge; there is a distinct transition from pedicel to calyx. Sepals unserrated, with a faint purple tinge. Flowering season is from late April to early May. 'Fukurokuju' has a triploid set of chromosomes (2n = 24).

Higurashi (synonym *Prunus serrulata* f. *amabilis* Miyoshi) is mentioned in the 1886 list of cherries along the Arakawa River and is an excellent form. It resembles 'Fukurokuju' in many respects, except that its leaves are strikingly often ovate, lacking the caudate tip, and in the flower season they are

Figure 111. Blossom of 'Fukurokuju' (left) and 'Hokusai' (right). Photo by author, 28 April 1996, Yūki Experimental Station of the Flower Association of Japan, Ibaraki Prefecture.

much farther out among the blossom than those of 'Fukurokuju'. Flowers of 'Higurashi' have about twenty petals.

Uzu-zakura (synonyms *Prunus serrulata* f. *spiralis* Miyoshi, 'Udzu-zakura') is mentioned in the 1886 list of cherries along the Arakawa River. The name means "eddy-cherry" and refers to the inner petals of the flowers that stand in an open, spiraled, fanlike movement. 'Udzu-zakura' is an old spelling. This cherry is often believed to be the same as 'Hokusai' or 'Fukurokuju'. Chadbund (1972), for example, mistakenly took 'Amabilis' (synonym 'Higurashi') and 'Spiralis' (synonym 'Uzu-zakura') as synonyms for 'Hokusai'. Ingram considered 'Uzu-zakura' merely an upright strain of 'Hokusai' and claimed that the petals showed the same wrinkled appearance when unfolding. Jefferson (1984) gave 'Hokusai' as a synonym for 'Udzu-zakura'. 'Uzu-zakura' does not, however, even vaguely resemble these cultivars, nor does it have any relation with 'Fukurokuju'. The latter has large flowers with at the most twenty petals at a diameter of 5 cm, whereas 'Uzu-zakura' has about thirty bifid, wrinkled petals 12–15 mm long, making for much

Figure 112. Sepals of 'Fukurokuju' (left) and 'Hokusai' (right). Photo by Arie Peterse, 28 April 1996, Yūki Experimental Station of the Flower Association of Japan, Ibaraki Prefecture.

smaller, compact flowers with a diameter of 3.0–3.5 cm. Furthermore, 'Uzu-zakura' has a pistil as long as the stamens, the pink color of the outer petals of its flowers is less outspoken than that of 'Fukurokuju', and it is clearly less spectacular, less floriferous, and less vigorous in growth habit (see also descriptions of Miyoshi 1916, Ohwi and Ohta 1973, and Kawasaki 1994). It is possible that a form of 'Fukurokuju' was brought to North America and Europe under the name of 'Udzu-zakura'.

'Goza-no-ma-nioi'

This cherry belongs to a group of Oshima cherry selections with white and fragrant flowers. It is given as *Prunus lannesiana* var. *speciosa* 'Gozanoma-nioi' comb. nov. by Kawasaki (1994). The *goza-no-ma* were the private rooms of the shogun or any other high-placed person. The cherry 'Goza-no-ma-nioi' first appears as a named cultivar in the beginning of the twentieth century. It has the same healthy and vigorous growth as the other fragrant forms of the Oshima cherry. The crown of older trees is a regular,

Figure 113. Healthy specimens of 'Hokusai' among the bulbs. Photo by Arie Peterse, 1996, Keukenhof, Netherlands.

Figure 114. 'Hokusai'. Photo by Arie Peterse, 4 May 1986.

dome-shaped umbrella, up to 8–10 m high, covered like 'Taki-nioi' with flowers, but not having the latter's cascading crown shape. The flowers of 'Goza-no-ma-nioi' appear at the same time as the brownish-red foliage and have five to seven petals with three to five petaloids. The oval, orbicular petals may show some fringes at the top end. Because of the semi-double flowers, the appearance of the tree as a whole is more white when it is in bloom than 'Taki-nioi'.

Prunus 'Goza-no-ma-nioi'

Description: Tree broad and vase-shaped, or umbrella-shaped, to 7 m. Color of the young foliage bronze brown, to brown red. Serration aristate. Stipules much furcated, 15–20 mm long. Corymbose inflorescence, with two to five flowers. Length of peduncles ca. 2.5 cm. Length of pedicels 2.0–2.5 cm. Flowers in bud with a pinkish hue; completely opened flowers are pure white, but show a red shade in the heart long before fading. Flower 4.2–4.8 cm in diameter, opening to a loose cup shape. Blossoms have a strong, sweet fragrance, reminiscent of crushed almonds. Petals five to six or even up to eight, with three or up to five petaloids, round or oval, slightly emarginate at the top, 18–20 mm long, 19–20 mm wide. There is

Figure 115. 'Goza-no-ma-nioi', double, scented flowers. Photo by author, 13 April 1997, Yūki Experimental Station of the Flower Association of Japan, Ibaraki Prefecture.

Figure 116. 'Goza-no-ma-nioi', tree shape. Photo by Arie Peterse, 30 April 1996, Mishima.

one pistil, perfect, 12–14 mm long, about as long as or shorter than the longest stamens. The calyx is funnel-shaped to campanulate, 7–8 x 4 mm, faintly purple; there is a distinct transition from pedicel to calyx. Sepals are wide-elongated; ca. 7×4 mm, unserrated (but with a rare tooth), faintly purple; an occasional flower has six sepals. Flowering season is early May in Tokyo. 'Goza-no-ma-nioi' has a diploid set of chromosomes ($2n = 16$).

'Hakusan-hata-zakura'

Hata-zakura means "flag cherry" and, in this situation, refers to the flaglike (vexillate) petals in the heart of the flower. Manabu Miyoshi and Ernest H. Wilson described a 'Hata-zakura' that they found around 1916 in the Arakawa River collection. Miyoshi (1916) described it as *Prunus serrulata* f. *vexillipetala* and in the original description spoke of "many" flaglike petaloids and ten petals. This cherry does not seem to exist any longer, and it certainly is not the famous one known at present as 'Hata-zakura'. Today's 'Hata-zakura' originated from a celebrated cherry still grown in the Hakusan Shrine in Tokyo, close to the Hakusan subway station of the Mita line. Miyoshi, who described it in 1936 as a white cherry with single flowers and some vexillate petaloids, applied the Japanese name 'Hakusan-hata-zakura' to it, which in daily use became 'Hata-zakura'. The Flower Association of Japan (1982) described the true 'Hakusan-hata-zakura' under the names 'Hata-zakura' and *P. lannesiana* 'Hatazakura'. It is rightfully named 'Hakusan-hata-zakura' though, as stressed by Kawasaki (1994), who gives it as *Prunus lannesiana* 'Vexillifera' stat. nov.

Another popular explanation of the name "flag cherry" leads us to Flag Cherry Temple, or Hata-zakura-dera, an old village temple, now within the city of Hitachi-Oota in Ibaraki Prefecture, northwest of Tokyo. According to local legend the warrior Yoshiie Minamoto (1039–1106) planted a flag staff in this place when preparing for an expedition to the East. The staff proved to be a fresh and sturdy cherry branch that quickly rooted and still can be seen in the temple as an old, many-branched clump. The 'Hata-zakura' now in cultivation does not originate from this temple, though, as explained above.

The branches of 'Hakusan-hata-zakura' spread upwards and could indeed serve as flag staffs. The flower buds have only a slight shade of pink that quickly fades to white with the opening of the blossoms. Flowers have five perfect petals and a few petaloids on a long filament. 'Hakusan-hata-zakura' resembles 'Ariake' somewhat, but in every respect is less outspoken and less robust.

Prunus 'Hakusan-hata-zakura'

Less current synonyms: flag cherry, flag staff cherry, 'Vexillifera', (not 'Hata-zakura')

Description: Tree broadly fastigiate. Young foliage light green, only partly developed in the flowering season. Serration single, at the base of the leaf with small, white glands. Stipules slightly divided, 10–15 mm long. Corymbose inflorescence, with three to four or up to five flowers. Peduncles 2.0–3.5 cm long. Pedicels 2–3 cm long. Flower in bud light pink, becoming practically white when completely opened. Flower 43–48 mm in diameter, spreading to an open plane, slightly fragrant. Petals five, with one to four petaloids, slightly emarginate at the top, 19–22 × 16–19 mm. Pistil one, rarely 2, perfect, 11–12 mm long, as long as or slightly shorter than

Figure 117. 'Hata-zakura' at the Hakusan Shrine was a celebrated cherry in Tokyo more than a century ago. Note the tiny white flag that stands on each flower. Woodblock print "Yawatamiya Kaicho Hatazakura," Utagawa Kuniyoshi (1798–1861).

Figure 118. 'Hakusan-hata-zakura'. Photo by author, 13 April 1997, Yūki Experimental Station of the Flower Association of Japan, Ibaraki Prefecture.

the longest stamens. The calyx is campanulate, 8–9 × 4 mm, with a distinct transition from pedicel to calyx, almost green. Sepals are elongated and triangular, 8 × 3 mm, unserrated. Flowering season is early May.

'Hoki-zakura'

Hoki-zakura means "broom-cherry." A *hōki* is a broom made of twigs bound tightly together on the stick, and that is indeed what 'Hoki-zakura' looks like in winter. This form of 'Taizan-fukun' has a slender calyx and smaller, less intensely pink flowers. In Japanese sources it is given as *Prunus ×miyoshii* Ohwi 'Miyoshii'. It has about thirty petals, or about half the number of 'Taizan-fukun', and abundant blossoms that, like those of 'Taizan-fukun', remain on the tree for a long time.

Prunus 'Hoki-zakura'
Synonym: *Prunus ×miyoshii* Ohwi 'Miyoshii'
   Description: Tree rather narrow and vase-shaped, with many thin branches, to 4 m high. Young foliage bronze-green to green, already unfolded in the flowering season. Serration clearly double and regular, without

Figure 119. 'Hoki-zakura', blossom. Photo by Arie Peterse, Wageningen Botanic Gardens of the Agricultural University, Netherlands.

glands. Only the petiole is distinctly pubescent. Stipules barely divided, 7–12 mm, short. Corymbose inflorescence, with two to four flowers. Peduncles 1–5 mm long, short, thick. Pedicels 2.0–2.5 cm long, distinctly pubescent. Flower in bud pink, becoming very light pink, almost white, when completely opened. The color is somehow dull(!). Flower 3.0–3.5 cm in diameter, fluffy as a powder puff. Petals about thirty, elliptic, pointed at the top, 13–15 × 5–7 mm. There is one pistil, perfect, 11–12 mm long; longer than the stamens. The number of stamens is very large. The calyx is funnel-shaped, 8 × 3 mm, glabrous, with a purple tinge; there is a distinct transition from pedicel to calyx. Sepals are triangular, 5 × 3.0–3.5 mm, with a slight reddish tinge, unserrated. Flowering season is from late April to early May.

'Horinji'

Hōrin-ji is the name of a temple in Kyōto, halfway up the hills of Arashi-yama, famous for their cherries. "New" cherry forms are often "discovered" in temple compounds, where they were planted long ago as a donation by nameless persons with, apparently, an eye for rare cherries. 'Horinji' originates from a tree on the grounds of this temple, as is reported in many documents from the late seventeenth century on, and reconfirmed by

Katen Mikuma (1803) and Miyoshi (1916), who both visited the temple to see its famous cherry. Yamada (1941) reported that no particular cherry tree was to be seen in the place, but that a specimen of 'Horinji' was found in the collection along the Arakawa River in Tokyo in the early 1920s. At that time various "Horinji" cherries, such as 'Edo-horinji', were already in cultivation, so cautiousness is required in checking the history of this cherry. The true 'Horinji' has been more or less forgotten in Japan. It is not described in the exhaustive study on flowering cherries by the Flower Association of Japan (1982). Other Japanese sources describing 'Horinji' refer to a wrongly labeled specimen of 'Ichiyo' in the Tama Forest Science Garden. *Prunus lannesiana* 'Horinji' is therefore 'Ichiyo', as supposed by Kawasaki (1994, p. 270) and confirmed by us in the field.

The same 'Horinji' that Ingram grew used to be in the Wageningen Botanic Gardens in the Netherlands but disappeared, and the tree in a Dutch nursery from which our description was derived has also unfortunately withered away. Considering its cultural value, 'Horinji' is one of the cherries that, assuming it still exists somewhere, urgently needs to be returned to the Hōrin-ji Temple or to a preservation collection in Japan. Ingram (1948) saw this cherry in Japan under the name 'Kabuto Zakura'.

'Horinji' resembles the Japanese mountain cherry and selections such as 'Arashiyama' and 'Tagui-arashi'. Its charming, light pink blossom comes in nodding corymbs of up to six flowers with about fifteen petals set tightly together. Its pedicels, calyx, and sepals are markedly purplish red, strikingly contrasting with the soft pink petals. The decorative pairing of pink and dark purple inspired Miyoshi (1916) to name it *Prunus serrulata* f. *decora*. The combination of a purple-red calyx and light pink flowers is found also in 'Taoyame', which has a larger, more spreading tree shape. 'Horinji' is suitable for the smaller garden: it is a small tree with erect, slightly stiff branches that are sparingly equipped with long, narrow leaves. Sure to be noticed are the bundles of pistils that appear in some flowers, although they are not mentioned in Miyoshi's description.

Prunus 'Horinji'
Less current synonym: *Prunus serrulata* f. *decora*

Description: Tree narrow and erect, to 5 m high. Young foliage green. Serration single with few small red glands. Fully developed leaves are remarkably narrow. Stipules slightly divided, 10–16 mm long. Corymbose

Figure 120. 'Horinji' in the garden formerly owned by Collingwood Ingram.
Photo by Arie Peterse, 8 May 1987, Benenden.

inflorescence, with four to five (sometimes as few as three or as many as six) flowers. Peduncles 2–4 cm long, sturdy. Pedicels 2.5–4.5 cm long. Flower in bud pink (RHS 65-D), becoming white with a slight pinkish shade when completely opened. Flower 4.5–5.0 cm in diameter, spreading to an open plane, not fragrant. Petals fourteen to fifteen, orbicular, also orbicular at the top(!), 19–21 × 15–20 mm. Pistil one, with a small ovary, plus one to fourteen supplementary pistils that stand in between the stamens(!); these extra pistils are 9–10 mm long, longer than the stamens. The calyx is broad funnel-shaped, 5 × 5 mm, with a smooth transition from pedicel to calyx, dark purple-red (RHS 59-B). Sepals are elongated, slightly narrower at the base, 8–9 × 4–5 mm, unserrated, also dark purple-red (RHS 59-B). Flowering season is from late April to early May.

Figure 121. 'Horinji', bundle of pistils in the heart of a flower. Photo by Arie Peterse, 17 May 1986, Wageningen Botanic Gardens of the Agricultural University, Netherlands.

Figure 122. 'Horinji', bundle of phylloid pistils in a flower. Drawing by Miss Els Gerhardt, 6 June 1957. Laboratory of Plant Taxonomy, Wageningen Botanic Gardens of the Agricultural University, Netherlands.

'Ichihara-tora-no-o' and 'Tora-no-o'

'Tora-no-o' has been used as a name for cherry cultivars for more than three centuries. One plant is described briefly in the *Kadan-kōmoku* (Flower bed catalog) of 1681, and the name appears since then in other historical Japanese plant lists. The word *tora-no-o,* from *tora* ("tiger"), *o* ("tail"), and the particle *no* ("of," "from," or the possessive), means tiger's tail. This word is found in the names of very distinctly different cherries.

Miyoshi (1916) described one "tiger's tail" under the name *Prunus serrulata* f. *caudata*. This 'Tora-no-o' formed a small tree with ascending branches. The flowers were single, white or light pink, and were set in corymbs with three or four together. The word *caudata* ("tailed") referred to the way of presenting the blossom. A description with photo in Kayama's 1933 survey of the cherries in the Hirano Shrine in Kyōto gives peduncles of 1 cm and pedicels of 5 mm. The photo shows that the foliage is later than the blossom. Another illustration with description is found in Ohwi and Ohta (1973). The inflorescences have short stalks and are set together rather tightly at the end of spurs that crowd only at the end of the branches. Miyoshi's 'Tora-no-o' is rarely seen in Japan.

'Beni-tora-no-o' was a pink "tiger's tail" sold to Western countries in a Japanese catalog of 1937 as 'Beni-toranowo'. Again, the flowers were described as "crowded at the tips of shoots" (Wada 1937). This cherry is found in a rare collection in Japan and is not extinct as Kawasaki (1994) believed. It is a dark pink version of Miyoshi's 'Tora-no-o'. 'Yae-beni-tora-no-o' is still in cultivation but has proved to be a form very close to, if not the same as, 'Edo-zakura'.

'Ichihara-tora-no-o' is quite spectacular and differs markedly from 'Beni-tora-no-o', 'Tora-no-o', or 'Yae-beni-tora-no-o'. It has double flowers in compact corymbs that, mixed with the foliage, completely cover the branches. Corymbs and foliage appear on spurs that are several years old, showing the marks of bud scales of previous years as rings on the twig. The spurs are regularly set on the upperside of the wide-reaching branches that barely ramify. White fluffs of blossom appear thus in a regular rhythm, alternating with the fresh green young foliage over the upperside of long branches. With a little imagination, one can see a perfect bigger-than-life-size tiger's tail of cherry blossom in it.

A 'Tora-no-o' with the same alternating colors is described in a 1713 book of humor called *Kokkei-zōdan*. 'Ichihara-tora-no-o' is quite spectacular compared to Miyoshi's 'Tora-no-o'. It is no surprise to find a detailed reference in a non-botanic source. The herbalist Matsuoka (1785) presented a 'Tora-no-o' with illustration in his cherry book, *Igansai-ōhin*, that fits well with 'Ichihara-tora-no-o' and has no relation to Miyoshi's 'Tora-no-o'. Therefore, it is tempting to let the written history of 'Ichihara-tora-no-o' begin with these eighteenth-century records.

Without reference to any older history though, this cherry was "discovered" in the village of Ichihara, north of Kyōto, in the early twentieth century. It was named 'Ichihara-tora-no-o' by Kōzui Ōtani (1876–1948), a priest of Nishi-honganji Temple in Kyōto, to distinguish it from Miyoshi's 'Tora-no-o'. This Ōtani was a friend of Tōemon Sano, who named the cherry *Prunus lannesiana* 'Ichihara'.

Apart from suggesting a "tiger's tail," 'Ichihara-tora-no-o' has a few other distinctive details. Its pink flower buds show the stigma and the end of the style sticking out very early, when the buds are still closed. The young green foliage, often with a bronze shade, indicates immediately that this cherry is a form of the Japanese mountain cherry. The fine, single serration and the whitish underside of the leaf blade are identical to that of Japanese mountain cherry. The influence is so obviously present in the leaves that this cherry is well classified as *P. serrulata* var. *spontanea* 'Ichihara' (following the Flower Association of Japan, 1982, after *Flowering Cherries of Japan,* 1973).

In winter this cherry is also remarkable because of its unusual branching with the many short spurs. The spurs carry a terminal bud giving a leaf sprout; about two to four lateral buds are flower buds. The blossoming on spurs, set on spreading branches, has a quality reminiscent of carefully trained fruit trees. Its overall presentation is similar to that of orchard scenes in impressionistic paintings. If in propagation it proves to be incompatible with rootstock of *Prunus avium,* a stock of the Japanese mountain cherry (*P. serrulata* var. *spontanea*) should give better results. *Prunus serrulata* 'Albo Plena', which plays an important role in the taxonomic discussion of the garden forms, is a toned-down strain of 'Ichihara-tora-no-o'.

Prunus 'Ichihara-tora-no-o'

Synonyms: 'Ichihara', *Prunus serrulata* var. *spontanea* 'Ichihara', (not 'Tora-no-o')

Description: Tree umbrella-shaped, with almost horizontally extending branches crowded with short twigs and spurs, to 5 m high. Spurs slow growing, showing rings of previous years; often withered black; one terminal tapered bud plus 2–5 lateral flower buds. Young foliage green with a bronze shade (RHS 146-B, 152-B), appearing with the blossom. Serration fine and mostly single. The upperside of immature leaves may show a few hairs on the central vein. The underside of mature leaves is markedly whitish. Inflorescence is a corymb or an umbel on a stalk, with three to four flowers making

Figure 123. 'Ichihara-tora-no-o'. Photo by author, 29 April 1996, Tama Forest Science Garden, Tokyo.

Figure 124. 'Ichihara-tora-no-o', tree shape. Photo by author, 28 March 1996, Kyōto Botanic Garden.

Figure 125. 'Ichihara-tora-no-o', typical spurs. Photo by author, 20 April 1996, Tama Forest Science Garden, Tokyo.

a rather compact cluster of flowers. Peduncles about 1.5 cm long. Pedicels 1.5–2.0 cm long. Bud scales and bracts red. Flower in bud pink, showing the stigma sticking out for a few days before they open, becoming pure white when completely opened(!). Flower about 3.5 cm in diameter, opening fluffy, disorderly, with upright petals in the heart. Petals are twenty to fifty, with sometimes a faint reddish shade on the outer side or at the edges; oval, elliptic, 12–14 × 9–10 mm, often with a notched tip. There is one pistil, longer than the stamens, always sticking out of the flower. Filament of the stamen extending above the yellow anther. The calyx is rather broad and funnel-shaped, 4 × 5 mm, with a reddish tinge. Sepals are elongated and triangular, 4 × 5 mm, occasionally serrated, with a reddish tinge. Flowering season is late April in Tokyo. (Compare this description with the one of *Prunus serrulata* 'Albo Plena' at the beginning of this chapter.)

'Ichiyo'

The Japanese 'Ichiyō' is written with the Chinese characters *ichi* ("one") and *yō* ("leaf"). The cherry was named *Prunus serrulata* f. *unifolia* by Miyoshi. The Latin *unifolia* ("one-leafed"), like the Japanese name, refers to the

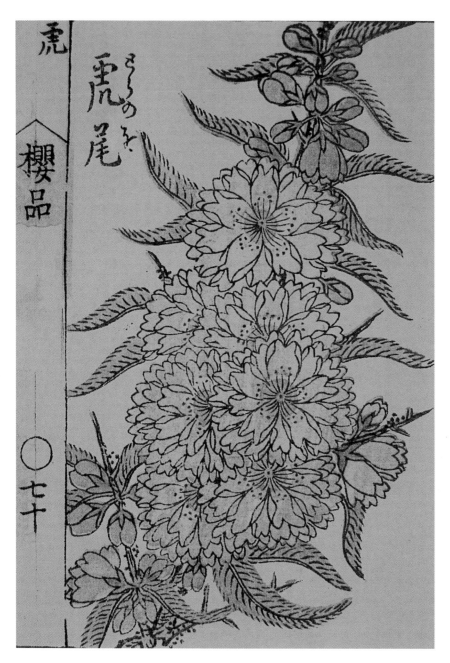

Figure 126. Eighteenth-century illustration of 'Tora-no-o' with a description that fits 'Ichihara-tora-no-o' ('Ichihara') rather than 'Tora-no-o' (*Prunus serrulata* f. *caudata*). From an 1891 reprint of Matsuoka (1758).

leaflike pistil in the heart of the flower. However, in a tree of 'Ichiyo' many flowers can be found with two pistils, of which the lower half is phylloid. The light shell-pink flowers turn to almost white when they fade. About twenty petals are regularly arranged in two tiers and make a saucer-shaped flower with a diameter of almost 5 cm. The flower resembles a ballerina's petticoat with the two green pistils forming the legs of the little figure. The mature leaves show long awns on the serration and an upperside that is deep green. The underside is light green without any whitish shade. This cherry is closely related to the Oshima cherry. It has the same kind of calyx, sepals, and bast coloring of the young twigs.

'Ichiyo' is found in Japanese collections since the early nineteenth-century garden of daimyo Ichihashi. It was introduced to Europe when Ingram, while visiting the Sakura Kwai in 1926, requested scions to be sent to his home in Kent.

The Flower Association of Japan (1982) and Kawasaki (1994) give *Prunus lannesiana* Wilson 'Hisakura' as the scientific name for 'Ichiyo'. "Hisakura" was proposed as a cultivar epithet in Germany by Koehne in 1902 in

Figure 127. 'Ichiyo', showing the spreading tree shape typical of the Oshima cherry (*Prunus serrulata* var. *speciosa*). Photo by Arie Peterse, 5 May 1987, Wageningen Botanic Gardens of the Agricultural University, Netherlands.

the midst of a confusing discussion, and when Wilson (1916) drew a wrong conclusion, it remained an accepted name. 'Ichiyo' will not be confused with 'Choshu-hizakura' if the scientific names of each are used; however, using the popular name "Hisakura" for either of these cherries will result in confusion. Jefferson (1984) gave 'Hizakura' as a synonym for 'Ichiyo', and the U.S. National Arboretum, Washington, D.C., documents 'Ichiyo' under the name 'Hizakura'. Nonetheless, the correct name is 'Ichiyo', and the Japanese "Hizakura" applies to other cherries such as 'Choshu-hizakura' or to forms related to the bell-flowered cherry. The name 'Hizakura' should not be used for 'Ichiyo'. (For more details on the confusion between 'Hizakura' and 'Ichiyo', see the discussion under 'Choshu-hizakura'.)

'Ichiyo' is a vigorous grower, though it tends to spread rather than grow very high. At a height of 6 m, it may attain a diameter of 8 m or more. This healthy, rather late flowering cherry is rarely planted in Western countries, although it makes a beautifully spreading, strong tree, perfect for a park or larger garden.

In ancient Japan, flowers of 'Ichiyo' were salted and pressed to be preserved. A few of these preserved flowers in a cup of boiling water made a hot drink with a delicate cherry fragrance.

Prunus 'Ichiyo'

Less current synonyms: *Prunus serrulata* f. *unifolia,* (not Hizakura)

Description: Tree broad and vase-shaped or table-shaped with a flattened crown, to 6 m high and 8–10 m wide. Young foliage bronze-green (RHS 152). Serration single or double with few glands. Foliage is well developed in the flowering season. Stipules fairly divided, 18–24 mm long. Corymbose inflorescence, with three to four flowers. Peduncles 1.3–3.0 cm long. Pedicels 2.5–3.5 cm long, not variable. Flower in bud pink, becoming very light pink (RHS 75-D) to almost white (RHS 155-D) when completely opened. Flower 4.5–5.0 cm in diameter, opening to a rather flat plane, with the petals nicely arranged around an open heart. Petals sixteen to twenty-two, with some petaloids, outer ones are orbicular 22 × 20 mm, inner ones oval 20 × 12 mm, slightly emarginate at the top, otherwise entire. Pistil one in 20 percent of the flowers, 2 in 80 percent, phylloid, second pistil sometimes abortive, 12–13 mm long, longer than the stamens. The calyx is funnel-shaped, 5 × 4–6 × 5 mm, with a faint purple tinge; there is a distinct transition from pedicel to calyx. Sepals are elon-

Figure 128. 'Ichiyo'. Photo by author, 13 April 1997, Yūki Experimental Station of the Flower Association of Japan, Ibaraki Prefecture.

gated and triangular, with a pointed top, 7–8 × 4.5–5.0 mm, unserrated, faintly purple. Young twigs have a chestnut-brown color. Flowering season is early May at about the same time as 'Kanzan'.

'Imose'

Imose (pronounced "eeh-mow-seh") is an old Japanese word meaning "man and woman" or "husband and wife." The word was also used to indicate the family bond between sister and brother, and was applied to this cherry because of its peculiar fruiting; it produces twin fruits, close together like a brother and sister, on one stalk.

'Imose' was originally found in the Hirano Shrine in Kyōto. The historical records of Hirano are scarce on its cherries, and 'Imose' appears—

although it might be much older—only in 1891 in written references (Kayama 1933). Ingram saw the tree at Hirano and managed to have grafting material sent to England; later he described it as *Prunus serrulata* 'Imosé'. An old clump with withered parts of a larger stub and some young and healthy stems at the side still remains in the Hirano Shrine, showing the original 'Imose' that formed the source of its cultivation in western countries. A young tree has since been planted there as a future replacement. In Japanese sources this cherry is called *P. lannesiana* 'Imose'.

'Imose' belongs to the large group of double-flowering, pink cherries, but has several characteristics that set it apart. The young foliage is remarkably pale copper-red in color, and later in the growing season its secondary shoots are salmon-pink. 'Imose' gives a healthy appearance with its

Figure 129. 'Imose', a second generation of the type tree from which Collingwood Ingram obtained grafting material. Photo by author, 22 April 1995, Hirano Shrine, Kyōto.

Figure 130. The always healthy glossy leaf and twin-fruits of 'Imose'. Photo by author, 6 May 1996, Hirano Shrine, Kyōto.

shining, grass-green foliage and rarely suffers from pests or diseases. The tightly connected twin fruits are typical and foreshadowed in the blossoming season when two perfect pistils may be seen in many flowers. The flowers are 4.0–4.5 cm in diameter, have twenty to twenty-five petals, and blossom in large, open corymbs. The outer whorl of petals can be helpful in identifying the cultivar as they sometimes show a green stripe at the back and then somehow come to resemble sepals. 'Imose' sheds its leaves very late; only in November do they turn yellow before falling.

Prunus 'Imose'

Less current synonym: Imosé

Description: Tree umbrella-shaped. Earliest, young foliage before the blossom, brownish red (RHS 164-A) to bronze-green (RHS 152-B); in the flowering season leaves are well developed and shiny as if sprayed with a synthetic leaf gloss(!). Serration single with dark red glands. Stipules slightly divided, 10–15 mm long. Corymbose inflorescence, with three to four flowers. Peduncles 1.5–4.0 cm long. Pedicels 1.5–3.0 cm long. Flower in bud purplish pink, becoming light pink to almost white (RHS 75-D) when completely opened. Flower 4.0–4.5 cm in diameter, opening to a rather flat plane, occasionally a few folded petals remain in the heart, especially with freshly opened flowers. Petals nineteen to twenty-three, oval, usually slightly emarginate at the top, 19–21 × 13–16 mm, one to five petaloids. Pistils usually two, perfect(!), 12–13 mm long, longer than the longest stamens. The calyx is funnel-shaped, 5 × 4 mm, short, with a faint purple tinge; there is a distinct transition from pedicel to calyx. Sepals are elongated and triangular, 7–8 × 3.0–3.5 mm, unserrated, with five supplemental sepal-like petals. Few typical twin fruits(!). Flowering season is late April.

'Ito-kukuri'

'Ito-kukuri' is an old cherry. It was illustrated in a Japanese cherry book of the mid-eighteenth century and mentioned in the *Kadan-kōmoku* (Flower bed catalog) of 1681. The name is a combination of *kukuri* ("bundle" or "bunch") and *ito* ("threads"), and means "bundled with a thread." This parallels the name under which Miyoshi described the cherry in 1916, *Prunus serrulata* f. *fasciculata;* the Latin word *fasciculata* means "bundled" or "(growing) in clusters." In Japan one finds it as *P. lannesiana* 'Fasciculata'.

The inflorescences are tightly set as fascicles (bunches of flowers at the end of the branches), an arrangement seen with other cherries as well. One corymb may have up to seven flowers, which must compete for space. A flowering branch looks as if it was artificially prepared for a floral show, with all the flowers bound with threads tightly to each other. This compact blooming poses a problem in wet springs. In these growing conditions, 'Ito-kukuri' might suffer from brown rot, a brownish withering of the flowers that may affect the twigs and show up the following year as cancerous spots on the branches. A few petals occasionally remain stuck in the calyx. Just before opening, the flower buds are a little inflated, somewhat spherical, and about 12 mm long. The unfolding foliage is yellowish green to bronze-green, closely resembling 'Edo-zakura', 'Okiku-zakura', and 'Yokihi'.

The cherry specialist Mr. Masatoshi Asari in the Matsumae region of

Figure 131. 'Ito-kukuri', the short flower stalks and the large number of flowers per corymb, make them compete for space. Photo by author, 13 April 1997, Yūki Experimental Station of the Flower Association of Japan, Ibaraki Prefecture.

緑
括

117

Figure 132. 'Ito-kukuri', showing the characteristic many flowers per corymb and the pointed buds with red stripes. From Miyoshi (1921b, no. 117).

Figure 133. An eighteenth-century illustration of 'Ito-kukuri', depicting the meaning of the name as a hanging "bundle of flowers." From an 1891 reprint of Matsuoka (1758).

Hokkaidō, made a few successful garden forms, such as 'Benigasa', with 'Ito-kukuri' as a parent. The latter's few but fertile seeds will explain some of the other resembling forms, including those mentioned above and others such as 'Azuma-nishiki', 'Beni-temari', 'Hakusan-o-demari', and 'Temari', which are rarely or never distinguished from 'Ito-kukuri'. The same holds true for cherries named 'O-demari' and 'Ko-demari' now, although in older sources these two differ considerably in the size of the flowers.

Prunus 'Ito-kukuri'
Less current synonym: 'Fasciculata'
   Description: Tree umbrella-shaped, to 5 m high; the few main branches that frame the crown are often bare from the base. Young foliage bronze-green (RHS 152-A), barely out when in bloom. Serration single or double, with glands to the top of the leaf. Stipules moderately to deeply bifurcated, 14–27 mm long. Corymbose inflorescence, with three to four or even seven flowers; sometimes more flowers, but then one to three are abortive. Peduncles 2.0–3.5 cm long. Pedicels 1.5–3.0 cm long. Flower buds dark pink and spherical. Flower with light pink (RHS 75-C, D) stripes when completely opened, 4.0–4.5 cm in diameter, with no distinct fragrance. Petals fifteen to twenty-four, orbicular or oval, slightly emarginate at the top, 16–20 × 12–16 mm, wrinkled and rumpled in appearance, often with a few half-expanded petals in the corolla. Pistil one, somewhat phylloid at the base in 80 percent of the flowers but with a normal stigma, 9–10 mm long, a little longer than or about as long as the stamens. The calyx has a campanulate or narrow-funnel shape, 7 × 3 mm, slightly purple, rather smoothly extending from the pedicel. Sepals are wedge-shaped, 8–9 × 3 mm, unserrated, sometimes with an extra sepal. Sensitive to brown rot. Flowering season is from late April to early May. 'Ito-kukuri' has a diploid set of chromosomes (2n = 16).

'Jo-nioi'

'Jo-nioi' ("supreme scent" or "first-class fragrance") was applied to this cherry for its striking fragrance. This cherry can also be recognized by an often-appearing, extra petaloid in the heart of the flower. It was described under the name *Prunus serrulata* f. *affinis* by Miyoshi in 1916, and its documented history appears to be no older than that. The single, white flowers combine with the fragrance to make an effective extra charm that will please anyone with a taste for simple beauty. 'Jo-nioi' forms an ascending-spreading tree with a flattened crown. The flowers are not very large but are so abundant that the crown of a tree in bloom looks like a huge, misty cloud of flowers. The stout corymbs are rather long and carry four to six flowers. Striking is the bright green of the young foliage and the many small, dark purplish cherries that appear after flowering. All this proves the close relation with the Oshima cherry. 'Jo-nioi' might have been discovered in the wild or in a nursery. Taking this parentage in account, Kawasaki (1994) named it *Prunus lannesiana* var. *speciosa* 'Affinis'.

Prunus 'Jo-nioi'
Less current synonym: 'Affinis'

Description: Tree broad and vase-shaped, with a flattened crown, to 7 m high. Color of the young foliage light green with a slight bronze hue. Ser-

Figure 134. 'Jo-nioi' is a spreading tree with a flattened crown. Photo by Arie Peterse, 1996, Keukenhof.

Figure 135. 'Jo-nioi' has single flowers, more meager in the Netherlands than the average Oshima cherry (*Prunus serrulata* var. *speciosa*), but nicely scented. Photo by Arie Peterse, 7 May 1986.

ration single with a few red glands at the base. Stipules deeply bifurcated, 12–18 mm long. Corymbose inflorescence, with four to six flowers (often rather in a peduncled umbel, with one flower halfway up the peduncle). Peduncles 2.5–3.5 cm long. Pedicels 2.5–3.5 cm long(!). Flowers in bud have a slight pinkish hue, becoming pure white when completely opened. Flower 4.0–4.5 cm in diameter, opening to a flat plane, with a strong, sweet fragrance reminiscent of crushed almonds. Petals five, with occasionally one to two small petaloids, oval, entire or sometimes emarginate at the top, 18–20 × 12–16 mm. There is one pistil, perfect, 9–10 mm long, clearly shorter than the longest stamens. The calyx is campanulate, 7–8 × 3.0–3.5 mm, faintly purple; there is a distinct transition from pedicel to calyx. Sepals are elongated, about 8 × 4 mm, unserrated (rarely dented at the top), faintly purple. Flowering season is early May. 'Jo-nioi' has a diploid set of chromosomes (2n = 16).

Figure 136. 'Jo-nioi'. Drawing by Mr. G. Langendijk, 29 April 1965, Laboratory of Plant Taxonomy, Wageningen Botanic Gardens of the Agricultural University, Netherlands.

Hosokawa-nioi, sometimes simply 'Hosokawa', was offered for export by Japanese nurseries in the early twentieth century. It has an erect tree shape when young, and its flowers resemble those of the Oshima cherry with their fresh-green long pedicels, calyx, and sepals. Each flower has three or more, rarely even six, erect flaglike petaloids in the heart, a distinguishing characteristic. 'Hosokawa-nioi' has a diploid set of chromosomes (2n = 16).

Nioi-zakura is a rarely seen fragrant selection of the Japanese mountain cherry. Its botany is as its parent: flowers have a diameter of about 4.8 cm, and petals are often fimbriate at the tip.

'Kanzan'

The name 'Kanzan' ("bordering mountain") is an old, poetic word. For Japanese writers in ancient times, the word led the reader's imagination to a homely, native land or the village of one's birth that lay in a valley. It suggested the prospect of viewing the whole valley when standing on the bordering mountain. In poems or literature, the mountain lies at the point where one enters the valley. Two bordering mountains that have served a strategic military role in Japan are the one at Ichi-no-seki in the north (called Kanzan) and another at Seki-gahara close to Nagoya (called Sekiyama).

Kan can also be read as *seki* ("border") and *zan* can be read as *yama* ("mountain"). Thus the cherry 'Kanzan' is also called 'Sekiyama' or 'Sekizan'. 'Kwanzan' is an obsolete spelling of 'Kanzan'. Why the name 'Kanzan' was applied to the cherry still remains a question.

'Sekiyama' is mentioned in the plant guide *Kadan-kōmoku* (Flower bed catalog) of 1681. Two hundred years later this cherry appeared again in lists of the cherry collection along the Arakawa River, near Tokyo. Today it is well known and often planted around Tokyo, but less common in other parts of Japan. Without doubt, it is the most popular cherry in Western countries and hardly needs an introduction. Some garden centers even sell it simply as 'Flowering Cherry'. The abundance of its blossom and its healthy, vigorous growth are superior. The pink-red buds expand to cyclamen-pink, double flowers. Miyoshi (1916) named this cultivar *Prunus serrulata* f. *purpurascens* after the purple flowers.

A full-grown tree is recognized from a distance because of its vase shape with branches bending inward as if forming a wine glass; it might reach up to 10 m high. The branches of older trees can become so heavy, certainly when in bloom, that they tend to hang, giving the tree a more saggy, umbrella-like shape.

Several strains of 'Kanzan' exist. A form known as 'Kurama-kanzan' has more open flowers. Other Japanese clones have mature leaves with an outspoken glaucous backside. Early in the twentieth century Japanese nurseries exporting to Western countries offered 'Kanzan' alongside 'Sekiyama' (or 'Sekizan'), presenting them as "only slightly different" without explaining the difference. Sometimes 'Kanzan' is sold as 'Hizakura', which creates confusion (see description of 'Choshu-hizakura' for a discussion of the name 'Hizakura'). French nurseries often sell 'Kanzan' as 'New Red'.

Figure 137. 'Kanzan'. Other clones have more petals in the heart so that the opening of the calyx is not visible. Photo by author, 27 April 1996, Kyōto Botanic Garden.

Prunus 'Kanzan'
Synonym: Sekiyama
Less current synonyms: Kwanzan, New Red, Sekizan, (not Hizakura)
   Description: Tree vase-shaped, later with hanging branches, to 10 m
high. Young foliage bronze-brown to bronze-green (RHS 152-A). Serration single and regular. Leaves that have just unfolded have on the serration tiny glands that quickly disappear. Foliage is well developed in the
flowering season. Stipules medium to deeply bifurcated depending on the
general vigor of the tree, 12–20 mm long. Corymbose inflorescence, with
three to five flowers. Peduncles 1.5–3.5 cm long. Pedicels 3.5–4.5 cm long.
Flower in bud pink-red, becoming pink (RHS 73-D) when completely
opened. Flower 4.5–5.0 cm in diameter, fuzzy and curly, with wrinkled
petals in the heart. Petals twenty-three to twenty-eight, ovate, sometimes
orbicular, usually slightly emarginate at the top, 19–23 × 13–17 mm. Pistils two, rarely three, phylloid, about 7 mm long, longer than the stamens.
At the end of flowering, stamens turn to a slight pink; the filament extends
above the anther, extension purplish red(!). The calyx is broad and funnel-
shaped, 3–4 × 4 mm, with a faint purple tinge; there is a distinct transition from pedicel to calyx. Sepals are elongated and triangular, 6.5–8.0 ×
3–4 mm, with a purple shade, basically unserrated, but a rare tooth can be
seen. Occasionally an extra, sixth sepal is found. Flowering season is early
May. 'Kanzan' has a diploid set of chromosomes (2n = 16).

Kirin (synonym *Prunus serrulata* f. *atrorubra* Miyoshi) is named for a mythical, fiery beast, the *kylin,* that announced the coming of a saint in ancient
Japan. In modern Japanese the same word *kirin* means "giraffe." The cultivar 'Kirin' is often confused with 'Kanzan' because of Miyoshi's (1916)
incomplete comparison of the two. The confusion prevails today and is remarkable, seeing how different the two cultivars are. 'Kirin' is a diploid
cherry with unquestionable horticultural merits, for instance, in its brown-
red young foliage dotted with the reddish-pink and double flowers. It is
rarely found, but when seen from a distance, it may be judged as a weaker
and less overdone version of 'Kanzan'. For one thing the tree is less vigorous
and for another it does not have the typical wine-glass shape of 'Kanzan'.
Looking closer at 'Kirin', one can immediately see that it has no relation to
'Kanzan', although the flowers of both are the same color of pink and have
the same phylloid pistils. The flowers of 'Kirin' are smaller, however, about

3.5 cm in diameter, and they are easily identified by the pedicel, calyx, and large sepals that are fresh green(!), whereas those of 'Kanzan' always show brownish or purplish tints and are smaller and narrower. 'Kirin's' sepals are wider, rather boat-shaped, and serrated(!). The unfolding foliage of 'Kirin' shows the main and lateral veins, as well as the finer veins at the edge of the leaf, as depressions in the upperside of the leaves. The young leaves of 'Kirin' show, therefore, a furrowed rumpling that is different from 'Kanzan'. Teeth of the more coarsely biserrated leaves of 'Kirin' point outwards in all directions when mature(!), which is quite different from the regular, neat, and mostly single serration of 'Kanzan'.

Figure 138. 'Kirin' as illustrated by Miyoshi, who neither observed nor described its sepals as serrated, although 'Kirin' clearly has serrated, fresh green sepals. From Miyoshi (1921b, no. 107).

Figure 139. The *kylin* beast as seen on labels of Kirin beer. With kind permission of Kirin Beer Company.

'Kenroku-en-kiku-zakura'

Many forms of chrysanthemum-flowered cherries originate from the Noto Peninsula and the neighboring valleys and city of Kanazawa in Ishikawa Prefecture (Kawasaki 1994). Until the mid-nineteeth century the region flourished through a thriving cargo-ship trade along the coasts of the Japanese archipelago, and even with Korea and China. Chrysanthemum-cherry imports from other regions, or maybe even from the continent, cannot be ruled out. A large number of these chrysanthemum cherries can be found in temple compounds, where they were planted long ago as a donation. Their names follow the pattern "The Chrysanthemum-Flowered Cherry of [Name of Temple]." Examples include 'Baigoji-juzukake-zakura', 'Hiuchi-dani-kiku-zakura', 'Keta-no-shiro-kiku-zakura', 'Raikoji-kiku-zakura', or 'Zenshoji-kiku-zakura'. Though long and cumbersome, these names are necessary to avoid misunderstandings in this group with its difficult classification.

Many temples and shrines thus have their unique chrysanthemum-flowered cherry, and it has been suggested that these were distributed in long-forgotten times by village people at marriages and other special occasions. The donation custom could explain the singular, isolated occurrence of chrysanthemum forms throughout mid-Japan. Looking more carefully, one can see that many of them are not unique but rather quite similar, if not exactly the same. Kimura Hisakichi (1968), for example, and the research published by the Kokuritsu Idengaku Kenkyujo (1995) concluded that 'Kinashi-chigo-zakura' (synonym 'Takamatsu-chigo-zakura'), 'Nison-in-fugenzo', and 'Kenroku-en-kiku-zakura' resemble each other very much, as well as a chrysanthemum form named 'Kokonoe' (not 'Kokonoe', synonym f. *homogena* Miyoshi, described as 'Kokonoye' by Ingram in 1948, nor 'Kokonoe' mentioned by Sano in 1970). A "Kiku-zakura" distributed by Mr. T. Sano is found in the collections of the Kyōto Botanic Garden and of the Flower Association of Japan. It is identical to the forms mentioned above. Practically speaking, all of these cherries must be grouped with 'Kenroku-en-kiku-zakura'. 'Kiku-zakura' (Chrysanthemoïdes) is in fact similar to this group, but differs in tree shape and details such as the receptacle.

'Kenroku-en-kiku-zakura' derives from a chrysanthemum-flowered cherry tree in the garden of Kenroku-en in Kanazawa. It was presented to a feudal lord of the Maeda clan who owned the garden, and was known long ago among local gardeners as *gosho-zakura* ("imperial palace cherry"). It might have been a donation from the palace in Kyōto, although no records exist. As an old, heavily branched tree it drew the attention of Miyoshi who obtained the natural monument status for it and described it in 1928 as *Prunus serrulata* f. *sphaerantha,* pointing to the spherical flowers in contrast to the caved-in powder puffs of 'Kiku-zakura'. Plucking off the petals of the flowers shows how this perfect ball shape comes about: the calyx has a protruding receptacle, fleshy as a miniature artichoke and best seen after the second-story flower finishes flowering. Recent Japanese sources give this cherry as *Prunus lannesiana* 'Sphaerantha'.

Miyoshi described this cherry from a very old tree, but it must be remembered that the number of petals in old trees is always extremely high, reaching 380 per flower. Younger trees have 150 to 200 petals per flower. The flowers are borne in peduncled umbels rather than in corymbs that are found on short, thick spurs with a leafy sprout from an end bud. The rather slow growth combined with abundant blossoms that take so much of the tree's energy result in mostly spurs with even more flower buds. The mostly single serration of mature leaves is another trait that is helpful in identification.

Probably since its days as an imperial palace cherry but certainly after its designation as a natural monument, it became a sought-after cherry. Plants named "Kiku-zakura" are mostly 'Kenroku-en-kiku-zakura' rather than 'Kiku-zakura' proper.

Figure 140. 'Kenroku-en-kiku-zakura', peduncled umbels. Photo by author, 24 April 1997, Kyōto Botanic Garden.

Prunus 'Kenroku-en-kiku-zakura'

Less current synonym: 'Sphaerantha'

Description: Tree small, spreading, to 4 m high. Young foliage comes out with the blossom, green to bronze-green, serration mostly single, no glands. Sometimes three to four nectaries, usually two on the petiole. Stipules green, 8–12 mm, sometimes divided, quickly shed. Inflorescence mostly a peduncled umbel of three flowers, often a fourth abortive flower on the peduncle(!). One or two flowers per inflorescence often only in bud stage and not developing(!). Peduncles 1–3 cm long, thick(!). Pedicels 3–5 cm long, or much longer. Flower in bud dark red (RHS 53-B, D), opening pink (RHS 62-C) or almost white. Rather than shedding petals, the flowers drop with the pedicel from the tree after flowering. Flower 3–4 cm in diameter, opening to a chrysanthemum-type flower ball, in its early stage with a dark pink heart because of the second-story flower still in bud stage. Partly and fully developed petals 150 to 200, or even up to 300, elliptic, some slightly emarginate at the top, well-developed petals 16–19×7–13 mm. In the heart of the flower one may notice second-story and third-story flowers, sometimes screwlike deformed; the heart is extremely variable in its developing. Small leaflike organs might be taken as deformed pistils. The calyx is a disk-shaped receptacle, not hollow, with a protrusion in the middle(!). Protrusion shows holes, or slits, sometimes spiraled. Sepals and accessory sepals are ovate or triangular, 5–7 × 3–4 mm, often with a purple shade, with small teeth. Flowering season is mid-May in Tokyo.

Hiyodori-zakura is found in the West as a name wrongly applied to some chrysanthemum forms. 'Hiyodori-zakura' is named after the *hiyodori*, a noisy, thrushlike Japanese bird that eats berries but in spring may be seen with the sparrows and white-eyes picking honey from the flowers. Most likely this bird does not visit or even like 'Hiyodori-zakura', which, being a chrysanthemum cherry, does not give any nectar. This cherry is rarely seen, but might be a very old cultivar as the name appears in the horticulture book *Kadan-jikin-shō* (Flower bed embroideries) of 1695. It was found in the city of Nanao near Kanazawa. Miyoshi named it *Prunus serrulata* f. *longipedunculata* in 1916, referring to the long flower stalks that, to be honest, can be quite short in warmer and drier climates. 'Hiyodori-zakura' forms a narrow, vase-shaped tree about 4 m high. It has erect branches; a few of these stand on the stem with a typical candelabrum-like bend. Even more characteristic of this cherry are the pubescent peduncles and pedicels, suggesting a parentage of *P. pseudo-cerasus* or *P. serrulata* var. *pubescens*. Among chrysanthemum cherries, only the closely related but rarely seen 'Ota-zakura' has some hair on its flower stalks. 'Hiyodori-zakura' forms in the heart of its flower a second-story flower that only opens a few days after the main flower.

Najima-zakura is a chrysanthemum form from the city of Kanazawa. It shows a perfect yellow ring of anthers in the heart of most flowers when

Figure 141. 'Hiyodori-zakura', pubescent pedicels. Photo by author, 19 April 1996, Yūki Experimental Station of the Flower Association of Japan, Ibaraki Prefecture.

they are expanding. The mature flowers are markedly different with their fifty to eighty stamens, and the receptacle is a hollow cup shape, with flower organs set on the inner side and sepals on the rim. 'Najima-zakura' has a diploid set of chromosomes (2n = 16).

Raikoji-kiku-zakura is a chrysanthemum-flowered cherry that originates from Raikō-ji Temple in the village of Fugeshi-gun, Ishikawa Prefecture. It has a fastigiate tree shape. The receptacle of the flower is disk-shaped, and it has no hole or depression as seen in the flowers of 'Kiku-zakura'.

Figure 142. 'Hiyodori-zakura'. From Miyoshi (1921b, no. 114).

Figure 143. 'Najima-zakura'. Photo by author, 19 April 1996, Yūki Experimental Station of the Flower Association of Japan, Ibaraki Prefecture.

'Kiku-shidare-zakura'

'Kiku-shidare-zakura' ("chrysanthemum weeping cherry') is listed among the cherries that were planted along the Arakawa River near Tokyo around the turn of the century. Miyoshi saw it and described it in 1922. At that time it was not a rare sight in gardens of northern Japan, having been brought there from nurseries in Kita-Kuwata, a village north of Kyōto in central Japan (Kayama and Kayama 1943).

The Flower Association of Japan (1982) classifies this cherry as a cultivar of the Japanese mountain cherry and describes it under *Prunus jamasakura* 'Plena-pendula'. Kawasaki (1994) supposes an influence of *P. serrulata* var. *pubescens* and gives it under the name *P. lannesiana* 'Plena-pendula'.

In nurseries in Western countries it is often grown on a stem of 1.5 to 1.8 m by training the top shoot along a stick. The abundant little globu-

Figure 144. 'Raikoji-kiku-zakura', a fastigiate chrysanthemum cherry, with a healthy growth on deep friable loam. Photo by Arie Peterse, 30 April 1996, Mishima.

lar, pink flowers resemble those of 'Asano'. The weeping chrysanthemum cherry has, like 'Ama-no-gawa' or *Prunus triloba,* become an almost commonplace garden plant.

In Britain a sport of 'Kiku-shidare-zakura' was introduced under the name 'Cheal's Weeping' in 1915. Its thinner branches hang down more steeply, and there are not as many blossoms.

Some nurseries sell this cultivar as Double Weeping Flowering Cherry, Shidare-zakura, *Prunus serrulata* 'Pendula', or even "Prunus pendula", leading to confusion with other weeping cherries, such as the forms of the true *Prunus pendula.* It is best to refrain from these names.

Prunus 'Kiku-shidare-zakura'
Synonym: Kiku-shidare
Less current synonyms: weeping Oriental cherry, 'Cheal's Weeping',
    P. chealii pendula, (not Shidare-zakura, not Prunus pendula, not
    double weeping flowering cherry, not *P. serrulata* 'Pendula')
Description: Tree with weeping branches pointing sideways, before they become hanging (drooping directly with 'Cheal's Weeping'). Young foliage light bronze-green (RHS 152-C) to bright green (RHS 144-A). Serration double with glands. Stipules deeply bifurcated, 12–22 mm long. Corymbose inflorescence, with three to five flowers. Peduncles short, 2–10 mm(!). Pedicels 2–4 cm long. Flower in bud deep pink, staying pink (RHS 65-B, C) when completely opened. Flower 3.0–3.5 cm in diameter, globular. Petals 75 to 125, elliptic, slightly crenate or entire at the top, 12–15 × 5–9 mm. There is one pistil, perfect, sometimes phylloid at the base, 10–12 mm long, longer than the very few stamens. The calyx is broad and funnel-shaped, 3 × 3–4 mm; it has a broad edge at the top where the petals are implanted; there is a distinct transition from pedicel to calyx. Sepals are triangular, 5 × 2.5 mm, unserrated, with one to five accessory sepal-like petals. Flowering season is from late April to early May.

'Kiku-zakura'

'Kiku-zakura' ("chrysanthemum cherry") suggests a cherry with flowers that resemble chrysanthemums. The word appeared in the Japanese song *Sakuragawa* ("The Cherry River"), dated 1675, and was later found among the names of cherries planted in the early nineteenth-century garden

Figure 145. 'Kiku-shidare-zakura' blossom (above) compared with 'Asano' (below). Photo by Arie Peterse, 6 May 1986.

Figure 146. 'Kiku-shidare-zakura'. Photo by Arie Peterse, 6 May 1986.

Yokuon-en in Tokyo. Since then, one finds many *kiku-zakura* in lists of cherry collections, often described in no more detail than as having red, pink, or white flowers, sometimes given as a weeping tree. Clearly in old Japan *kiku-zakura* was simply used as a general name for cherries with many-petaled flowers; however, one clearly defined clonal cultivar 'Kiku-zakura' exists.

Chadbund (1972) found 'Kiku-zakura' not very abundant in its flowering, nor vigorous in its growth. Ingram (1948) was somewhat condescending in his description of the flower as a "densely packed, rounded boss" in which "the petals are so numerous, and so closely crowded together, that the natural shape of the flower is entirely lost—indeed, they form such a congested mass of petals that one might almost suppose that they had been artificially tied with the idea of making a sort of floral ball." He thought it a "shy flowerer, but also a slow and stubborn grower." Considering these comments, it is difficult to find any praise for 'Kiku-zakura'. Nonetheless, the trees seen in Japan are certainly charming: the flowers do not smother the tree, as is seen with 'Kanzan' for instance, but are dotted throughout the tree in hanging blooms, giving it a picturesque appearance.

The correct soil is critical to 'Kiku-zakura', which prefers a rich and airy loamy soil. Under such conditions it grows quite vigorous to about 6 m with a few leader branches on a short stem.

Figure 147. 'Kiku-zakura', blossom and foliage. The slightly whitish underside of a mature leaf can be seen in the lower right corner. Photo by Arie Peterse, 29 April 1996, Tama Forest Science Garden, Tokyo.

When the buds develop, the corymb shows a strong resemblance to a little sprig of dark pink chrysanthemums. The thick, glabrous, sometimes shiny pedicels and the way they fit into the calyx with its many accessory sepals are all very much chrysanthemum-like. Only the bracts and bractlets betray the *Prunus* affiliation. Later in the season the petals are completely out, reflexing over the calyx and covering the sepals. A characteristic of this garden cherry, late in the flowering season, is a small depression or hole in the middle of the disk-shaped receptacle; it is visible after all petals (and sometimes other warty little things) have been plucked off. The shape of the receptacle gives the flowers a caved-in powderpuff shape.

Because of the strong resemblance of the young flowers to chrysanthemums, this cultivar was named 'Kiku-zakura', despite the possible confusion with the loosely used general term *kiku-zakura*. Miyoshi described it as *Prunus serrulata* f. *chrysanthemoïdes,* and it is also found described under *P. lannesiana* 'Chrysanthemoïdes'. The origin of its cultivation is a tree that stood in the courtyard of the former Sixth High School in Okayama, Japan. Thus, this cherry sometimes is seen in Japan under the name 'Rokkō-giku' ("Six-High-chrysanthemum").

Prunus 'Kiku-zakura'

Less current synonyms: 'Chrysanthemoïdes', Rokkō-giku

Description: Tree quite vigorous, ascending, to 6 m high. Young foliage almost completely out in the flowering season, green (RHS 146-A), serration mostly double, with glands. Underside of mature leaves somewhat whitish green. Stipules divided a bit, 10–15 mm. Corymbose inflorescence, with three to five flowers per corymb; occasionally a three-flower umbel. Peduncles 1.0–1.5 cm long, thick. Pedicels 2.5–3.5 long, occasionally a little twisted, not straight, shiny. Flower in bud dark red (RHS 53-B, D), turning purplish pink (RHS 64-D) when first opening, to pink (RHS 65-B) when completely opened. Flower 3–4 cm in diameter, opening to a chrysanthemum-type flower with a depression in the heart. Developed petals seventy to ninety or up to 180, elliptic, some slightly emarginate at the top, 14–17 × 7–10 mm. In the heart of the flower one may notice a cluster of undeveloped petals and carpels, sometimes with a few perfect stamens, sometimes with leafy sepals; in later blooming flowers the heart is sometimes developed as a second-story flower with more petals (total up to 180); the heart is extremely variable in its developing. No pistils. The calyx is a disk-shaped receptacle, not hollow, with a depression or hole in the middle(!). Sepals are triangular, 6 × 3–4 mm, with a purple shade, unserrated, with about five to ten outer petals developing as accessory sepals. Flowering season is late April in Tokyo, a little earlier than 'Hiyodori-zakura'.

'Mikuruma-gaeshi'

'Mikuruma-gaeshi' ("court carriage returned") has several interpretations. One often-heard explanation claims an imperial traveler ordered his carriage to return for a second look after passing a cherry of great beauty. According to some authors the traveler was the emperor Go-Mizuno-o (1596–1680), who is well remembered in horticultural circles for having commanded the construction of great gardens in Kyōto, some of which are still well kept. Another interpretation speaks of noblewomen picnicking under a cherry so beautiful that they decided to stay longer than planned and sent their carriage back. Historically documented, though, is the explanation that, after passing by an unknown but beautiful cherry, courtiers in a carriage quarreled over whether it was a single or a double cherry (Matsuoka 1758). One of them was sure to have seen single flowers, and the other was convinced they were double. To solve the dispute, the carriage was ordered to return so the courtiers could take another look. The cherry proved to have both single and a few double flowers.

Miyoshi named this cherry *Prunus serrulata* f. *diversiflora,* meaning "with diverse flowers," since single and double flowers are found on a tree. Another popular name for it is 'Yae-hitoe' ("double-single"), again pointing to the flowers. In reality, the word *double* is saying too much for these flowers that, at most, have seven or eight petals. Many other single cherries also have a few flowers with more petals, and it is not an exclusive characteristic for 'Mikuruma-gaeshi'.

Two other synonyms are 'Kirigaya' or 'Kirigayatsu', both of which are written with Chinese characters that translate as "valley of *Paulownia* trees." The latter name appeared in Japanese written sources in the early fifteenth century (Yamada 1941, pp. 122–123). From these sources, one must conclude that 'Mikuruma-gaeshi' is one of the true classics among the flowering cherries. Its beauty lies in the abundantly produced, large, and pink flowers. Sano IV (1961) reported they were 6 cm in diameter; indeed, well over 5 cm is typical. Since the beginning of the twentieth century 'Mikuruma-gaeshi' has been offered by Japanese nurseries for export. In Japan one finds it as *Prunus lannesiana* 'Mikurumakaisi'.

'Mikuruma-gaeshi' barely ramifies, making a broad crown with few, heavy branches. To encourage more branching, it is best to prune the tree when it is still young. The branches have many spurs that produce rather compact clusters of many, soft pink flowers, more than 5 cm in diameter. Because they blossom on short spurs, the flowers may suffer from brown rot. The branching and flowering on the spurs give young, blooming trees the appearance of a vase of flowering branches, an image that becomes less apparent when the tree ages. Although the semi-double, pink flowers of cherries such as 'Ito-kukuri' and 'Okiku-zakura' resemble those of 'Mikuruma-gaeshi', the latter is clearly superior because of its shapely branches and its much larger flowers with a delicate fragrance. Because of its broad shape, this cultivar needs space to grow. It is not suitable as a roadside tree, but shows to full and splendid advantage in parks or larger gardens.

The name 'Mikuruma-gaeshi', with its story, is so attractive that it has been applied to other unrelated cherries as well. At Kyōto's Ninna-ji Temple, for instance, one may come across several forms of 'Omuro-mikuruma-gaeshi', probably mutant forms discovered among plants that were raised from layer-stools of 'Omuro-ariake' in the temple compound. Another, rare garden cherry, 'Gosho-mikuruma-gaeshi', has ten to fifteen petals in fragrant flowers.

Prunus 'Mikuruma-gaeshi'

Less current synonyms: 'Diversiflora', Kirigaya, Kirigayatsu, Kuruma-gaeshi, 'Mikurumakaisi', Yae-hitoe

Description: Tree broad and vase-shaped, with only a few main branches, many spurs. Young foliage bronze-green (RHS 152-A, B). Serration single without glands. Stipules slightly divided, 17–20 mm long. Corymbose inflorescence (occasionally more umbellate), with three to four flowers (often one abortive). Peduncles 2.0–2.5 cm long, sturdy. Pedicels short(!), only 1.5–1.8 cm long. Flower in bud light pink, becoming white with a pink shade (RHS 76-D) when completely opened. Flower 5.0–5.5(–6.0) cm in diameter, opening to a flat plane, medium fragrance. Petals five, occasionally with a few extra petaloids, ovate, usually slightly emarginate at the top, 23–25 × 18–20 mm. Pistil one, perfect, 11–12 mm long, as long

Figure 148. 'Mikuruma-gaeshi'. Flowers develop better under more favorable growing conditions. Photo by Arie Peterse, 4 May 1986, Wageningen Botanic Gardens of the Agricultural University, Netherlands.

as the stamens. The calyx has a long funnel shape, 7.5 × 5.0 mm, with a faint purple tinge. Sepals are elongated and triangular, 9–11 × 4.0–4.5 mm, unserrated, green. Flowering season is from late April to early May. 'Mikuruma-gaeshi' has a diploid set of chromosomes (2n = 16).

'Ojochin'

'Ojochin' (*ō-jōchin* is "large lantern") refers to the Japanese bulbous lantern made of paper that is glued on a frame of thin bamboo sticks. As for the cherry 'Ojochin', the inflated, bulgy flower buds at the point of bursting into bloom are rather large for a garden cherry and are likened to miniature paper lanterns dangling from the tree. Miyoshi described this cherry under the name *Prunus serrulata* f. *bullata;* his *bullata* points to the buds inflated in their prime. In Japan one finds this cultivar as *P. lannesiana* 'Ojochin'.

'Ojochin' appears from the late seventeenth century in written sources in Japan and was exported by Japanese nurseries from the end of the nineteenth century. Both 'Senriko' and 'Ariake' resemble 'Ojochin', but the latter is distinguished because it is not fragrant. Kawasaki (1994) places the three in the same group of garden forms supposedly influenced by 'Mazakura'.

'Ojochin' is a vigorous, broad and vase-shaped tree, and gives with its ascending branches a rather coarse appearance. The shape of the tree and the size of the flowers are reminiscent of 'Tai-haku', but the flowers of 'Ojochin' have a pink tinge in bud and they often have a few extra petals, sometimes up to ten, therefore clearly differing from the pure white and always single flowers of 'Tai-haku'. Remarkable are the plump and ovate winter buds of 'Ojochin'. Young leaves have a bronzelike color, are remarkably bristled, and, once developed, many of them lack the acuminate top. A rare garden

Figure 149. 'Ojochin', large, fluffy buds. Photo by author, 12 April 1997, Tama Forest Science Garden, Tokyo.

大提燈

五

Figure 150. Artistic representation of 'Ojochin'. Woodblock print in Takeda

form 'Higurashi' as well as 'Fugenzo' may show this deviating leaf shape, but the latter less frequently than 'Ojochin' or 'Higurashi'.

Prunus 'Ojochin'

Less current synonym: *Prunus serrulata* f. *bullata*

Description: Tree umbrella-shaped, to 8 m high and 10 m wide. Young foliage slightly bronze. Serration single, remarkably coarse and with awn-tipped teeth. Fully developed leaves often lack the acuminate top. Teeth without glands. Stipules medium divided, 13–19 mm long. Corymbose inflorescence, with three to five or even seven flowers. Peduncles 1.5–4.0 cm long. Pedicels 1.5–2.5 cm long. Flower in bud soft pink, becoming practically white with a light pink shade when completely opened. Flower 5.0–5.5(–6.0) cm in diameter, large, opening to a flat plane with slightly folded petals. Petals five, occasionally one to three or up to six petaloids extra, orbicular and wavy at the edge, emarginate at the top, 23–28 × 20–25 mm. Pistil one, perfect, about 12 mm long, as long as or slightly longer than the longest stamens. The calyx is campanulate to funnel-shaped, 7 × 5 mm, with a faint pink tinge; there is a distinct transition from pedicel to calyx. Sepals are elongated, narrowing to the base, 12 × 6 mm (at the base 4.5 mm), with a faint pink tinge, unserrated. Flowering season is from late April to early May. 'Ojochin' has a triploid set of chromosomes (2n = 24).

'Okiku-zakura'

'Okiku-zakura' (*ō-kiku-zakura* is "big chrysanthemum-cherry") is rarely mentioned in any Japanese source, is never described, and is named only in lists of large collections like the one of Chōjagamaru (ca. 1842), or ranked as "rare and newly formed" in the source *Sakura-bon* (1910). The Yokohama Nursery Company offered it for export in the 1930s. Trees are not found in Japanese collections at present, but may be seen in the Rombergpark in Dortmund, Germany, in the Belgian arboreta at Hemelrijk and Kalmthout, and in the Belmonte Arboretum in Wageningen, Netherlands. Jefferson (1984) says it is in cultivation in the United States.

One would expect a big chrysanthemum-cherry to have large flowers tightly set with many petals, as is typical of chrysanthemum-flowered cultivars, but 'Okiku-zakura' has in fact no more than about twenty petals. The flowers are of a perfect shape, showing themselves at their best when half-opened among buds that are at the brink of bursting. At this time the large buds are soft pink with darker stripes. The flowers, about 5 cm in diameter, appear in tight bunches on the spurs at the end of the twigs. This way of flowering makes 'Okiku-zakura' sensitive to brown rot in damp or rainy weather, and in regions with wet springs this affliction can be considered characteristic for this cherry.

Ingram (1929, 1948) named this cherry *Prunus serrulata* 'Okiku' and described it as ugly and beautiful at the same time. Without any mercy he compared it with "a beautifully dressed and heavily beringed woman of an uncertain age and unattractive figure." Indeed the barely ramifying, bare skeleton of 'Okiku-zakura' contrasts violently with the perfectly shaped flowers. In Ingram's description the sepals are finely serrated, something that is not always seen on every flower.

Ingram reported that 'Ito-kukuri' resembles 'Okiku-zakura' but has fewer petals. The 12-mm long buds of 'Ito-kukuri' are more spherical than

Figure 151. 'Okiku-zakura', most beautiful just before the flowers open. Photo by Arie Peterse, 7 May 1986, Wageningen Botanic Gardens of the Agricultural University, Netherlands.

the 15-mm long, more egg-shaped buds of 'Okiku-zakura', which Ingram found "square-shouldered" or broadly angular at the base. Otherwise, the slightly inflated, dark pink buds are characteristic for both cherries.

Prunus 'Okiku-zakura'
Less current synonym: Okiku
Description: Tree broad and vase-shaped, airy, to 5 m high. Young foliage light bronze-green (RHS 152-C) to green. Serration single, rather coarse and with long awns, without glands. Stipules medium to deeply bifurcated, 13–23 mm long. Corymbose inflorescence, with three to five flowers. Peduncles 1.5–3.5 cm long. Pedicels short(!), 1.5–2.0 cm long. Flower in bud purplish pink (RHS 76-B), becoming light pink-purple on the underside (RHS 75-C) and almost white in the heart when completely opened. Buds elongated to ovate, angular just before opening. Flower 4.8–5.3 cm in diameter, not flat, somewhat disorderly. Petals nineteen to twenty-four, with two to seven petaloids, orbicular, emarginate at the top and sometimes a little crenate, 18–23 × 13–20 mm. Pistil one, rarely two, phylloid in 75 to 80 percent of the flowers, 9–10 mm long, longer than the longest stamens. The calyx is funnel-shaped, 5–6 × 4.5–5.0 mm, with a faint purple tinge; there is no distinct transition from pedicel to calyx. Sepals are elongated and triangular, 8–9 × 3.5 mm. Flowering season is from late April to early May.

'Oshokun'

The cherry 'Oshokun' appears in Japanese lists of cultivars from the late eighteenth century on, sometimes given as 'Shokun-zakura', and was found, for instance, in the garden Yokuon-en in the first quarter of the nineteenth century. It appears in the literature since then and was offered for export by Japanese nurseries in the 1930s. Nevertheless, it seems to be practically extinct today. It has become one of the phantom cherries that haunts cherry books, mostly because of the imagery that evokes its name. It is mentioned here in the hope that a labeled tree shows up in a forgotten collection somewhere in the world.

Ōshōkun is the Japanese name of a Chinese noblewoman of famed beauty, Wang Zhaojun. In 33 B.C. the horsemen tribe Hsiung-nu threatened the Chinese Han empire from the Mongolian plain in the north. To appease the barbarians, it was decided to present a noblewoman to their leader Tanyu when he came to the palace for negotiations. Ōshōkun became the diplomatic present. Shortly after her departure with Tanyu and his men to the wintry desert plains, she committed suicide with a poisonous drink. It was rumored that the grass that grew on her grave the next spring was fresh and green, whereas everywhere else it was yellow and dry.

Such is the story of Ōshōkun as it appears in official history books, but her tragic death also became a popular theme among poets and writers who worked out history through literature with all the qualities of veritable drama. In these versions Ōshōkun is presented as a lowerclass woman, chosen by the emperor by mistake and only because she had not paid a bribe. The emperor planned to give a noblewoman in name only, choosing instead from the countless women of lesser rank living in and around the palace. Privately, he was determined to send the most ugly one as the barbarians would not see the difference anyway. Because he was the emperor, he could not appear face to face with women of such low rank, so he commanded his court painter Mao to paint as many women as possible. Mao saw an opportunity here and demanded large bribes from any woman in front of his easel if she wanted to be depicted beautifully. Ōshōkun, who was self-confident about her beauty, thought it not necessary to pay. Mao got angry and painted the ugliest face he had ever painted. Because of her most ugly portrait, Ōshōkun was elected. When the announcement was made, she was led before the emperor Yuan Ti. Her delicate beauty shocked the emperor with distress, but the choice had already been announced. He could do nothing else than to give her to Tanyu as was agreed. The victim of intrigue and of her own pride and beauty, Ōshōkun committed suicide in the remote desert.

How do beauty, bribes, and suicide relate to the cherry 'Oshokun'? Indeed, it is the victim of its own beauty, according to Ingram (1948), who thought it suffering for being beautiful. He valued the pure and deep, blushing pink of the blossom as probably the most lovely among all flowering cherries.

Miyoshi also pointed to its conspicuous beauty by incorporating the word *conspicua* in his name, *Prunus serrulata* f. *conspicua*. Despite this beauty, the flowers seem to have appeared in such an abundance that only misshapen spurs were produced. After twenty years Ingram's tree was not any taller than about 2 m. In his description the flowers are "carmine red" in

王昭君

Figure 152. The lady Ōshōkun (Wang Zhaojun) in a Chinese picture book, wearing a winter dress and fur hat. Adapted from a classic set of "pictures of beautiful women" (*meirentu*) in *Zhongguo gudian huadian*.

bud and quickly expand to "a lovely malmaison pink" set together in multi-flowered bunches, usually at the end of the twigs. The medium-sized flowers have short peduncles. The young foliage is bronze to brown-green; developed leaves are glabrous and have a silken texture. Flowering occurs in the second half of April. Miyoshi (1916) spoke of twelve to fifteen sturdy petals, but Ingram mistakenly spoke of single flowers.

Tōemon Sano IV, who grew the tree when his book appeared in 1961, adds that the dark brown foliage is barely out at the time of the blossoming, that the flower has about thirteen petals which are divided in two at the top, and that the pistil is slightly longer than the stamens. Sano's illustrator shows 'Oshokun', though not very detailed, as a cherry with flowers of a rather intense pink that is less intense than 'Kanzan' and resembles 'Fukurokuju'. Sepals are not serrated in this picture and are, like the calyx and pedicel, green. Flowers are borne on a thick twig. Adding this to the relevant details of Miyoshi's original description, 'Oshokun' is described as below.

Prunus 'Oshokun'

Less current synonym: *Prunus serrulata* f. *conspicua*

Description: Tree small, with a flattened crown. Young foliage dark brown to brownish green, barely out in the blossoming season. Mature leaves 10 × 6.5 cm with a tip of 2.5 cm. Serration single with finely tipped teeth. Corymbose inflorescence, with three to five flowers. Peduncles 1.3 cm long. Pedicels 1.5–1.8 cm long. Corymb about 4.5 cm long. Calyx 6 × 4 mm, green. Sepals 6 × 4, green, unserrated. Flower diameter about 4 cm. Petals about sixteen, 18 × 16 mm, in two tiers—an outer red tier and an inner reddish tier, bifid at the apex. Flower in bud red, conical, obovate. Pistil longer than the longest stamens. Flowering season is late April.

'Pink Perfection'

'Pink Perfection' is a prudish name compared to the rich poetic names of other Japanese cherries, but it applies perfectly to the pink flowers of this cultivar. When only some of the flowers are out among the red buds, the pure pink blossom shows to utmost advantage. Among the old garden forms, only 'Daikoku' can match this perfect pink.

'Pink Perfection' was secured by the British nursery of Waterer Sons and Crisp in 1935. It was a seedling of 'Shogetsu', and the pollen parent is like-

Figure 153. 'Oshokun'. From Sano IV (1961).

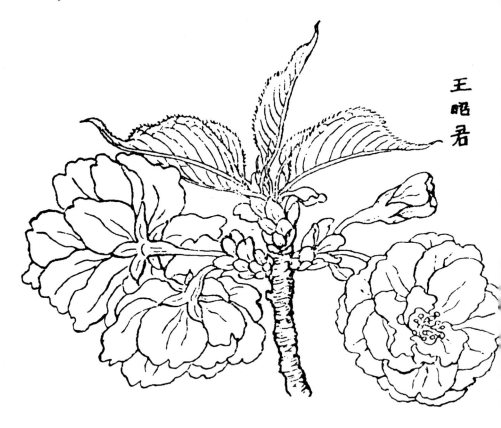

Figure 154. 'Oshokun'. From Miyoshi (1938).

ly to have been 'Kanzan'. From its female parent, 'Pink Perfection' inherited the long, somewhat airy corymbs, and from its male parent it inherited the deep and perfect pink color. The young foliage shows a color that is clearly intermediate between the green of 'Shogetsu' and the coppery brown of 'Kanzan'. The double flowers have about thirty petals and are more than 5 cm in diameter. The shape of a young tree is often disorderly. The thin and hanging branches, often bare for the most part, give the tree an untidy, twiggy appearance. A better branching can be obtained by regularly pruning the tree. Older trees often have a fountainlike shape, showing ascending branches in the middle of the crown and letting the outer,

Figure 155. 'Pink Perfection', perfectly pink blossom. Photo by Arie Peterse, Keukenhof.

thinner branches hang a little on the outer side. 'Pink Perfection' is not a vigorous grower, so it is best grafted high on a stock of *Prunus avium,* if one wants a proper tree of it. It is quite popular as a garden tree in Europe and North America. Although some other successful Western crosses of Japanese cherries equally well deserve to be described in detail, we give 'Pink Perfection' here as an example.

Prunus 'Pink Perfection'

Description: Tree to 5 m high, making a globular crown with often hanging, thin twigs. Young foliage light bronze-green to green. Serration double, only at the base with glands. Stipules medium divided, 11–16 mm long. Corymbose inflorescence, with three to seven flowers. Peduncles 3–4 cm long. Pedicels 2.5–5.5 cm long(!). Flower in bud red (RHS 63-A)(!), becoming pink (RHS 73-C, D) when completely opened. Flower 5.0–5.5(–6.0) cm in diameter, disorderly, often with some imperfect petals in the heart. Petals twenty-eight to thirty-two (sometimes as few as twenty-

Figure 156. The twigs of 'Pink Perfection' hang a little at the end in older trees. Photo by Arie Peterse, 7 May 1985, Wageningen Agricultural University, Netherlands.

four and as many as thirty-six), obovate, 21–25 × 17–25 mm. Pistils two to four, phylloid, about 10 mm long, longer than the stamens. The filament is elongated above the anther. The calyx is saucer-shaped, 3–4 × 5–8 mm (short). Sepals are elongated and triangular, 9–10 × 4–5 mm, clearly serrated(!). Flowering season is from late April to early May.

'Shibayama'

'Shibayama' ("grass hill") points to Shibayama at Fuji-Susuno where this cherry was originally found. The botanical writer Matsuoka (1758) lists in his book, *Igansai-ōhin,* a cherry 'Shibayama Zakura', adding 'Washi-no-o' as synonym. Today, these two are understood as being clearly different

Figure 157. 'Shibayama' as seen in Kyōto. Photo by author, 15 April 1995, Hirano Shrine, Kyōto.

forms. 'Shibayama' was offered for export in the early twentieth century and was described by Wilson (1916), who had seen some trees in Nara and Kyōto. In Japan one finds it as *Prunus lannesiana* 'Shibayama'.

'Shibayama' is related to *Prunus serrulata* var. *pubescens:* its parts are sparsely pubescent, but there is some variability in this, as well as in some of the other plant characteristics. It is easily grown from seed, but as can be expected from a flowering cherry, it is not true to seed and various clones exist. The pubescence of the flower stalks may vary, for instance, as well as the color of the flowers, and the fragrance may be lacking. The markedly long pedicels, however, are always present, and the heart and the stamens of the flower turn to a beautiful violet-purple just before the petals are shed, giving the heart of the flower a red shade. This reveals, according to Kawasaki (1994), a parentage of the Fuji cherry, which shows the same change in color.

Figure 158. 'Shibayama' as seen in Tokyo. Photo by author, 12 April 1997, Tama Forest Science Garden, Tokyo.

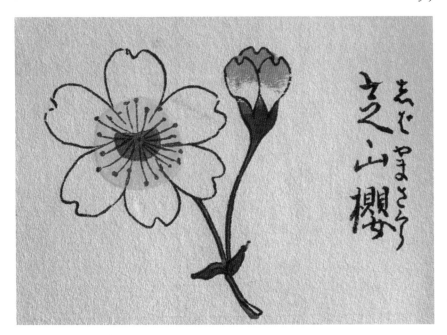

Figure 159. 'Shibayama' was one of the standard garden forms to which others were compared in early cherry botany. From an 1891 reprint of Matsuoka (1758).

Prunus 'Shibayama'

Description: Tree vase-shaped, to 8 m high. Young foliage bronze to green when unfolding; mature leaves sometimes show hairs on the main vein, serration double and coarse, sometimes like the Fuji cherry. Petiole with sporadic hairs. Corymbose inflorescence, with two to four flowers. Peduncles rather short, 1.0–1.5 cm long, thick, often flattened. Pedicels markedly long, 3–4 cm(!). Both occasionally slightly pubescent. Bud scales are orbicular, with few hairs. Flower in bud white with a little pink, becoming white (RHS 155-D) when completely opened, showing a purplish tinge in the heart (RHS 76-D) at the end of blooming. Flower 4.0–4.5 cm in diameter, opening to a flat plane, with a pleasant crushed-almondlike fragrance. Petals five, round, with wrinkles and irregular fringes at the top, about 15 mm in diameter. There is one pistil, perfect, a little shorter than the longest stamens. The calyx is campanulate, 6 × 3 mm, with a purplish shade and occasionally a few hairs at the upper end; there is a distinct transition from pedicel to calyx. Sepals are triangular, 7 × 4 mm, entire or with a few small teeth, pubescent, green. At the end of flowering the filaments of the about forty stamens turn purplish red, with the lower part of the petals. Flowering season is from mid- to late April in Tokyo.

'Shirotae'

Shirotae is the Japanese name of a white cloth made from fibers of the bast of the paper-mulberry (*Broussonetia papyrifera*). It is perfectly white, like the clothlike, thin, and smooth petals of the cherry 'Shirotae'. This cultivar was among those planted at the beginning of the nineteenth century in the garden Yokuon-en of Matsudaira and appeared since then in Japanese collections. Referring to the white (Latin *albidus*) flowers, Miyoshi described this cherry in 1916 as *Prunus serrulata* f. *albida*. In the early twentieth century it was exported to Europe and North America as 'Mount Fuji'. The snow-capped mountain with its perfect cone shape was a preeminent symbol of the exotic Land of the Rising Sun. The name appealed to the fashionable Western public, but can lead now to confusion with the Fuji cherry (*P. incisa*).

Figure 160. 'Shirotae', broad and spreading tree shape. Photo by Arie Peterse, 7 May 1986, Opheusden, Netherlands.

Today in its homeland as well as in the West, 'Shirotae' is one of the better known cultivars thanks to its abundant and beautiful flowers, healthy and vigorous growth, and remarkably broad tree shape. If it gets the room it deserves, it is without doubt the most gorgeous white-flowering cherry. Older trees show an overwhelming bloom that is richer than other white cherries, such as 'Tai-haku' or 'Washi-no-o'. The flowers are, at 5 cm in diameter, among the largest of the flowering cherries, and somewhat resemble a rambling rose. They have a crushed almond fragrance. Outer petals may have a faint pink shade on the outside. Kawasaki (1994) supposes a parentage of 'Mazakura', as for the triploids 'Washi-no-o' and 'Ariake'.

Typical of 'Shirotae' are the large, pale-green leaves that have a serration tipped with long awns. To take full advantage of the splendid spreading habit of this cherry, it is recommended to work it on a high rootstock and give the tree room to display its wide-reaching branches. If the stock is not

Figure 161. 'Shirotae' flowers have thin, clothlike petals with a faint pink coloring on the outer petals. Petaloids develop as perfect petals under better climatic conditions. Unfolding foliage shows long bristles on the serration. Photo by Arie Peterse.

too vigorous, the crown of the tree will come up in the middle and make a dome shaped like Mount Fuji. 'Shirotae' is not suitable as a roadside tree, but is perfect for a park or larger garden.

Prunus 'Shirotae'

Less current synonyms: *Prunus serrulata* f. *albida, (not* Fudschijama-
    Kirsche, not Mount Fuji, not Mount Fuji cherry)
Description: Tree broad, umbrella-shaped with a flattened crown, to 5 m high and 10–12 m wide. Young foliage green (RHS 146-B), well developed in the flowering season. Serration single, without glands but with extremely long teeth(!). Lower stipules slightly divided, 2–3 cm long. Corymbose inflorescence, with four to six flowers (to eight flowers in some young trees). Peduncles 2.5–5.0 cm long, sturdy, up to 3 mm thick(!). Pedicels 1.5–3.5 cm long. Flower in bud white with a faint pink tinge, becoming pure white (RHS 155-D) when completely opened. Flower 5.0–5.5 cm in diameter, fuzzy and curly, with pleasant almondlike fragrance. Petals five, with one to six extra (approximately petaloid) petals, orbicular, slightly emarginate at the top, 22–24 × 19–21 mm, smooth, thin. There is one pistil, perfect, 11–12 mm long, a little shorter than the longest stamens. The calyx is campanulate, 9 × 4 mm, with a faint purple tinge; there is a distinct transition from pedicel to calyx. Sepals are elongated and triangular, at the base a little narrow, with a few teeth or green hairs. Flowering season is from late April to early May. 'Shirotae' has a triploid set of chromosomes (2n = 24).

'Shogetsu'

Due to a misunderstanding in its history, this superb cherry became known as 'Shimidsu-zakura' in the West.

Miyoshi described it as *Prunus serrulata* var. *superba* and 'Shogetsu' in 1916. 'Shogetsu' appeared with 'Miyako' in early-twentieth-century lists of Japanese cultivar collections, such as *Okashū* of 1904 and at Arakawa in 1912, showing that these were two forms. Wilson described this 'Miyako' very briefly under the name *P. lannesiana* f. *miyako;* it is now extinct.

Along with 'Miyako', a second, now extinct cherry, 'Oku-miyako', was offered for export by Japanese nurseries in the early twentieth century. This cherry was described by Miyoshi as *P. serrulata* f. *longipes* in 1916. It had light pink flowers in 8.5-cm long corymbs that were not nodding, but stood sideways (which makes *longipes* not the most adequate epithet); its flowers had about ten petals and a slight fragrance reminding him of freesia's.

Neither 'Miyako' (an old name for the imperial capital Kyōto) nor 'Oku-miyako' ("deeply hidden in Miyako") are connected to any particular cherry today, but sometimes are used incorrectly as synonyms for 'Shogetsu'. Because 'Oku-miyako' and 'Miyako' were different plants, their names should not be used for 'Shogetsu'.

More confusion was raised by Ingram, who described a cherry he received as 'Shogetsu' from the Arnold Arboretum, Jamaica Plain, Massachusetts, under the names 'Oku-miyako' and *Prunus serrulata longipes* in 1925. A year later when he visited the Sakura Kwai, apparently realizing that something was wrong, he requested scions of 'Shogetsu' to be sent from Japan to his home in Kent, England. Because he could not fit this true 'Shogetsu' plant in Miyoshi's description of 'Oku-miyako', which he (Ingram) apparently had misunderstood earlier, Ingram later repaired his mistake by introducing a new name for his "longipes": 'Shimidsu-zakura', or *P. serrulata* 'Shimidsuii'. Ingram (1941) gives the impression that his struggling with the German (of Miyoshi 1916) created the misunderstanding in the first place.

To complicate the situation, Jefferson (1984) took 'Shogetsu' (synonym *P. lannesiana* Wilson 'Superba') to be a different cherry from 'Miyako' that he considered synonymous to 'Oku-miyako', *P. serrulata* f. *longipes,* and *P. serrulata* Shimidsuii), thus introducing a different confusion.

Shimidsu is an old spelling for Shimizu, and was chosen by Ingram to honor Mayor Kengo Shimizu, who arranged for the planting of an important collection of cherries along the Arakawa River in his village of Kōhoku near Tokyo. The undertaking, begun in 1886, saved many cherry cultivars from extinction, as related in an earlier chapter.

The word *shōgetsu* translates as "moonlight on the pine trees," leaving the reader free to his or her poetic imagination. No dictionary gives any further explanation for the word. The cultivar 'Shogetsu' is described in Japan under the name *Prunus lannesiana* Wilson 'Superba'.

In spite of the confusing history surrounding its name, the identity of 'Shogetsu' is not in doubt. It is a superb garden cherry with large and showy, loosely hanging corymbs. The inflorescences with three to six flowers can be up to 15 cm long. With 'Fugenzo', it is one of the latest-blooming flowering cherries; in more temperate climate zones it might be in full bloom as late as the first week of June. The 5-cm large, double flowers are light pink in bud, but expand to a pure, snow-white. The hanging flowers, when completely opened, may be likened to little ballerinas, with the green legs below their petticoats formed by phylloid carpels, of which two are often found. The petticoat is represented by the white tiers of petals. 'Ichiyo' flowers also resemble ballerinas, but the petals of 'Shogetsu' are frilled and pleated—certainly observed at the end of the flowering season—and suggest the petticoat idea even stronger. 'Ichiyo' flowers one or two weeks earlier and its corymbs are considerably shorter.

'Shogetsu' is not a vigorous grower and makes a spreading, often flattened crown, with thinner, slightly hanging branches at the outer sides. Young foliage is green, apparently delicious and greedily attacked by bugs and caterpillars. In spite of this minor drawback, it is a well-known and popular cherry.

Figure 162. 'Shogetsu' has a spreading tree shape. Photo by Arie Peterse, 15 May 1985, Opheusden, Nursery Peterse, Netherlands.

Figure 163. The corymbs of 'Shogetsu' have long flower stalks. Photo by Arie Peterse, 12 May 1986, Opheusden, Nursery Peterse, Netherlands.

Prunus 'Shogetsu'

Less current synonyms: 'Shimidsu-zakura', 'Superba', (not 'Miyako', not 'Oku-miyako')

Description: Tree umbrella-shaped, making a globular crown, somewhat flattened at the top, to 5 m high. Young foliage green (RHS 144-A), well developed in the flowering season. Serration double or single, with awn-tipped teeth, without glands. Stipules deeply bifurcated, 12–17 mm long. Corymbose inflorescence, with four to six flowers. Peduncles 3–6 cm long. Pedicels 3.5–5.0 cm long. Corymb to 15 cm long(!). Flower in bud light pink, becoming pure white when completely opened. Flower 4.5–5.0 cm in diameter, fuzzy and curly, usually open in the heart. Petals twenty-two to twenty-five (sometimes as few as twenty and as many as twenty-eight), oval, obovate, emarginate and slightly notched at the top, 19–21 × 12–17 mm, with folds. The flowers that open first usually have more petals. A few petaloids. Pistils two, rarely three, phylloid, 5–6 mm long, as long as or longer than the longest stamens. The calyx is wide and funnel-shaped, 3–4 × 3–4 mm, short(!); there is an indistinct transition from pedicel to calyx. Sepals are 7–8 × 4–5 mm, green, usually clearly serrated. Flowering season is from early to late May. 'Shogetsu' has a diploid set of chromosomes (2n = 16).

'Shujaku'

Shujaku is the name of a mythical phoenix, the fire bird, one of the four gods of the Far-Eastern compass. According to diviners of ancient times, the fire bird Shujaku guarded the south. Three other gods guarded the east, west, and north. With the founding of Kyōto in the eighth century, the southern gate of its imperial palace became the gate of Shujaku, and the wide avenue that led from it to the south was called Shujaku Avenue. In the natural sciences of that time, the southern direction of the fire bird Shujaku related to the sun and associated with the color red. An old word for red ink is *shu*, written with the same Chinese character as in the bird's name. Thus, this cherry was named for the color of its blossom, which, though not exactly fire-red, is most characteristic and unique among the cultivars of *Prunus serrulata*. The cherry 'Shujaku' appears from about the 1830s in lists of Japanese cherry collections and is today rather well known in its homeland. It was offered for export in the 1930s by the Hakoneya nursery (Wada 1937).

Figure 164. The fire bird Shujaku, which came to resemble the peacock in later history, is shown here as it appeared in a poetry collection, *Ise-shū*. Sixteenth century, Nishi-honganji Temple, Kyōto.

'Shujaku' (sometimes spelled as 'Suzaku' or 'Sujaku') makes with its spreading and ascending branches a tree of about 4–5 m high and wide. The strikingly delicate shell-pink (RHS 62-B) of the blossom in its prime is always a convincing point in classifying this cherry among other semi-double or double pink cherries. When standing under the tree, one views the flowers hanging as little saucers on their slender stalks in a nice contrast of colors with the fresh green or light bronze of the young leaves. Pedicels are very thin and compel the buds and flowers to dangle in the slightest breeze. The somewhat bell-like shape of the flowers led Miyoshi (1916) to describe this cherry as *Prunus serrulata* f. *campanuloïdes*. In Japan one finds it as *P. lannesiana* 'Shujaku'.

Prunus 'Shujaku'

Less current synonyms: *Prunus serrulata* f. *campanuloïdes,* Sujaku, Suzaku
    Description: Tree ascending and vase-shaped, with slender branches, to 5 m high and 5 m wide. Young foliage light green with a bronze shade

Figure 165. 'Shujaku' has hanging corymbs on thin stalks and somewhat campanulate flowers. Photo by Arie Peterse, 29 April 1996, Tama Forest Science Garden, Tokyo.

(RHS 144-A, 152-A). Serration single, awn-tipped. Stipules only slightly divided, 10–15 mm long. Corymbose inflorescence, with three to four or even five flowers. Peduncles 1.5 cm long. Pedicels 2.5–4.5 cm long, thin(!). Flower in bud deep pink, becoming a delicate shell-pink (RHS 62-B) when completely opened. Flower 3.5–4.0 cm in diameter, expanding to almost flat and open but always somewhat bell-shaped. Petals five to six or even up to twelve, orbicular or oval, emarginate at the top, 18–19 × 14–17 mm. There is one pistil, perfect, 8–10 mm long; about as long as the longest stamens. The calyx is narrow campanulate, 6–7 × 3 mm, with a faint purple tinge; there is a distinct transition from pedicel to calyx. Sepals are elongated and triangular, 6–7 × 2–3 mm, unserrated. Fruits blackish. Flowering season is from mid- to late April in Tokyo, a little earlier than 'Kanzan'.

'Sumizome'

The Japanese *sumizome* is a poetic word that means "dyed black" or "stained with ink." It has many connotations. Usually it is understood as the black of the garments of priests or the dark color of mourning robes, therefore pointing to a gloomy black or gray. The meaning extends as far as a gloomy dusk or the precarious uncertainty of human life.

The word *sumizome* entered cherry history long ago. According to an ancient legend, an important Minister Mototsune Fujiwara died early in 891 A.D. He was buried in the lonely fields of Fukakusa and a poem was recited at the grave:

> Oh, cherries of Fukakusa's fields
> You must lament his death
> Your blossom will be gloomy gray this spring.

The "gloomy gray" is conveyed by the word *sumizome*. The fields of Fuka-kusa were deserted and shaggy with many wild cherries. The poetical arti-fice lies in the connection of the gloominess of the place to the sharply contrasting bright beauty of cherries in flower. The poet is not suggesting that the cherries should change color nor that they are black; rather it was his wish that their bloom would be felt by all people as a gloomy reminder of the uncertainty of life. The story became the theme of a famous Noh theater piece in later centuries.

Today in southern Kyōto, two railway stations are named Fukakusa and Sumizome, respectively. Not far from the latter station is the modest Sumi-zome Temple where, according to a notice on the premises, stands the third generation of the original 'Sumizome' cherry. It is a single, white cherry with an unpretentious show of blooms shortly before the green foliage ap-pears. It seems to be merely a selected wild form of the Oshima cherry.

From the end of the seventeenth century until the nineteenth, the Sumi-zome District was famous among traveling merchants as a stop-over with tea houses and brothels. The origin of a garden cherry 'Sumizome' must be thought of as belonging to this period. As the name of a cherry variety, 'Sumizone' appears for the first time in a Japanese balalaika songbook dated 1701. In the nineteenth century it appears in lists of specialized col-lections in Japan. For example, in the *Zoku kafu* of 1804, an extended ver-sion of the 1803 list of cherries grown in the garden of the daimyo Seihō Ichihashi, three double cherries named 'Sumizome' are found. Appealing names were sometimes applied more than one time to unrelated cherries.

Miyoshi described a 'Sumizome' similar to the one in the Sumizome Temple under the name *Prunus serrulata* f. *subfusca* in 1916. It has small, white, single flowers, usually in two-fold, short-stalked inflorescences. Without its name plate, such a tree would be considered as just another Oshima cherry. Apart from the tree at Sumizome Temple, this form does not need to be kept in cultivation.

Another 'Sumizome' was brought from Japan to the Arnold Arboretum, Jamaica Plain, Massachusetts, by Wilson, who described it in 1916. He speaks of white, single, or almost single flowers that are very large and fragrant, different from the form as it was described by Miyoshi. The description is too short and is at present not fixed to an extant tree.

Years later Ingram received material from the Arnold Arboretum, but found it to be semi-double and pink. It, too, was something other than the cherry that either Miyoshi or Wilson had described as 'Sumizome'. Ingram (1929, 1948) relates that it exactly resembled "so far as my memory serves" the 'Sumizome' plants that he had seen in Japan. He concluded that there are two types of 'Sumizome' and described the semi-double pink cherry from the Arnold Arboretum as *Prunus serrulata sumizome* Ingram nov.

Figure 166. Ingram's 'Sumizome' with dark spot in the heart of the flower at the end of flowering. Photo by Arie Peterse, 1997, Opheusden, Nursery Peterse, Netherlands.

comb. This very successful semi-double, pink cherry was offered for export by the Yokohama Nursery Company in the 1930s, and can still be found in the West. A tree labeled "Taoyame" that stands today at the little shop of the Hirano Shrine, Kyōto, appears to be Ingram's semi-double, pink 'Sumizome', but Kayama's (1933, p. 17) description of the Hirano 'Taoyame' does not cover 'Taoyame' proper, nor this tree at the shop. 'Taoyame' proper is no longer seen at the Hirano Shrine.

The 'Sumizome' of Ingram has soft pink flowers with a diameter of more than 5 cm, somewhat resembling 'Fukurokuju'. Ingram likened them to the flowers of 'Hokusai', which is closely related to 'Fukurokuju'. The flowers have an open heart, and the ovary is visible. Petals are thick, sturdy, and wrinkled. Both Ingram and Chadbund (1972) found the flowers to be fragrant. The young foliage is bronze-green, and the tree has an ascending vase shape, not as large as 'Fukurokuju' though. A purplish stain in the heart of the flowers appears before they fade to complete dark pink. This characteristic of the flowers may help as an aid to memorize the name 'Sumizome' (dyed black), although the name has another origin.

Care should be taken not to confuse Ingram's 'Sumizome' with the Oshima-type 'Sumizome'.

Prunus 'Sumizome' (Ingram)

Synonyms: *Prunus serrulata sumizome* Ingram, Ingram's Sumizome

Description: Tree vase-shaped and ascending to 6 m high. Young foliage bronze-green to dark green (RHS 146-A). Serration often double, coarse, with a few small white glands at the base. Some leaves are orbicular in shape(!). Stipules medium to deeply bifurcated, 1.5–3.0 cm long. Corymbose inflorescence, with three to five flowers. Peduncles 2.0–4.5 cm long, thick and sturdy(!). Pedicels 1.5–3.5 cm long. Flower in bud purple-pink, turning pink to white (RHS 75-D) when completely opened, fading to purple-pink at the end of blooming, darker in the heart. Flower about 5 cm in diameter, disorderly with a few petals standing upright in the heart. Petals fourteen to seventeen, with one to three petaloids, orbicular, usually slightly emarginate at the top, 20–23 × 17–21 mm, much rumpled, even more than with 'Fukurokuju' or 'Hokusai'. There is one pistil, perfect, 10–11 mm long, usually longer than the longest stamens. Stamens are short, 4–6 mm. The calyx is broad and funnel-shaped, 6 × 4–5 mm, with a faint purple tinge; there is a distinct transition from pedicel to calyx.

Sepals are elongated and triangular, 10–11 × 4.5–5.0 mm (rarely narrower at the base), green, unserrated. The inflorescences give a robust appearance. Flowering season is from late April to early May.

'Tagui-arashi'

The name *Tagui-arashi* is written with two Chinese characters that can also be read as *rui* and *ran*. Thus 'Ruiran' and 'Tagui-arashi', or even 'Rui-arashi', are synonyms of a linguistic origin. *Tagui* means "a kind of" and *arashi* refers to Arashiyama, a scenic area west of Kyōto. This cultivar, therefore, literally an "Arashi type," was one of the cherries selected from the hills of Arashiyama. It is a single-flowered cherry that has red-brown foliage developing in a nice contrast with the white or slightly pink-shaded blossom. A similar spring show is offered by such cherries as 'Bendono' and 'Arashiyama'.

Manabu Miyoshi described a slightly different 'Tagui-arashi' under the name *Prunus serrulata* f. *similis;* the Latin *similis* points—as does the Japanese *tagui*—to a resemblance in the botanic sense. This form had large flowers with a diameter of 5 cm on thick pedicels.

'Tagui-arashi' appears among the cherries that were planted along the Arakawa River near Tokyo, according to a list made in 1886. Since then it has always been a collector's item rather than a popularly known cultivar. The single, light pink flowers are of value and the plant's rather uncultivated appearance gives it an unpretentious beauty that matches a more naturalistic approach to gardening. The young foliage is brown-green and leaves are singly serrated; the underside of the mature leaf shows a slight whitish shade, betraying its family relation with the Japanese mountain cherry.

Prunus 'Tagui-arashi'
Less current synonyms: Ruiran, Rui-arashi, *Prunus serrulata* f. *similis*

Description: Tree broad and vase-shaped, to about 7 m high. Young foliage deep bronze-green to green (RHS 175-B, 152-A), only partly developed in the flowering season. Serration rather fine, single and with glands. Stipules barely divided, 13–15 mm long. Corymbose inflorescence, with three to five flowers. Peduncles 1.0–2.5 cm long. Pedicels 1.7–2.3 cm long. Flower in bud light pink, becoming white with a shade of pink (RHS 76-C) when completely opened. Flower about 4 cm in diameter, opening to a flat plane, with faint fragrance. Petals five, with rarely a few petaloids,

Figure 167. 'Tagui-arashi', flowers and young foliage. Photo by author, 13 April 1997, Yūki Experimental Station of the Flower Association of Japan, Ibaraki Prefecture.

oval, slightly emarginate at the top, 17–19 × 12–14 mm. There is one pistil, perfect, 12 mm long; it is as long as or shorter than the longest stamens. Calyx 7.5 × 4 mm, with a purple tinge; there is a distinct transition from pedicel to calyx. Sepals are elongated and triangular, 7 × 3 mm, occasionally with a few teeth. Remarkable is the bright red of the bracts and bractlets. The heart of the flower turns at the end of flowering to a purplish shade of pink. Flowering season is late April. 'Tagui-arashi' has a diploid set of chromosomes (2n = 16).

Koshio-yama has close family ties with 'Tagui-arashi'. It was described as *Prunus serrulata* f. *communis* by Miyoshi. The cultivar was named after Koshioyama, six kilometers southeast of Arashiyama, where it was selected from the wild cherries, according to the encyclopedia *Kokon-yōran-kō* (Yashiro 1821–1841). Like Arashiyama, Koshioyama also was famous for its cherries since ancient times. The cultivar 'Koshio-yama' is distinguished from 'Tagui-arashi' in minor details. The underside of its leaves is rather whitish and the upperside is, like 'Bendono', shiny. Its calyx is short (5 mm), and its flowers have slight pink shading; they are almost white. 'Koshio-yama' has a diploid set of chromosomes (2n = 16).

'Tai-haku'

'Tai-haku' is written with the Chinese characters *tai* ("thick" or "big") and *haku* ("white"). Indeed the flowers are remarkably big and white. Ingram tells the story of a Mrs. Freeman of Sussex, England, who, when visiting France in 1899, heard about some magnificent cherries from a Frenchman who had seen the trees in Japan. She wrote to a Japanese friend of the Frenchman and received back several plants, some previously unknown in England. When Ingram visited the elderly Mrs. Freeman in 1923, he noticed one of these cherries had been planted among vigorous shrubs where it was unable to compete and was obviously dying. Only a few blossoms could be seen on one or two branches, but they were of such exceptional size and beauty that Ingram asked for a few twigs of bud wood. From this tiny sample, thousands of trees were propagated and eventually grown in Europe, North America, South Africa, New Zealand, and Australia. In this way, Ingram would later write, "the loveliest of all Japanese *sato-zakura* was miraculously saved from extinction." But the story does not end there.

Figure 168. 'Koshio-yama' (left) and 'Bendono' (right). From Miyoshi (1921b, nos. 86 and 87).

Two years after obtaining Mrs. Freeman's material, Ingram returned to Japan to search for new cherries. His host, Mr. Taka Tsukasa, introduced him to the aging Mr. Seisaku Funatsu of Kōhaku, the garden cherry specialist who also collected antique scroll paintings and colored drawings of flowering cherries. One of these illustrations depicted Mrs. Freeman's cherry with its large white flowers and young copper-colored leaves. Mr. Funatsu explained that the cherry had been grown in Kyōto but was now lost to cultivation. Before Ingram could send plant material to him, Mr. Funatsu died; however, Masuhiko Kayama, a cherry researcher in Kyōto, received scions from Ingram that were grafted by Tōemon Sano. In this way this cherry was reintroduced to Japan in 1932. It was named 'Tai-haku' by Ingram's host, Prince Taka Tsukasa.

Ingram described this cherry as *Prunus serrulata* 'Tai-haku'. In Japan one finds it as *P. lannesiana* 'Taihaku'. It must be concluded that when 'Tai-haku' reached Europe earlier, that is before 1900, it was under a different name. The older history of 'Tai-haku' is not clarified yet, but it is possible that a forgotten garden form will yet show up in Japan and prove to be the same. The Jindai Botanical Park gives 'Koma-tsunagi' as a synonym for 'Tai-haku' (see Tōkyō toritsu Jindai Shokubutsu Kōen 1991, p. 155). Indeed

Figure 169. 'Tai-haku' has erect flowers on sturdy stalks. Photo by author, 18 April 1996, Kyōto Botanic Garden.

the two are much alike, confirmed by Mr. T. Kawasaki (personal communication). 'Koma-tsunagi' originates from Shōren-in Temple in Kyōto and was offered for export in the 1930s.

Prunus 'Tai-haku'

Less current synonyms: great white cherry, taihaku

Description: Tree umbrella-shaped and broad, to 8–10 m high and 10 m wide. Young foliage brown to bronze-green (RHS 152-A). Serration single, long bristles without glands. Stipules slightly divided, 2–3 cm long. Corymbose inflorescence, with three to four flowers. Peduncles 1.5–2.5 cm long. Pedicels 1.5–3.5 cm long. Flowers in bud have a slight pink tinge, becoming white (RHS 155-D) when completely opened. Flower 5.5– 6.0(–7.0)

Figure 170. 'Tai-haku' makes large, spreading limbs as it ages. Photo by author, 3 March 1997, Arboretum Kalmthout, Antwerp Province, Belgium.

cm in diameter(!), opening to a flat plane. Petals five, rarely petaloids, orbicular, emarginate at the top, occasionally fimbriate, 30–33 × 24–28 mm. There is one pistil in most flowers, absent in others, perfect when present, 15–16 mm long, longer than the longest stamens. The calyx is campanulate, 8 × 4–5 mm, with a purple tinge. Sepals are elongated and triangular, 12–14 × 5 mm, occasionally with a few teeth. Flowering season is late April.

'Taizan-fukun'

The story is told about a certain Minister Narinori Fujiwara in ancient Japan, who loved cherry trees so much that he had his residence in the capital completely planted with them. The place became even more famous and popularly known as the Cherry Estate after the writer Ki no Tsurayuki (872?–945 A.D.) came to live there. An early fourteenth-century version of the old Japanese Heike Tale, as well as a Noh theater song of later date, tells us that this minister was disappointed with the brevity of the flowering season of his cherries. To relieve the problem he began to pray three times a month to the Chinese god Taizan Fukun (*Heike Monogatari, Engyō,* quoted by Yamada 1941). The prayers were heard, and a celestial nymph was sent to investigate. Seeing cherries so beautiful, the nymph could not contain herself and broke off a spray of a tree, bringing it back to the other world. There she appeared before Taizan Fukun, who reproached her for damaging such a beautiful cherry. However, seeing the blossom and hearing her story, he was delighted over the ardent but delicate wish of the minister. From that time on the Cherry Estate trees flowered every year for thirty-seven days.

The story became famous through the Noh theater piece, and the god's name was applied to the cherry. This cherry name appears for the first time in a list of the early seventeenth century, and was clearly described and illustrated by Matsuoka in 1758. It is quite old and was cultivated in a broad region of Japan, mainly on the Japan Sea side of the main island of Honshū, but also in Tokyo, Kyōto, and their surroundings.

The small, compact, double flowers and the pubescent leaf stalks and flower stalks of this cherry seem to point in the direction of *Prunus pendula*. Many flowers seem to be set on umbels. Looking closely, however, one sees that the inflorescences are not umbellate but set on short peduncles or even perfectly corymbose. Also the shape of the flower and the leaf, as well as the tree shape, resemble the other forms usually related to *P. serrulata*. 'Taizan-fukun' has, like 'Shibayama' or 'Takasago', some pubescent parts, but this characteristic alone is not reason enough to group such pubescent cherries under a different species name, as some authors have proposed.

Miyoshi (1916) described 'Taizan-fukun' as *Prunus fruticosa* f. *ambigua* for its uncertain, ambiguous classification. It was described as a hybrid of *P.* ×*subhirtella* and *P. pseudo-cerasus* Lindley under the name *P.* ×*miyoshii* 'Ambigua' by Ohwi and Ohta (1973).

'Taizan-fukun' is a shrub with ascending growth and pink, double flowers set on slender branches. In winter, the broomlike shape of this cherry with its many branches, thinner than the average garden cherry, is characteristic. 'Taizan-fukun' is easily propagated from side shoots that develop from superficial roots. This method has induced mutant forms over the centuries of its cultivation so that one may come across different strains of 'Taizan-fukun', such as 'Hoki-zakura'. In fact, 'Asano' could also very well be such a strain.

The best, most floribund forms of the Japanese 'Taizan-fukun' have a widely funnel-shaped calyx, showing in a cross section a triangle with equal sides; in this hollow calyx many undeveloped petals are stuffed together, as if they could not find their way out while expanding. Other forms of 'Taizan-fukun' have a more slender calyx. 'Taizan-fukun' has pale pink flowers about 3 cm in diameter with approximately fifty to sixty petals. The young foliage is bronze-green and expands to relatively small, mature leaves. The bast of two-year-old branches peels off slightly. The broom-like shape of the tree has advantages for private and narrower gardens. The blossoming of 'Taizan-fukun' is quite abundant and, like its form 'Hoki-zakura', it keeps its flowers for a long time.

Prunus 'Taizan-fukun'

Less current synonym: *Prunus* ×*miyoshii* 'Ambigua'

Description: Tree rather narrow and vase-shaped, with many thin branches(!), to 4 m high. Young foliage shiny green to bronze-green (RHS 146-A), already unfolded in the flowering season. Leaves fully developed are relatively small, 4–10 × 3–4 cm. Serration double, with short awns.

Figure 171. 'Taizan-fukun'. Photo by Arie Peterse, 29 April 1996, Tama Forest Science Garden, Tokyo.

Figure 172. 'Taizan-fukun' in an old woodblock print, showing the typical branching of this garden form. From an 1891 reprint of Matsuoka (1758).

Petiole pubescent(!). Stipules divided, 7–9 mm, short. Corymbose inflorescence, with two to four flowers. Peduncles short, 4–8 mm. Pedicels 1.5–2.5 cm long, not very pubescent. Flower in bud pink, becoming light pink (RHS 65-D) when completely opened. Flower 2.5–3.5 cm in diameter, fluffy as a powder puff. Petals about forty-five to sixty, oval to elliptic, pointed at the top, 12–14 × (3–)7–9 mm. Many undeveloped petals stuffed inside the calyx. There is one pistil, perfect, 8–11 mm long; longer than the stamens. Number of stamens is very large, forty to fifty. The calyx is widely campanulate or funnel-shaped, 5 × 5 mm, glabrous, with a purple tinge; there is a smooth transition from pedicel to calyx. Sepals are triangular, 4 × 3–4 mm, with a slight reddish tinge, unserrated. Flowering season is from mid- to late April in Tokyo.

'Takasago'

A peculiar double pine, growing intertwined in Takasago, made that city famous. According to a legend, the tree was married to another pine in nearby Ōsaka. Through a Noh theater song on this theme, the pines became a well-known symbol for faithful matrimony lasting into venerable old age. The Takasago Noh song is still sung at wedding parties to wish newlyweds a long-lasting, loyal marriage, and a popular wedding present in many Japanese households is a pair of dolls representing the Takasago couple as a gray-bearded Darby and a gray-haired Joan. Apart from its pines, the city is also known for its cherry blossoms, though it has not generated new forms.

The origin of the cherry name 'Takasago' is more complicated. 'Takasago' became a poetic epithet in stereotyped, traditional poetry. For example, a poetry card game known as *hyakunin-isshu* has been played in Japan for generations. In this very popular game a poem on Takasago takes flowering cherries as theme rather than the famous pines, and here lies the origin of the cherry name.

'Takasago' appears in lists of cherries in more recent times, but 'Naden', a synonym, is found in older lists from the mid-eighteenth century on. 'Nanden' ("southern sky") is another synonym. 'Takasago' was imported by Robert Fortune and marketed by the Standish Royal Nursery at Ascot, England. It was formerly known as *Cerasus sieboldii rubraplena*, Von Siebold's cherry, or *Prunus sieboldii* (see Carrière 1866). Be that as it may,

Miyoshi (1916) stated that he "discovered" 'Takasago' in the Arakawa River collection at Kōhoku.

Confusingly enough, there exists also a 'Naten', a nonpubescent cherry written with the same characters as 'Naden' and sometimes pronounced as 'Naden'; it is very similar to 'Gosho-zakura'. Both have five flowers in a peduncled umbel (see Kokuritsu Idengaku Kenkyūjo 1995, pp. 51, 58).

'Oh-nanden' ("great southern hall"), described by Wilson, is the same as 'Nanden' ("southern hall"), which was shortly described as f. *sericea* by Miyoshi; there is no relation with the cherries above nor with 'Takasago'; both 'Oh-nanden' and 'Nanden' were purplish pink, semi-double forms and are now probably extinct (see Kawasaki 1994, pp. 285—286).

Typical of the cherry 'Takasago' is the downy pubescence on many plant parts that at first is reminiscent of *Prunus tomentosa*. One may take the long beard of Takasago's Darby and the white hair of Takasago's Joan as an aid to memorize the name. Those who have seen *P. apetala* can see its parental influence in 'Takasago'. Various authors have suggested such a connection because the pubescence of the leaf and petiole, and the young sprouts of both are very similar.

The dense pubescence of 'Takasago' induced some botanists to distinguish it as a separate species. Wilson (1916) gave it as *Prunus sieboldii,* after an extremely short mention in *Gartenflora* by Wittmack (1902). Miyoshi (1916) and Ingram (1948) listed it under *P. serrulata,* and Bean (1976), who usually followed Ingram, gave it as *P. sieboldii* (Carrière) Wittmack. Recent Japanese sources give 'Takasago' as *P.* ×*sieboldii* Wittmack 'Caespitosa'. Apart from its striking pubescence, though, 'Takasago' has no characteristics that distinguish it from typical *P. serrulata* forms.

'Takasago' has three to six light pink, semi-double flowers in its corymbs. The young leaf sprouts are a peculiar light red to orange-bronze, turning green when expanding; then the leaves show a tip typical of *Prunus serrulata* forms. 'Takasago' is an abundantly blooming cultivar with a slow growth, making a vase-shaped shrub or small tree. In midsummer without flowers, it is quickly identified by the rough pubescence on both sides of the leaves. Most likely several clones are in cultivation, since forms with accessory sepals are found alongside forms with the usual five sepals.

'Takasago' is a healthy plant and proved fertile as a parent of 'Matsumae-hayazaki' and other forms obtained in the Matsumae region of Hokkaidō by the cherry specialist Mr. Masatoshi Asari.

Figure 173. 'Takasago' has downy sprouts and pubescent pedicels. Photo by author, 13 April 1997, Yūki Experimental Station of the Flower Association of Japan, Ibaraki Prefecture.

Prunus 'Takasago'

Less current synonyms: 'Caespitosa', Musha-zakura, Naden, Nanden,
  Prunus ×*sieboldii* Wittmack 'Caespitosa', Von Siebold's cherry
Description: Tree vase-shaped, eventually about 7 m high and 6 m wide. Young foliage light red-bronze just after appearing, quickly turning to green (RHS 152-A, 144-A); leaves well developed in the height of the flowering season. Serration single or sometimes double, with small, light pink glands to the top of the leaf. Petiole and leaf blade velvety-pubescent(!). Stipules slightly divided, short, about 8 mm long. Corymbose inflorescence, with three to six flowers that point sideways. Peduncles 1.5– 4.0 cm long. Pedicels 1.5–4.0 cm long. Both flower stalks distinctly pubescent. Flower in bud pink, becoming light pink (RHS 75-D) to almost white when completely opened. Flower 3.5–4.0(–4.5) cm in diameter, opening to a rather flat plane, with a slight scent. Petals ten to thirteen, including a few petaloids, oval, slightly emarginate at the top, 16–19 × 12–13 mm. There is one pistil (rarely an extra pistil without an ovary), perfect, with a few hairs at

the base(!), 10–12 mm long, about as long as the longest stamens. The calyx is thickly funnel-shaped or campanulate, 6–7 × 3.5–4.0 mm, pubescent, with a darker shade than the pedicel; there is a distinct transition from pedicel to calyx. Sepals are elongated, 7 × 4 mm, narrowing a little towards the base, unserrated, with a faint purple tinge. Some forms have five distinct accessory sepals, 5 × 2 mm. Flowering season is late April. 'Takasago' has a triploid set of chromosomes (2n = 24).

'Taki-nioi'

'Taki-nioi' is written with two Chinese characters. The first, *taki* ("waterfall"), refers to the way in which the horizontally feathering branches are held up, producing out of the heart of the tree layer upon layer that make up its cascading crown. The second, *nioi* ("fragrance") refers to the pure white, small, single flowers that send forth a sweet odor reminiscent of crushed almonds. In older trees the pleasantly fragrant blossom is presented in clouds on top of each other, giving a scented blossom cascade.

The name 'Taki-nioi' appears in lists of cherry collections since the beginning of the twentieth century, often written differently: *Roko, Taki-niowasu,* or *Rōkō* ("incense waterfall"). Miyoshi described it as *Prunus serrulata* f. *cataracta,* which captured the idea of falling water, but not exactly the idea of cascading.

'Taki-nioi' is rare in Japanese and European collections, but an old tree is found in the garden of the conservator of the Rombergpark in Dortmund, Germany. It is likely that this tree was planted by German horticulturist Gerd Krüssmann, author of the *Manual of Cultivated Broad-Leaved Trees and Shrubs* and other works.

The picturesque beauty of 'Taki-nioi' in bloom resembles that of 'Jonioi', another of the fragrant cherries (*nioi-zakura*), but its young foliage is bronze-brown instead of green. Assuming the likely parentage of the O-shima cherry, Kawasaki (1994) presented this cherry as *Prunus lannesiana* var. *speciosa* 'Cataracta' comb. nov.

'Taki-nioi' is rarely offered for sale by nurseries, rarely seen, and hardly known. However, it has several attractive features: a lovely cascading shape; healthy growth; abundant little white flowers that contrast nicely with the bronze-brown foliage appearing late in the cherry season; and a sweet scent that surrounds the tree with a waterfall of fragrance.

Figure 174. 'Taki-nioi'. Photo by Arie Peterse, 15 May 1986, Dortmund.

Prunus 'Taki-nioi'

Less current synonym: 'Cataracta'

   Description: Tree broad and vase-shaped with a flattened crown, to 6 m high. Young foliage bronze-brown. Serration single and with small light pink glands on the teeth. Stipules deeply bifurcated, 16–20 mm long. Corymbose inflorescence, with five to six flowers. Peduncles 2–3 cm long. Pedicels 2–3 cm long. Flower in bud slightly pink, becoming pure white. Occasionally the petals do not touch each other when the flower is completely opened. Flower 4.0–4.5 cm in diameter, opening to a flat plane, not perfectly symmetrical, with a distinct fragrance not as strong as that of 'Jo-nioi'. Petals five, oval-elliptic, slightly emarginate at the top, 21–22 × 13–14 mm. There is one pistil, perfect, 8–9 mm long, shorter than the stamens. The calyx is campanulate, 6 × 3.5 mm, with a faint purple tinge. Sepals are elongated and triangular, 9–10 × 3.0–3.5 mm, occasionally with a single tooth. Flowering season is from early to mid May. 'Taki-nioi' has a diploid set of chromosomes (2n = 16).

Surugadai-nioi is named after the hill Surugadai in the Kanda District of Tokyo, from which one could look over the city and see Mount Fuji in the distance. This nineteenth-century selection of the Oshima cherry is listed, for instance, in 1886 in the collection planted along the Arakawa River. In the 1920s and 1930s it was offered for sale in the export catalogs of Japanese nurseries such as the Yokohama Nursery. It has single, white, and not too large flowers that appear a little before the foliage unfolds. Once the flowers are in full bloom, the foliage also is out. The rather narrow petals show one or more folds lengthwise on the middle vein. 'Surugadai-nioi' flowers at about the same time or a little later than 'Taki-nioi'. Like 'Taki-nioi', it shows branching in horizontally feathering twigs, but it is less outspoken and its foliage is not as deep bronze-brown. 'Taki-nioi' is clearly the better tree because of its more abundant bloom and the better covering with flowers of the cascading boughs.

'Taoyame'

'Taoyame' became more widely known in the nineteenth century. It was found among the cherries planted in the compound of the Hirano Shrine, a Shinto temple in Kyōto known to have kept a cherry collection since at

Figure 175. Reddish-bronze foliage with aristate serration accompanies a fine fragrance in 'Surugadai-nioi'. Photo by author, 29 April 1996, Tama Forest Science Garden, Tokyo.

least the early seventeenth century. Ingram explains that he received scions of this tree from a certain Count Kujuji and thus imported the cultivar to England. This would have been Count Tsuneo Kajūji (1882–1936), a prominent nobleman who had connections in the imperial palace, studied the cherries he collected, and prepared an illustrated catalog of them (*Koto-meibokuki,* 1925).

Ingram (1948) described this cherry as *Prunus serrulata* 'Taoyoma Za-kura'. "Taoyoma" is simply a spelling error: the 'Taoyoma Zakura' that one finds in Europe is the same as the 'Taoyame' in North America and Japan. In Japan one finds this cherry as *P. lannesiana* 'Taoyame'.

Taoyame is an old and elegant Japanese word that means something like "a graceful maiden." Seeing the tree, it is quite obvious that this word is a well-chosen name for this garden form. Young foliage of 'Taoyame' appears with the blossoms and is perhaps the darkest red-brown (RHS 165-A, 199-A) of all Japanese flowering cherries. It contrasts superbly with the shell-pink flowers that have a calyx, sepals, and peduncle that are equally deep wine-red, like the petioles of the young leaves. In this coloring it re-

Figure 176. 'Taoyame' makes a regular crown and must be a good avenue tree. Photo by author, 28 April 1996, Yūki Experimental Station of the Flower Association of Japan, Ibaraki Prefecture.

Figure 177. 'Taoyame', contrasting blossom and dark foliage, suggesting Japanese mountain cherry parentage. Photo by Arie Peterse, 28 April 1996, Yūki Experimental Station of the Flower Association of Japan, Ibaraki Prefecture.

sembles 'Horinji', though 'Taoyame' is much healthier and grows more vigorously, making a broad, large shrub to about 7 m high. The crown is well balanced with regularly spaced limbs and branches.

'Taoyame' shows a variability in the number of petals. Trees may have single flowers, though there are always more semi-double flowers, with an average of at least eight petals. Other trees have eight to twelve or even fourteen petals per flower. The number of petals does not make for a very sure characteristic in identifying this cultivar, but the combination of all other details is so specific that 'Taoyame' is easily identified. Ingram (1948) placed it very high on his list of best varieties; anybody seeing 'Taoyame' in full splendor will agree.

Prunus 'Taoyame'

Less current synonym: Taoyoma

Description: Tree making a broad, ovate crown, to 7 m high. Young foliage very dark brown-red(!) (RHS 165-A, 199-A). Serration double and single, teeth with small dark red glands, up to the top of the leaf. Stipules medium divided, 12–16 mm long. Corymbose inflorescence, with three to four flowers. Peduncles 1.5–2.5 cm long. Pedicels 2–3 cm long. Flower in bud pink, becoming light pink (RHS 62-D) when completely opened. Flower 4.5–5.0 cm in diameter, opening to a flat plane. Petals five to fifteen, orbicular to ovate, slightly emarginate at the top, 19–23 × 16–20 mm. There is one pistil, perfect, 10–12 mm long; about as long as the longest stamens. The calyx is funnel-shaped, 5–6 × 4.0–4.5 mm, rather short(!), with a dark purplish-red tinge (RHS 60-C). Sepals are elongated and triangular, 8–9 × 4 mm, with a dark purplish-red tinge, not completely unserrated, with a few teeth. Tips of the sepals turn upwards(!). Flowering season is early May.

'Ukon'

Given the enormous variability of the native Japanese cherries, it is no surprise that forms with greenish or even green flowers are found, such as the very outspoken green 'Gyoiko', the creamy green 'Ukon', and the slightly paler 'Asagi'. The three forms are very old and appear in a description of the cherries at Ninna-ji Temple, found in a tourist guide of Kyōto called *Miyako meisho zue* and dated 1780. 'Asagi' appears as a cherry cultivar even a century earlier in the Japanese horticultural book *Kadan-kōmoku* (Flower bed catalog) of 1681. Other greenish forms of less interest can be found at present in specialized collections.

'Ukon' is a superior cherry among the greenish or cream-flowered forms. The Japanese word *ukon* ("turmeric") refers to a powder ground from the dried root of an Indian plant of the ginger family, *Curcuma longa,* which is also called *ukon* in Japanese. Turmeric is used as an ingredient for curry powder and in the past was known as a dyestuff for bright yellow colors. The flowers of the cherry 'Ukon' are uniquely yellowish, but certainly not the bright yellow of turmeric; the color is closer to a greenish-creamy white (RHS 145-C) and easily identifies this cultivar.

'Ukon' was among the early introductions of cherries to Europe and was at the end of the nineteenth century known by the cumbersome Latin name *Cerasus Sieboldi flore luteo virescenti pleno* ("Siebold's cherry with the double, yellow-green flowers"). In 1903 it was described in the German horticultural magazine *Gartenflora* (with illustration Tafel 1513, p. 169) by Albert Wagner as *Prunus serrulata* f. *grandiflora.* Three years later, Miyoshi described 'Ukon' again as *P. serrulata* Lindley f. *viridiflora,* and in 1916 he revised it as *P. serrulata* Lindley f. *luteo-virens,* in combination with a description of the cherry 'Asagi' as *P. serrulata* Lindley f. *luteo-virens* subf. *luteoides.* In Japan one finds it as *P. lannesiana* 'Grandiflora'.

Several clones of 'Ukon' are in cultivation. One with greenish-yellow petals that are more obovate and deeply notched is often found (and sometimes called 'Kizakura') in and around Kyōto. The heart of its flower turns purplish pink at the end of flowering. A form with more cream-yellow flowers and orbicular petals is the standard, found around Tokyo and in Europe. The 1822 catalog *Hana-no-kagami* (A paragon of flowers) illustrates six green or creamish garden forms.

Kayama (1931), quoting the source *Zōho-kadan-taikan-goshū, ni,* described 'Asagi-zakura' as a pale form of 'Kizakura': "Double, big flowers hanging in a bunch. Light color, pale yellow, a slight yellow tint it has, which is uncommon. There is also a single form." 'Kizakura' can be found in several Kyōto collections.

In *Igansai-ōhin* (Matsuoka 1758) an illustration and short description of a 'Kaba-zakura' are found, giving 'Kizakura' as synonym. Ingram (1925, 1929), followed by Russell (1934), named a green-pigmented flowering cherry 'Kaba-zakura', which must be the same as Matsuoka's cherry. *Kaba* in this name is written with a Chinese character that is used for the birch tree. (*Kaba-zakura* is also the name for the glossy, chestnut colored bark of certain cherries used in decorative crafts.) This character *kaba* also indicates a mixed color of yellow (*ki*) and red (*aka*). Ingram found the young leaves of 'Kaba-zakura' bronze as in 'Ukon'. A range from cream to green would run as 'Ukon'—'Asagi'—'Kizakura' (synonym 'Kaba-zakura')—'Gyoiko', taking the color of the flowers in their prime.

What is understood at present as 'Kaba-zakura' in Japan is quite different: a white-flowered *Prunus* ×*media* Miyoshi Media, a hybrid of the Japanese mountain cherry (*P. serrulata* var. *spontanea*) and the Edo-higan cherry (*P. pendula* f. *ascendens*). The origin of this cultivar is an old tree in a temple compound in Kitamoto, Saitama Prefecture, legally preserved as a natural monument (Kawasaki 1994). The *kaba* in this name is written with a different Chinese character, the one for bulrush (*gama*) that is also used for certain willow species.

But let us return to 'Ukon'. The true 'Ukon' is an excellent cultivar with its 5-cm large, greenish-creamy flowers that contrast beautifully with the

Figure 178. 'Ukon', peculiar blossom and foliage. Photo by author, 'Ki-zakura'-form of 'Ukon', 25 April 1996, Kyōto Botanic Garden.

bronze-green young foliage. It makes a vase-shaped tree, but needs to be pruned a little when young to encourage it to ramify. It blooms about a week earlier than 'Gyoiko' and at about the same time as 'Kanzan' and 'Mikuruma-gaeshi'. In autumn 'Ukon' gives its encore with a purplish-brown or purplish-red autumn foliage. Among the old garden cherries, it has proved to be one of the hardiest for climatic and soil conditions. 'Ukon' certainly needs to be remembered whenever one considers planting a flowering cherry.

Prunus 'Ukon'

Less current synonym: *Prunus serrulata* f. *grandiflora*

Description: Tree broad and vase-shaped, to 8 m high and 15 m wide. Young foliage green with a little bronze. Leaves unfolding in the flowering season. Serration single, occasionally double, with a few small glands on teeth at the base of the leaf. Stipules medium to deeply bifurcated, 1.5–2.0 cm long. Corymbose inflorescence, with four to five flowers. Peduncles 2.5–4.0(–6.0) cm long. Pedicels 2–5 cm long. Flower in bud green-yellow, becoming green-yellow to cream (RHS 145-C) when completely opened. Flower 5.0–5.5 cm in diameter, fluffy. Petals nine to fifteen, orbicular, slightly emarginate at the top, 20–25 × 16–20 mm. There is one pistil,

Figure 179. 'Ukon' has reddish bracts and pedicels. Photo by Arie Peterse, 6 May 1985, Wageningen Botanic Gardens of the Agricultural University, Netherlands.

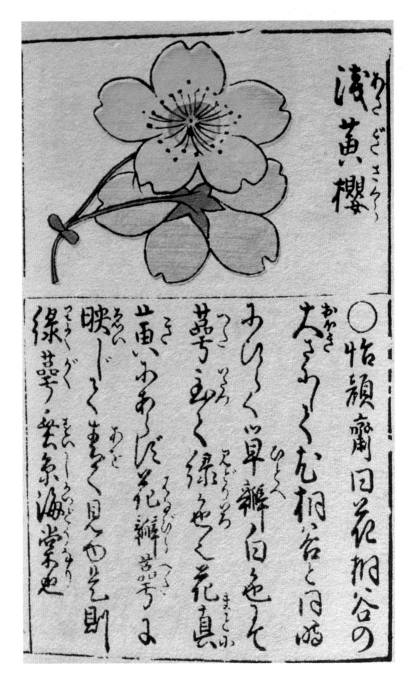

Figure 180. 'Asagi', a pale-yellow form from the early eighteenth century. From an 1891 reprint of Matsuoka (1758).

perfect, 13–14 mm long; distinctly longer than the longest stamens. The calyx is broad and funnel-shaped, 6 × 4 mm; there is a distinct transition from pedicel to calyx. Sepals are elongated to elongated-triangular, 10–11 × 4–6 mm, with a faint purple tinge, usually with a few teeth, and occasionally with 1–4 accessory sepals. Flowering season is from late April to early May. 'Ukon' has a diploid set of chromosomes (2n = 16).

Asagi ("shallow-yellow") is a strain of 'Ukon' with lighter flowers. They are "greenish yellow slightly tinged with pink, and single" in a Japanese export nursery catalog of 1937 (Wada 1937). Ingram (1948) added that the cream-tinged flowers of 'Asagi' are of a better shape than those of 'Ukon' and nearly single. 'Asagi' flowers earlier than 'Ukon', but makes a less vigorous, less handsome tree. Sano IV (1961) counted eight to twelve petals per flower. Today 'Asagi' is rarely cultivated in Japan, and it must be rare or extinct in Western countries as well.

Gyoiko, spelled "Gioiko" in an older romanization, has flowers that are unusual for their colors: green, white, and pink. The name translates as

Figure 181. From a distance the green blossom of 'Gyoiko' hardly shows among the green foliage. Photo by Arie Peterse, 1 May 1996, Ninna-ji, Kyōto.

"colored court-robes" (*kō Gyo-i*) and refers to the green, white, and purple found in robes of the women at the imperial court in ancient Japan. The petals are grass-green in color with a contrasting narrow, white stripe, occasionally provided with an extra pink stroke. Miyoshi (1916) named this cultivar *Prunus serrulata* f. *tricolor,* referring to the three colors. The flowers appear a little later than those of 'Ukon', and they are a curiosity. When expanded, the outer petals are reflexed, resulting in a not-so beautiful flower shape. Seen from a distance, the flowers are so green that the vase-shaped tree does not seem to be in bloom. Nonetheless, this cherry is a necessity for the collector and, as there are many collectors, it is not rare. 'Gyoiko' has a diploid set of chromosomes (2n = 16). Some trees reportedly have grown a chimerical branch with 'Ukon' flowers.

'Washi-no-o'

Washi-no-o ("eagle's tail") was the name of a hillside in the city of Kyōto, which was famous for its cherries from the thirteenth to about the end of the fifteenth century. The hillside was south of the present-day Maruyama Park, which is now famous for its large weeping cherries. The hillside has become a built-up part of the town known as Washinoo-chō.

The cherry 'Washi-no-o' is an old cultivar and was named after the hillside. It was described in the *Kadan-kōmoku* (Flower bed catalog) of 1681 and appears since then in old lists of cherries. Miyoshi described it as *Prunus serrulata* f. *arguta* in 1916. In Japan one finds it as *P. lannesiana* 'Washinowo'.

It was a favorite among the export products of the Yokohama Nursery Company from the late nineteenth century until about the 1930s. It is rarely lacking in collections outside Japan, although there are better cultivars that deserve to be planted as often as 'Washi-no-o'. It is a healthy plant with a vigorous and robust growth. The flowers are usually single, and the inflorescences with three to four flowers are set on a short peduncle. The petals can be large, about 2 cm as a rule, but Sano IV (1961) speaks even of 3.2 cm. The petals give a waxy, sturdy impression; they have wrinkled undulations in the surface, and the edges are wavy, retuse, or unevenly divided. They are reminiscent of the petals of 'Ariake', and for both of these triploids an influence of 'Mazakura' has been suggested by Kawasaki (1994).

Figure 182. 'Washi-no-o'. Photo by author, 13 April 1997, Yūki Experimental Station of the Flower Association of Japan, Ibaraki Prefecture.

Prunus 'Washi-no-o'

Less current synonyms: *Prunus serrulata* f. *arguta,* 'Washinowo'

Description: Tree umbrella-shaped, with heavy limbs, to 10 m high and 15 m wide. Young foliage light brownish or brownish green when unfolding with the flowers. Serration double, aristate. Stipules much divided, 10–15 mm long. Corymbose inflorescence, with three to four flowers. Peduncles short (!), 0.7 cm long. Pedicels 1–2 cm long. Flower in bud white with a little pink, turning white (RHS 56-D) when completely opened. Flower 4.0–4.5 cm in diameter, opening to a flat plane, somewhat fragrant. Petals five or even up to eight, rarely with a few petaloids, round or slightly ovate, 18–20 × 16–19 mm, with irregular wrinkles and undulations at the emarginate, occasionally fimbriate, top end(!). There is one pistil, perfect, 12–13 mm long, about as long as the longest stamens. The calyx is campanulate, 8 × 4 mm, with a deep red shade; there is a distinct transition from pedicel to calyx. Sepals are elongated and triangular, 7 × 4 mm to 9 × 4.5 mm, some serration, or a few teeth, reddish. Styles have a rather large stigma. Flowering season is from mid- to late April. 'Washino-o' has a triploid set of chromosomes (2n = 24).

'Yae-akebono'

The Japanese word *akebono* ("daybreak") carries literary connotations in Japan because of a classic poetic phrase, the opening sentence of a famous diary (*Makura Sōshi*, by a noblewoman, Shōnagon Sei, ca. 1002 A.D.). The diary begins with *Haru ha akebono,* which translates as "Spring means morning twilight." The promising, pinkish-orange twilight of spring associates nicely with a cherry.

There are two plants with the name 'Akebono': a rather recent cultivar of *Prunus ×yedoensis* that was developed in the United States, and a cherry mentioned in seventeenth century Japanese sources, which was described as *P. serrulata* f. *lucifera* by Miyoshi, but is now believed to be extinct. 'Yae-akebono' ("the double daybreak cherry") is more recent and was found among the cherries along the Arakawa River at the end of the nineteenth century. It was also offered for export in Japanese catalogs; its flowers are described as "very large, semi-double, rose, fragrant" by the Hakoneya nursery (Wada 1937).

'Yae-akebono' is one of the semi-double, pink-flowered cherries that is very similar to 'Fukurokuju', as was shown by Kawasaki (1994), who gives it as *Prunus lannesiana* 'Versicolor'. Apart from minor variations in millimeters, the main difference Kawasaki found was that the sepals of 'Yae-akebono' have some serration. 'Yae-akebono' also has, according to Kawasaki, slightly fewer petals than 'Fukurokuju'. Miyoshi described it under the name *P. serrulata* f. *versicolor* and gives twelve petals for the flowers of both forms. His Latin *versicolor* means that the color of the flowers is not uniform. Indeed the inner petals are various shades of pink, presenting flowers between an almost pure white and a light pink. The outer petals,

Figure 183. 'Yae-akebono'. Photo by Arie Peterse, 29 April 1996, Tama Forest Science Garden, Tokyo.

though, are always the same kind of light pink as 'Fukurokuju'. The flowers of the latter seem a little less disorderly.

The flowering season of 'Yae-akebono' is about the third week of April. It makes a healthy tree of a somewhat irregular outline, because of the few bent, heavy branches that support the crown.

Prunus 'Yae-akebono'

Less current synonyms: Yaye-akebono, *Prunus serrulata* f. *versicolor*

Description: Tree broad and spreading, to 8(–12) m high. Young foliage green to bronze-green (RHS 146-A). Serration single with small glands. Foliage is not yet well developed in the flowering season. Stipules slightly divided, 12–17 mm long. Corymbose inflorescence, with two to four flowers. Peduncles short, 0.5–1.0 cm long. Pedicels 1.5–2.5 cm long. Flower in bud purplish pink (RHS 63-D), becoming pale pink (RHS 62-D) to almost pure white when completely opened; petal edges have a slightly darker color. Flower about 5 cm in diameter, opening to a flat plane, with the opening of the ovary always visible, no distinct fragrance. Petals fourteen to sixteen (sometimes as few as ten), orbicular, uniform, usually slightly emarginate at the top, 20–25 × 17–27 mm, starchy-rumpled in appearance when the flower first opens. There is one pistil, perfect, 10–11 mm long, as long as or slightly longer than the longest stamens. The calyx is broadly campanulate, 6 × 5–6 mm, with a faint purple tinge; there is a distinct transition from pedicel to calyx. Sepals are a little narrower at the base, but not as distinctly as with 'Hokusai'; 6–9 × 4–5 mm, occasional serration at the edge, and with a faint purple tinge. Flowering season is mid-April in Tokyo.

'Yae-murasaki-zakura'

'Yae-murasaki-zakura' ("double purple cherry") was selected by Manabu Miyoshi from among seedlings of 'Murasaki-zakura' ("purple cherry") with which he was experimenting in the Cherry Garden of the Botanical Gardens of the Tokyo University at the beginning of the twentieth century. Miyoshi named his discovery *Prunus serrulata* f. *purpurea* (subf. *plena*). One often finds it as *P. lannesiana* 'Purpurea-plena'. Its female parent, 'Murasaki-zakura', is in cultivation and resembles 'Choshu-hizakura' and other cherries related to the Japanese mountain cherry.

'Yae-murasaki-zakura' is a nice cultivar, and if any cherry should be brought into prominence among those that are unjustly only seen in spe-

Figure 184. 'Yae-murasaki-zakura' makes a low, spreading tree. Photo by Arie Peterse, 11 May 1986, Hemelrijk, Belgium.

Figure 185. Most flowers of 'Yae-murasaki-zakura' are set in peduncled umbels.
Photo by Arie Peterse, 11 May 1986, Hemelrijk, Belgium.

Figure 186. 'Yae-murasaki-zakura' (no. 79, left) grown from seed of 'Murasaki-zakura' (no. 78, right). Miyoshi reported this cultivar to be the first filial generation of *Prunus serrulata* f. *purpurea*. From Miyoshi (1921b).

cialized collections, then this should be the one. It flowers in an abundance rarely seen in other cherries. Its growth is slow; the tree attains a height of less than 3 m after twenty years, making it an excellent choice for the small garden. In spite of its profuse blossoming and slow growth, it always has a healthy appearance, and it has in early spring beautifully bright-red flower buds. All these qualities recommend this cultivar for the retail trade.

The inflorescences of 'Yae-murasaki-zakura' often have three to four flowers set together at the end of the peduncle. The occurrence of these peduncled umbels, rather than the usual corymbs, is typical for this cultivar. The flowers are 3.5–4.0 cm large, have eight to fourteen petals, and carry a pleasant scent that is clearly discernible. The young foliage is coppery-red, bronze-green to green.

Prunus 'Yae-murasaki-zakura'
Synonym: 'Purpurea-plena'
Less current synonym: *Prunus serrulata* f. *purpurea* (subf. *plena*)

Description: Tree remarkably broad umbrella-shaped, 3–4 m high and 8 m wide, slow grower. Young foliage coppery-red to dark green (RHS 174-A to 146-A). Serration single, truly regular and distinctively fine(!)

teeth with small, dark red glands up to the tip of the leaf. Stipules deeply bifurcated, 9–14 mm long. Corymbose inflorescence; but often also as an umbel on a rather long peduncle that has one flower halfway; three to five flowers per inflorescence, but usually 4. Peduncles 2.5–4.0 cm long. Pedicels 2.0–3.5 cm long. Flower in bud purplish pink, becoming a fairly saturated pink (RHS 75-C) that turns to a more violet hue (RHS 84-C) when completely opened. Flower 3.5–4.0 cm in diameter, opening loose and fluffy, with a rather distinct fragrance. Petals eleven to fourteen, occasionally with one to three petaloids, oval to orbicular, deeply emarginate at the top, 17–19 × 10–13 mm. There is one pistil, perfect, 10–11 mm long; as long as the longest stamens. The calyx is campanulate, 7–8 × 3 mm, with a faint purple tinge; there is no distinct transition from pedicel to calyx. Sepals are elongated and triangular, 7–8 × 3.0–3.5 mm, with a faint purple tinge, unserrated. Flowering season is from late April to early May.

'Yokihi'

Yōkihi is the Japanese pronunciation of the Chinese characters that form the name of Yang Kuei-fei (719–756 A.D.), a historical woman of famed beauty at the Chinese imperial court. She was a beloved concubine of the emperor Hsüan Tsung (in power 713–742) of the T'ang dynasty and became famous as Yōkihi through a poem, titled *Zhang Henge* (in Japanese, *Chōgonka*, 806), by the poet Bo Juyi (772–846). This classic Chinese poem inspired much Japanese literature of later ages. Yōkihi is presented as an intelligent woman, excelling all other noblewomen in dance, music, verse, and song. In a period of turmoil she was killed by competitors who considered her too self-conceited.

The cherry 'Yokihi' is often believed to have originated in Nara. For the Japanese, this city and its culture have a Chinese ring, as Nara was founded and constructed after Chinese city planning models in the early eighth century with help of Chinese artisans. However, 'Yokihi' is not found in any source earlier than the *Kadan-kōmoku* (Flower bed catalog) of 1681. It appears since then in lists of collections.

Like 'Oshokun', 'Yokihi' echoes a historical Chinese idea of feminine beauty, and the two cultivars responded to aesthetic ideals associated with China. The blushing pink of the blossom of both (a little more intense with 'Oshokun' according to old descriptions) and the abundance of the many-petaled flowers set in lush clusters were considered very "Chinese" by the Japanese of the time, resembling for instance the gorgeous flowers of Chinese tree peonies. For its botany and horticultural merits, though, 'Yokihi' resembles 'Edo-zakura' and 'Ito-kukuri'. It is distinguished from the two by its fewer flowers per cluster: in a corymb 'Yokihi' has three or four flowers about 4 cm in diameter. The flowers are pink in bud, paling to whitish light pink when opened completely. The inner tier of petals is a noticeably lighter shade than the outer row. The outer petals have a clearly darker pink hue at the top edge. The scales of the flower buds and leaf buds are large. 'Yokihi' grows into a tree of moderate size.

Ingram imported 'Yokihi' to England. Miyoshi (1916) referred to it under the name *Prunus serrulata* Lindley f. *mollis*. One finds it also as *P. lannesiana* 'Mollis'.

Figure 187. 'Yokihi'. Photo by Arie Peterse and Wybe Kuitert, 28 April 1996, Yūki Experimental Station of the Flower Association of Japan, Ibaraki Prefecture.

Figure 188. Two types of 'Yokihi'. Woodblock print in Takeda (1902–1907).

Prunus 'Yokihi'

Less current synonym: 'Mollis'

Description: Tree vase-shaped to broadly vase-shaped, small, to about 6 m high. Young foliage light to bronze-green (RHS 152-A). Serration single, teeth with small glands. Stipules not divided, awn-tipped with small, red glands, 12–17 mm long. Corymbose inflorescence; three to four or even five flowers per inflorescence. Peduncles short, 0.5–1.5 cm long. Pedicels 1.5–3.0 cm long. Flower in bud pinkish red to pink, becoming light pink to very light pink (RHS 76-D) when opened, and fading with a darker pink in the heart of the flower. Flower 3.4–4.0 cm in diameter, opening loose and fluffy, slightly fragrant. Petals fourteen to seventeen (up to twenty-one), wavy, somewhat elliptic to orbicular, emarginate at the top that occasionally has a few extra indentations, 16–19 × 14–16 mm. Pistil one, usually perfect, 7–9 mm long, rarely phylloid, longer than the stamens. The calyx is funnel-shaped, about 7 mm long, flattened on one side; there is no distinct transition from pedicel to calyx. Sepals are elongated and triangular, 5 × 2.5–3.0 mm, with a faint pink shade, unserrated. Flowering season is mid-April in Tokyo.

APPENDIX 1

Metric System Tables

Millimeters/Inches
1 mm = ca. 1/25 of an inch
10 mm = ca. 2/5 of an inch

Centimeters/Inches or Feet
1 cm = ca. 2/5 of an inch
10 cm = ca. 4 inches
100 cm = 40 inches or 3 feet

Meters/Inches or Feet
1 m = 40 inches or 3 feet
10 m = 30 feet
100 m = 300 feet

Celsius/Fahrenheit
0°C = 32°F
18°C = 0°F

Conversion Formulas
mm = inches $\times$ 25
cm = inches $\times$ 2.5
cm = feet $\times$ 30
m = feet $\times$ 0.3
°F = $(9/5 \times °C) + 32$

Cherry Names in Japanese

In horticultural books and nursery catalogs in Japan, plant names are usually given in the phonetic alphabet. Trees in cherry collections or botanic gardens are often labeled only with Chinese characters used in the Japanese language.

ROMAN	PHONETIC	CHARACTERS
Akebono	アケボノ	曙
Amagi-yoshino	アマギヨシノ	天城吉野
Ama-no-gawa	アマノガワ	天の川
Amerika	アメリカ	
Anzu	あんず	杏
Arashiyama	アラシヤマ	嵐山
Ariake	アリアケ	有明
Asagi	アサギ	浅黄
Asahiyama	アサヒヤマ	旭山
Asano	アサノ	浅野
Azuma-higan	アズマヒガン	東彼岸
Azuma-nishiki	アズマニシキ	東錦
Baigoji-juzukake-zakura	バイゴジジュズカケザクラ	梅護寺数珠掛桜
Bendono	ベンドノ	弁殿
Beni-fugen	ベニフゲン	紅普賢
Beni-higan-zakura	ベニヒガンザクラ	紅彼岸桜
Beni-shidare	ベニシダレ	紅枝垂れ
Beni-temari	ベニテマリ	紅手毬
Beni-tora-no-o	ベニトラノオ	紅虎の尾
Beni-yama-zakura	ベニヤマザクラ	紅山桜
Botan-zakura	ボタンザクラ	牡丹桜
Chi-shima-zakura	チシマザクラ	千島桜
Choji-zakura	チョウジザクラ	丁子桜
Choshu-hizakura	チョウシュウヒザクラ	長州緋桜
Daikoku	ダイコク	大黒

ROMAN	PHONETIC	CHARACTERS
Edo-higan	エドヒガン	江戸彼岸
Edo-zakura	エドザクラ	江戸桜
Endo-zakura	エンドウザクラ	遠藤桜
Ezo-yama-zakura	エゾヤマザクラ	蝦夷山桜
Fudan-zakura	フダンザクラ	不断桜
Fugendo	フゲンドウ	普賢堂
Fugenzo	フゲンゾウ	普賢象
Fuji-kiku-zakura	フジキクザクラ	富士菊桜
Fuji-zakura	フジザクラ	富士桜
Fukurokuju	フクロクジュ	福禄寿
Fuyu-zakura	フユザクラ	冬桜
Ganjitsu-zakura	ガンジツザクラ	元日桜
Gosho-zakura	ゴショザクラ	五所桜
Gosho-zakura	ゴショザクラ	御所桜
Goten-nioi	ゴテンニオイ	御殿匂い
Goza-no-ma-nioi	ゴザノマニオイ	御座の間匂い
Gyoiko	ギョイコウ	御衣黄
Hakone-zakura	ハコネザクラ	箱根桜
Haku-fugen	ハクフゲン	白普賢
Hakusan-hata-zakura	ハクサンハタザクラ	白山旗桜
Hakusan-o-demari	ハクサンオオデマリ	白山大手毬
Hata-zakura	ハタザクラ	旗桜
Higan-zakura	ヒガンザクラ	彼岸桜
Higo-yoshino	ヒゴヨシノ	肥後吉野
Higurashi	ヒグラシ	日暮らし
Hi-kan-zakura	ヒカンザクラ	緋寒桜
Hime-fuji-zakura	ヒメフジザクラ	姫富士桜
Hime-midori-zakura	ヒメミドリザクラ	姫緑桜
Hirano-nioi	ヒラノニオイ	平野匂い
Hiyodori-zakura	ヒヨドリザクラ	鵯桜
Hizakura	ヒザクラ	緋桜
Hoki-zakura	ホウキザクラ	箒桜
Hokusai	ホクサイ	北斎
Horinji	ホウリンジ	法輪寺
Hosokawa-nioi	ホソカワニオイ	細川匂い
Ichihara-tora-no-o	イチハラトラノオ	市原虎の尾
Ichiyo	イチヨウ	一葉
Imose	イモセ	妹脊
Inu-zakura	イヌザクラ	犬桜
Ise-zakura	イセザクラ	伊勢桜
Ito-kukuri	イトククリ	糸括り
Itozakura	イトザクラ	糸桜
Jo-nioi	ジョウニオイ	上匂い

ROMAN	PHONETIC	CHARACTERS
Jugatsu-zakura	ジュウガツザクラ	十月桜
Kaba-zakura	カバザクラ	樺桜
Kaba-zakura	カバザクラ	蒲桜
Kabuto-zakura	カブトザクラ	
Kan-hi-zakura	カンヒザクラ	寒緋桜
Kanto-ariake	カントウアリアケ	関東有明
Kanzan	カンザン	関山
Karami-zakura	カラミザクラ	唐実桜
Kasumi-zakura	カスミザクラ	霞桜
Ke-yama-zakura	ケヤマザクラ	毛山桜
Kenroku-en-kiku-zakura	ケンロクエンキクザクラ	兼六園菊桜
Kiku-shidare-zakura	キクシダレザクラ	菊枝垂れ桜
Kiku-zakura	キクザクラ	菊桜
Kinashi-chigo-zakura	キナシチゴザクラ	鬼無稚児桜
Kinki-mame-zakura	キンキマメザクラ	近畿豆桜
Kinugasa	キヌガサ	衣笠
Kirigaya, Kirigayatsu	キリガヤ、キリガヤツ	桐ヶ谷
Kirin	キリン	麒麟
Kizakura	キザクラ	黄桜
Koba-zakura	コバザクラ	小葉桜
Ko-demari	コデマリ	小手毬
Ko-fugen	コウフゲン	紅普賢
Ko-higan-zakura	コヒガンザクラ	小彼岸桜
Kokonoe	ココノエ	九重
Komame-zakura	コマメザクラ	小豆桜
Koma-tsunagi	コマツナギ	駒繋ぎ
Koshio-yama	コシオヤマ	小塩山
Koshi-no-higan	コシノヒガン	越しの彼岸
Kumagai-zakura	クマガイザクラ	熊谷桜
Kurama-yama	クラマヤマ	
Kurama-zakura	クラマザクラ	鞍馬桜
Mame-zakura	マメザクラ	豆桜
Matsumae-hayazaki	マツマエハヤザキ	松前早咲き
Mazakura	マザクラ	真桜
Mikuruma-gaeshi	ミクルマガエシ	御車返し
Mine-zakura	ミネザクラ	峰桜
Miyama-zakura	ミヤマザクラ	深山桜
Mochi-zakura	モチザクラ	餅桜
Musha-zakura	ムシャザクラ	武者桜
Murasaki-zakura	ムラサキザクラ	紫桜
Naden	ナデン	南殿、奈天
Nadeshiko	ナデシコ	撫子
Najima-zakura	ナジマザクラ	名島桜

ROMAN	PHONETIC	CHARACTERS
Nanden	ナンデン	南殿
Nara-no-yae-zakura	ナラノヤエザクラ	奈良の八重桜
Naten	ナテン	奈天、南天
Nioi-zakura	ニオイザクラ	匂い桜
Nison-in-fugenzo	ンソンインフゲンゾウ	二尊院普賢象
Niwa-zakura	ニワザクラ	庭桜
O-eshiki-zakura	オエシキザクラ	御會式桜
O-nanden	オオナンデン	大南殿
Ojochin	オオジョウチン	大堤燈、大堤灯
Okame	オカメ	
Okiku-zakura	オオキクザクラ	大菊桜
Oku-miyako	オクミヤコ	奥都
Omoigawa	オモイガワ	思い川
Omuro-ariake	オムロアリアケ	御室有明
Oshidori-zakura	オシドリザクラ	鴛鴦桜
Oshima-zakura	オオシマザクラ	大島桜
Oshokun	オウショウクン	王昭君
O-yama-zakura	オオヤマザクラ	大山桜
Ota-zakura	オオタザクラ	太田桜
Raikoji-kiku-zakura	ライコウジキクザクラ	来迎寺菊桜
Ranzan	ランザン	嵐山
Roko	ロウコウ	滝香
Ruiran	ルイラン	類嵐
Ryoku-gaku-zakura	リョクガクザクラ	緑萼桜
Ryukyu-kan-hi-zakura	リュウキュウカンヒザクラ	琉球寒緋桜
Sakigake	サキガケ	魁
Sato-zakura	さとざくら	里桜
Sekiyama	セキヤマ	関山
Sendai-shidare	センダイシダレ	仙台枝垂れ
Sendai-zakura	センダイザクラ	仙台桜
Senriko	センリコウ	千里香
Shibayama	シバヤマ	芝山
Shidare-higan	シダレヒガン	枝垂れ彼岸
Shidare-yoshino	シダレヨシノ	枝垂れ吉野
Shidare-zakura	しだれざくら	枝垂れ桜
Shima-zakura	シマザクラ	島桜
Shiogama	シオガマ	塩釜
Shirayuki	シラユキ	白雪
Shiro-fugen	シロフゲン	白普賢
Shiro-higan-zakura	シロヒガンザクラ	白彼岸桜
Shirotae	シロタエ	白妙
Shiro-yama-zakura	シロヤマザクラ	白山桜
Shogetsu	ショウゲツ	松月

ROMAN	PHONETIC	CHARACTERS
Shujaku, Suzaku	シュジャク、スザク	朱雀
Somei-yoshino	ソメイヨシノ	染井吉野
Sumizome	スミゾメ	墨染め
Sumomo	すもも	李
Surugadai-nioi	スルガダイニオイ	駿河台匂い
Tagui-arashi	タグイアラシ	類嵐
Tai-haku	タイハク	太白
Taizan-fukun	タイザンフクン	泰山府君
Takane-zakura	タカネザクラ	高嶺桜
Takamatsu-chigo-zakura	タカマツチゴザクラ	高松稚児桜
Takasago	タカサゴ	高砂
Takigi-zakura	タキギザクラ	薪桜
Taki-nioi	タキニオイ	滝匂い
Tanabata	タナバタ	七夕
Taoyame	タオヤメ	手弱女
Temari	テマリ	手毬
Tora-no-o	トラノオ	虎の尾
Tsukushi-zakura	ツクシザクラ	筑紫桜
Uba-higan	ウバヒガン	姥彼岸
Uba-zakura	ウバザクラ	姥桜
Ukon	ウコン	鬱金
Ume	うめ	梅
Umineko	ウミネコ	海猫
Uzu-zakura	ウズザクラ	渦桜
Wakaki-fudan-zakura	ワカキフダンザクラ	若木不断桜
Washi-no-o	ワシノオ	鷲の尾
Yae-akebono	ヤエアケボノ	八重曙
Yae-beni-oshima	ヤエベニオオシマ	八重紅大島
Yae-beni-tora-no-o	ヤエベニトラノオ	八重紅虎の尾
Yae-hitoe	ヤエヒトエ	八重一重
Yae-murasaki-zakura	ヤエムラサキザクラ	八重紫桜
Yae-zakura	やえざくら	八重桜
Yama-zakura	ヤマザクラ	山桜
Yokihi	ヨウキヒ	楊貴妃
Yokohama-hizakura	ヨコハマヒザクラ	横浜緋桜
Yono-no-yae-zakura	ヨノノヤエザクラ	予野の八重桜
Yoshino	ヨシノ	吉野
Zensho-ji-kiku-zakura	ゼンショウジキクザクラ	善正寺菊桜

Glossary

Acuminate. Tapering to a point.

Aristate. A kind of serration in which the teeth of a leaf end in long, slender bristles; bristled.

Beni. A Japanese word always translated as "red" in English, though pink would be more appropriate. In ancient Japan, *beni* referred to the red dye derived from safflower (*Carthamus tinctorius*).

Bifid. Having two divisions.

Botan-zakura. Double-flowered cherries. Also the name of a specific cultivar.

Brown rot. A brownish withering of the flowers in damp or rainy weather.

Calyx. The outer, tubular case that holds a flower.

Caudate. Tapering to a long tail-like part. Refers to the leaf tip.

Chrysanthemum cherries. Refers to cherries with more than 100 petals per flower, though fewer are typical in less-than-ideal growing conditions.

Ciliate. Having a fringe of fine hairs.

Corymb. A broad cluster of flowers on stalks of various lengths, branching off at various points from a main flower stalk.

Corymbose. Having flowers in corymbs.

Crenate. See **retuse**.

Cuneate. Wedge-shaped. Refers to the leaf base.

Daimyo. A feudal governor, vassal to the shogun.

Fastigiate. Having a growth habit that results in an erect, narrow crown.

Fimbriate. Having many deep indentations, fringed.

Glabrous. Hairless.

Glaucous. Showing a whitish surface.

Inflorescence. The arrangement of flowers in a cluster.

Ito-zakura. Thread (or weeping) cherries. Also a folk name of a specific botanic cherry.

Kiku-zakura. Chrysanthemum-flowered cherries. Refers to cherries with more than 100 petals per flower. Also the name of a specific cultivar.

Kiku-zaki-zakura. Chrysanthemum-flowered cherries. Refers to cherries with more than 100 petals per flower.

Hanami. Literally, "viewing the flowers." Refers to the spring picnics under cherry trees, popular in Japan.

Mature. Fully developed.

Natural Monument. In Japan, some remarkable thing in nature, often a singular specimen of an old tree, sometimes planted to memorialize some heroic or imperial event, having a legal preservation status.

Nectary. A gland that secretes nectar, found on the leaf stalk or at the base of the leaf.

Nioi-zakura. Scented (or fragrant) cherries. Also the name of a rarely seen but fragrant selection of the Japanese mountain cherry.

Noh theater. Highly abstracted, traditional Japanese drama with dance and song.

Obovate. Upside-down egg-shaped.

Obtuse. Having a rounded end, with no tip. Refers to leaves.

Orbicular. Round.

Ovate. Egg-shaped.

Pedicel. A subordinate flower stalk holding one flower.

Peduncle. The main flower stalk (holding pedicels that hold flowers).

Perfect. Fully developed. Refers to a pistil having a completely developed ovary with style and stigma.

Petaloid. A stamen that has developed into a petal. It stands on a short stalk that is a rudimentary part of the thread of the stamen.

Petals. Colored leaflike parts that make the disk of a flower.

Petiole. The leaf stalk.

Phylloid. Leaflike. Refers to pistils.

Pubescent. Covered with hairs.

Retuse. Emarginated; indented at the top.

Sakura Kwai. A cherry club founded in 1917 in the Tokyo Imperial Hotel.

Sato-yama. Literally a "village mountain." A forest used by local villagers to obtain fruits and timber for household use.

Sato-zakura. Garden (or cultivated) cherries.

Second-story flower. A small flower completely furnished with sepals, petals, stamens, and pistils in the heart of a larger (main) flower. Commonly found in chrysanthemum cherries.

Sepal. One of usually five leaflike appendages of the calyx in a cherry flower that envelop the petals.

Serrate. Notched like a saw.

Shogun. Japanese feudal leader-general, having absolute, virtual power.

Stipule. A small leaflike appendage at the base of the petiole.

Trifid. Having three divisions.

Two-story flower. A flower that consists of a smaller flower, complete with sepals, petals, stamens, and pistils, in the heart of a larger (main) flower. Commonly found in chrysanthemum cherries.

Umbel. A cluster of flowers with stalks of approximately the same length that spring from one point on the twig.

Umbellate. Having flowers in umbels.

Urceolate. Pitcher-shaped.

Vexillate. Flaglike. Refers to petaloids, standing as little flags on a pole.

Yae-zakura. Double-flowered cherries. Refers to cherries with about twenty-five to fifty petals per flower.

Yama-zakura. Mountain (or wild) cherries. Also the folk name of a specific botanic cherry.

Bibliography

Akisato Ritō. 1780. *Miyako meisho zue* (in Japanese). 6 vols. Ōsaka.
————. 1799. *Miyako rinsen meisho zue* (in Japanese). 6 vols.
Andō Tooru. 1989. *Nihon no Sakura* (in Japanese). Andō Tooru Shashin-shū, Gurafikkusha, Tokyo.
Anichi Sakura Tomo no Kai (Asociación Argentina Japonés de los Amigos de Sakura). 1990. *Aruzenchinkoku ni okeru Nihon Zakura (Sakura en la Argentina)* (in Japanese, with Spanish captions).
Arai, Seitaro. 1904. *Special Offer of Japanese Bulbs, Plants, Seeds!* Yokohama, Japan.
Arends, G. 1990. "*Prunus*-Onderstammen" (*Prunus* rootstocks, in Dutch). *Dendroflora* (Boskoop) 27: 51–55.
Asari M. 1983. Section in *Sekisetsuchi.kanreichi ni okeru sakura no meisho zukuri no tame no chōsa kenkyū hōkokusho* (Report on research and investigations concerning the constructing of cherry parks in cold northern regions and districts with deep snow, in Japanese), pp. 81–97. Nihon Hana no Kai (Flower Association of Japan), Tokyo.
Bean, W. J. 1976. *Trees and Shrubs Hardy in the British Isles.* Vol. 3, *N–RH.* 8th ed. London.
Böhmer, L. 1894. *Price list of Japanese Bulbs, Plants, Seeds, etc., Exported by L. Böhmer & Company Nurserymen & Florists.* Nos. 4, 5, & 28. Bluff, Yokohama, Japan, 1894.
————. 1901–1902. *Wholesale Catalog of Japanese Lily Bulbs, Iris, Peonies, and Other Japanese Flower Roots, Seeds, General Nursery Stock and Florists' Supplies.* L. Böhmer & Company Horticulturists & Nurserymen, Bluff, Yokohama, Japan.

Chadbund, Geoffrey. 1972. *Flowering Cherries.* Collins, St. James Place, London.

Chugai Shokubutsu Yen. 1931. *Descriptive Catalog of Seeds of Forest and Ornamental Trees for 1931–1932.* Chugai Shokubutsu Yen, Yamamoto, Kawabegun, near Kobe, Japan.

Du Cane, Florence. 1908. *The Flowers and Gardens of Japan* (with paintings of Ella du Cane). London.

Fairbank, J. K. 1953. *Trade and Diplomacy on the China Coast.* Stanford.

Flore des Serres et des Jardins de l'Europe. 1845–1880. Gand, red. Louis Van Houtte.

Flower Association of Japan (Nihon Hana no Kai) (comp.). 1982. *Manual of Japanese Flowering Cherries.* Trans. from *Sakura no hinshū ni kansuru chōsakenkyū hōkoku.* Tokyo.

The Garden. 1873, 1876, 1890, 1896.

The Gardener's Chronicle. 1861, 1894–1905. London.

Gartenflora, Allgemeine Monatschrift für Garten- und Blumenkunde. 1902. 8 vols. Deutschen Dendrologischen Gesellschaft, Stuttgart, Vols. 11, 12, 31, 51. Berlin.

Gashu Kuhei. 1976. *Sekai no Nihon-zakura* (Japanese cherries of the world, in Japanese). Seibundō Shinkōsha, Tokyo.

Hayashi Yasaka, Azagami Chikara, and Hishiyama Chūzaburō (eds.). 1995. *Nihon no jumoku* (Trees of Japan, in Japanese). Yama Kei Karā Meikan, Tokyo.

Hearn, Lafcadio. 1894. *Glimpses of Unfamiliar Japan.* London and Boston. Reprinted, 1907, Leipzig.

Hiroe Minosuke. 1976. *Sakura to Jinsei* (Flowering cherries and a human life, in Japanese). Meigen Shobō, Tokyo.

Honda Masaji, and Hayashi Yasaka. 1974. *Nihon no Sakura* (Flowering cherries of Japan, in Japanese). Seibundō Shinkōsha, Tokyo.

Honda Masaji, and Matsuda Osamu (Tsukamoto Yotaro, ed.). 1982. *Hana to ki no bunka, Sakura* (Culture of flowers and trees, flowering cherries, in Japanese). Ie no Hikari Kyōkai, Tokyo.

Inamura Toku. 1981. *Tsurezure Gusa Yōkai.* Yūseidō Shuppan, Tokyo.

Igansai Matsuoka, see Matsuoka Gentatsu.

Ingram, Collingwood. 1925. "Notes on Japanese Cherries." *Journal of the Royal Horticultural Society* (London) 50: 73–99.

————. 1929. "Notes on Japanese Cherries—II." *Journal of the Royal Horticultural Society* (London) 54: 159–180.

————. 1941. "Corrections in the Names of Japanese Cherries." *The Gardeners' Chronicle* (27 December): 240.

————. 1942. "Cherry Hybrids." *The Gardeners' Chronicle* 2914 (112) (31 October): 163.

————. 1948. *Ornamental Cherries.* London, New York.

Itō Ihee III. 1695. *Kadan-jikin-shō* (Flower bed embroideries, in Japanese).

Itō Ihee IV. 1710. *Zōho-jikinshō,* 1710.

Itō Tokutarō. 1906. *Saishin shokubutsugaku kyōkasho* (Newest botany text book, in Japanese). Sanseidō, Tokyo.

Jacques, A. 1832. *Cerisier Parmentier à fleurs doubles.* Ann. Soc. Roy. Hort. Paris 11: 75–76.

Jefferson, Roland M., and Alan E. Fusoni. 1977. *The Japanese Flowering Cherry Trees of Washington, D.C.— A Living Symbol of Friendship.* U.S. Department of Agriculture, National Arboretum Contribution No. 4, Washington, D.C.

Jefferson, Roland M., and Kay Kazue Wain. 1984. *The Nomenclature of Cultivated Japanese Flowering Cherries (Prunus): The Sato-zakura Group.* U.S. Department of Agriculture, National Arboretum Contribution No. 5, Washington, D.C.

Kaempfer, E. 1712. *Amoenitatum Exoticarum,.* book 5. Lemgo, Germany.

Kaneko Takashi. 1992. "Somei-yoshino no kigen" (The origin of *Prunus* ×*yedoensis,* in Japanese). *Puranta* 20 (March): 21–24.

Kawasaki Tetsuya. 1982. "Classification of Japanese Cherry Trees." In *Manual of Japanese Flowering Cherries,* comp. Flower Association of Japan, pp. 1–49. Tokyo.

————. 1991. "Tōa ni okeru sakura azoku no bunpu to Nihonsan sakura no jiseishū no bunrui" (Distribution of East Asian cherries and classification of Japanese indigenous, wild cherries, in Japanese). *Sakura no Kagaku* 1: 28–45.

————. 1994. *Nihon no Sakura* (Flowering cherries of Japan, in Japanese). Yama-kei serekushon.

Kayama Masuhiko. 1931. *Ōmuro no sakura* (Flowering cherries of Ōmuro, Ninna-ji, in Japanese). Dai-honzan Ninnaji, Kyoto.

————. 1933. *Hirano no sakura* (Flowering cherries of the Hirano Shrine, in Japanese). Hirano-jinja Samusho, Kyoto.

————. 1938. *Kyoto no Sakura, daiisshū* (Flowering cherries of Kyoto, in Japanese), vol. 1. Kyoto.

Kayama Masuhiko and Kayama Tokihiko. 1943. *Sakura* (Flowering cherries, in Japanese). Kyoto.

Kimura Hisakichi. 1968. "Ishikawa-ken ni mirareta yamazakurakei kikuzaki no sakura ni tsuite," "Kanazawa no kikuzaki meizakura sanpin," and "Kikuzakikei sakura no hana no keishitsu to shinka ni tsuite" (three articles on chrysanthemum-flowered cherries, in Japanese). In *Kyoto Engei dai 57 shū,* pp. 31–82. Kyoto Engei Kurabu.

Kitamura F., et al. 1984. "Sakurarui no taikansei ni kansuru jikenteki kenkyū" (Experimental research on the hardiness of flowering cherries, in Japanese). *Zōen Zasshi* 47(5): 112–116.

Kobayashi Yoshio. 1992. *Sakura no hinshū* (Varieties of flowering cherries, in Japanese). *Puranta* 20 (March): 9–14.

Koehne, E. 1909. "Die in Deutschland eingeführten japanischen Zierkirschen" (Japanese ornamental cherries imported in Germany, in German). *Mitteilungen der Deutschen Dendrologischen Gesellschaft* 18: 161–179.

————. 1909. "*Prunus japonica, glandulosa* und *humilis.*" *Mitteilungen der Deutschen Dendrologischen Gesellschaft* 18: 179–181.

Koidzumi, G. 1913. "Conspectus Rosacearum Japonicarum." *Journal of the College of Science of the Imperial University of Tokyo* 34 (28 October), art. 2.

Kokuritsu Idengaku Kenkyūjo (kanshū). 1995. *Idenken no Sakura* (The flowering cherries of the National Genetics Research Institute, in Japanese). Idengaku fukyūkai, Mishima.

Kōnomori S. 1985. *The Sakura, tsuzuku Somei-yoshino-zakura no kigen.* Privately published, Tokyo.

Krüssmann, G. 1986. *Manual of Cultivated Broad-Leaved Trees and Shrubs.* Vol. 3, *Pru–Z.* Timber Press, Portland, Oregon.

Kyoto Engei Kurabu (Kyoto Garden Club). [1681] 1932. *Kadan-kōmoku* (Flower bed catalog, in Japanese). Reprint, Kyoto.

————. [1695] 1933. *Kadan-jikin-shō* (Flower bed embroideries, in Japanese). Reprint, ed. by Kayama Masuhiko, Kyoto.

Lavallee, A. 1880–1885. *Icones arborum et fruticum in hortis Segrezianis collectorum* (Illustrations of trees and fruit trees collected in the garden at Segrès, in Latin). Paris, Librairie J. B. Bailliere et fils.

Lombarts, P., and H. J. Van de Laar. 1990. "*Prunus* Keuringsrapport" (*Prunus* test report, in Dutch). *Dendroflora* (Boskoop) 27: 7–50.

Matsuoka Gentatsu (also known as Matsuoka Joan or Igansai Matsuoka). 1758. *Ōhin* (also known as *Igansai-ōhin,* Igansai's cherries, in Japanese). Facs. reprint, Bunkyūdō, Tokyo, 1891.

Matsuoka, Joan, see Matsuoka Gentatsu.

Meyer, et al. 1993. *A Catalog of Cultivated Woody Plants of the Southeastern United States.* U.S. National Arboretum, Washington, D.C.

Miyoshi Manabu. 1916. "Japanische Bergkirschen, ihre Wildformen und Kulturrassen" (Japanese mountain cherries, their wild forms and cultivars, in German). *Journal of the College of Science of the Imperial University of Tokyo* 34 (10 March), art. 1.

———. 1921a. *Ōka gaisetsu (Sakura ni kansuru tosho kaidai ryaku)* (An overview of materials relating to flowering cherries, in Japanese). Unsōdō, Kyoto.

———. 1921b. *Ōka zufu* (Figures of flowering cherries, in Japanese but with Latin names). 2 vols. Unsōdō, Kyoto.

———. 1924(?). *Koganei Ōka Zusetsu, daiisshū* (Illustrated records on the flowering cherries at Koganei, in Japanese), vol. 1. Tokyo Shiyakusho.

———. 1938. *Sakura* (Flowering cherries, in Japanese). Tokyo.

———. 1941. *Sakura, Japanese cherry.* Tourist Library, vol. 3, rev. ed. Tokyo.

Mizuno Katsuhiko. 1997. *Sakura Zukan, Kyōto.* Tankōsha, Kyoto.

Mizuno Motokatsu. 1681. *Kadan-kōmoku* (Flower bed catalog, in Japanese).

Morohashi Tetsuji. 1968. *Daikanwa jiten* (dictionary). Daishūkan shoten.

Nagasawa, N. (ed.). 1969. *Keitai, Shinkanwa chūjiten* (dictionary). Sanseidō, Tokyo.

Nihon Kokugo Daijiten (dictionary). 1976. 20 vols. Shogakkan, Tokyo.

Nihon Hana no Kai (Flower Association of Japan). 1982. *Sakura no hinshū ni kansuru chōsa kenkyū hōkoku.* Tokyo.

Nihon Sakura No Kai. 1990. *Nihon no Sakura, Sakura Meisho 100 sen,* (Flowering cherries of Japan, a selection of 100 famous cherry sites, in Japanese). Zaidan Hōnin Nihon Sakura no Kai, Tokyo.

Nippon Engei Kaisha. 1910–1911. *Wholesale Catalog.* Kawanishi-mura, Ikeda, Settsu, Japan.

Numata, M. (ed.). 1974. *The Flora and Vegetation of Japan.* Amsterdam, London, New York.

Ogasawara Ryō. 1994. *Sakura* (Flowering cherries, in Japanese). NHK Shumi no Engei/Sagyō 12 ka getsu, vol. 19. Nihon Hōsō Shuppan Kyōkai, Tokyo.

Ohba Hideaki. 1992a. *Sakura no bunrui no muzukashisa* (On the difficult taxonomy of flowering cherries, in Japanese). *Puranta* 20 (March): 4–8.

———. 1992b. "Japanese Cherry Trees under the Genus *Cerasus* (Rosaceae)." *Journal of Japanese Botany* 67(5) (1 October): 276–281.

Ohwi Jisaburō. 1965. *Nihon Shokubutsushi* (Flora of Japan, in Japanese). Rev. ed. Tokyo.

Ohwi Jisaburō, and Ohta Yoai. 1973. *Nihon Sakura Shū* (Flowering cherries of Japan, in Japanese). Tokyo.

Peterse, Arie. 1987. *Japanse sierkersen, verslag van een doctoraal onderzoek 1986* (unpublished thesis on ca. 50 *P. serrulata* cultivars, in Dutch). Wageningen Agricultural University.

Rehder, A. 1940. *Manual of Cultivated Trees and Shrubs Hardy in North America.* 2nd ed. New York.

Revue Horticole. 1866; 1872, 1873, 1875; 1876, 1877, etc. Paris, red. Edouard André.

Royal Horticultural Society. 1996. *Colour Chart.* Wisley.

———. 1830– . *Transactions, Journals and Proceedings of the Royal Horticultural Society.* London.

Russell, Paul. 1934. *The Oriental Flowering Cherries.* U.S. Department of Agriculture, Circular No. 113 (March), Washington, D.C.

Saitama-Engei & Company. 1913. *Wholesale Trade List.* Saitama-ken, Japan.

Saito Shōji. 1978. "Sakura," Section in *Nihonteki shizenkan no kenkyū, gekan* (Research on the Japanese view on nature, in Japanese), pp. 133–148. Yasaka Shobō, Tokyo.

———. 1980. *Nihonjin to sakura* (The Japanese and their flowering cherries, in Japanese). Kōdansha, Tokyo.

Sakura No Kwai. 1918–1921. *Sakura* (official organ of the "Sakura-no-Kwai," in Japanese with some English articles), vols. 1–4. Tokyo Teikoku Hotel.

Sano Tōemon IV. 1961. *Sakura; Flowering Cherries of Japan* (in Japanese, with English title). Mitsumura Suiko Shoin, Kyoto, Tokyo.

———. 1970. *Sakura kashō* (Scribbles on flowering cherries, in Japanese). Seibundō Shinkōsha.

Sano Tōemon V. 1990. *Sakura taikan* (Broad view on flowering cherries, in Japanese). Shikōsha, Tokyo.

———. 1993. *Kyo no Sakura* (Flowering cherries of Kyoto, in Japanese). Shikōsha, Kyoto.

———. 1995. *Sakura, Sano Tōemon 'Sakura korekushon' no sekai* (The world of Sano's flowering-cherry collection, in Japanese). Tokyo.

Satō Taihei. 1935. *Sakura no Nihon*, pp. 352–355. Tokyo.

———. 1937. *Sakura to Nihon minzoku* (Flowering cherries and the Japanese race, in Japanese). Daitō shuppansha, Tokyo.

Seidensticker, E. G. (trans.). 1982. *Murasaki Shikibu, The Tale of Genji.* Rutland, Tokyo.

Shimmura, I. 1935. *Ji-en* (dictionary). Hakubunkan, Tokyo.

Suzuki and Iida. 1897. *The Wholesale Price List of Bulbs, Plants and Seeds for 1897*. No. 3. Nakamura, Yokohama, Japan.

Takaghi & Company. 1899. *Wholesale Price List of Lily Bulbs, Cycas revoluta, Plants, Eularia, and Seeds.* Tokyo.

Takagi Kiyoko. 1979. *Sakura hyakushu* (Hundred flowering cherries, in Japanese). Tanka Shinbun Sha, Tokyo.

Takagi Tokumitsu. 1995. *Ennai de mirareru Sakura no kaisetsu* (Description of the flowering cherries found in the botanical garden, in Japanese). Higashiyama Shokubutsuen, Nagoya.

Takeda Suika. 1902–1907. *Sakura* (Flowering cherries, in Japanese). In the series *Kōko ruisan engei burui, nana shūme* by Sugimura Kosugi. Kōkosha, Tokyo.

Tama Shinrin Kagakuen. 1995. *Sakura gaido* (Guide to the cherry collection of the Tama Forest Science Garden, in Japanese). Daiichi Puranningu Senta, Tokyo.

Tōkyō toritsu Jindai Shokubutsu Kōen (Tokyo Metropolitan Jindai Botanical Park). 1991. *Shokubutsu Mokuroku* (List of plants).

Uehara Keiji. 1961, 1977. *Jumoku dai zusetsu* (Illustrated tree encyclopedia, in Japanese), vol. 2. Ariake Shobō, Tokyo.

Van Trier, H. 1990. "Small Flowering Ornamental Cherries In Arboretum Kalmthout." In *The International Symposium on Flowering Cherries,* pp. 151–153. Takatoh.

Wada, K. 1937. *Japanese Garden Treasures* (Catalog of Hakoneya Nurseries). Numazushi, Japan.

Wagner, Albert. 1902. "Hizakura." *Gartenflora* 890: 49.

Whitehouse, W. E. 1932. "Training the Kwanzan Cherry Tree." *National Horticultural Magazine* (Washington, D.C.) 16 (October): 236–248.

Wilson, Ernest Henry. 1916. *The Cherries of Japan.* Publications of the Arnold Arboretum, No. 7 (30 March), Cambridge.

Wyman, D. 1937. "Japanese Flowering Cherries." *The Gardener's Chronicle* 41 (March): 143–144.

Yamada Takaō. 1941. *Ōshi* (History of flowering cherries, in Japanese). Sakura shobō, Tokyo.

Yamamoto S., and Takahashi R. 1991. "Satoyama ni okeru yamazakura gunseichi no seiritsu katei ni tsuite" (Establishment of cherry-dotted coppice in the countryside, in Japanese with English summary). *Zōen Zasshi* 54(5): 173–178.

Yashiro Hirokata. 1821–1841. *Kokon-yōran-kō,* (Notes on the survey of old and new, in Japanese). Reprint, Kokusho Kankōkai, Tokyo, 1906.

Yokohama Nursery Company. 1899, 1906, 1907, 1908, 1911–1912, 1913, 1913–1914, 1917–1918, 1922–1923, 1924, 1926–1927, 1927–1928, 1928–1929, 1930–1931. *Descriptive Catalogs.* Released from the nursery at Nos. 21–35 Nakamura (-machi, Naka-ku), Yokohama, Japan.

Cherry Name Index

For quick and handy reference to the names in this volume, the generic *Prunus* (or *Cerasus*) has been deleted from this index as well as, in general, the single quotation marks for cultivars, the hybrid sign, and abbreviations such as var., f., and so forth. Complete, taxonomically correct names with authors are found at the descriptions.

This index includes popular names in quotation marks, synonyms from nursery catalogs, and some frequently seen but obsolete spellings. Homonyms (same name applied to different cherries) are listed with all appropriate cross-references. Names only of historic interest are found in the general index.

Bold-faced page numbers indicate the main descriptions.

General Index